Praise for
When
Gifted Kids
Don't Have
All the Answers

"This book belongs in the canon of gifted literature. Every teacher, parent, or mental health professional working with the gifted should have a well-worn, dog-eared copy on his or her desk. Its readability, practical advice, and unique voice make it a must own. Five stars and two thumbs up."

—Lisa Van Gemert, youth and education ambassador, Mensa Foundation

"An excellent resource for advocates—both teachers and parents— offering practical and insightful strategies on how to answer information seekers and critics alike about gifted children and their education."

—Lisa Conrad, founder and blogger at Gifted Parenting Support, and moderator of Twitter's Global Gifted & Talented Chat (#gtchat)

"Jim and Judy are on target! This book really does help students, parents, educators, and friends of gifted people understand that being gifted is truly a blessing, not a burden."

—Patti Rendon, gifted and talented coordinator in Edinburg, Texas

"Galbraith and Delisle successfully ┆ research and practice to make a pos⸱ for gifted young people. This text is a th⸱ ┆terly essential collection of information a⸱ ┆t gifted kids and the adults in their liv⸱

—Colleen Harsin, director of the Davidson Academy

When Gifted Kids Don't Have All the Answers

How to Meet Their Social and Emotional Needs

Judy Galbraith, M.A.
Jim Delisle, Ph.D.

free spirit
PUBLISHING®

Library of Congress Cataloging-in-Publication Data
Galbraith, Judy.
    When gifted kids don't have all the answers : how to meet their social and emotional needs / Judy Galbraith, M.A. and Jim Delisle, Ph.D. — Revised & updated edition.
            pages cm
    Previous edition entered under: Delisle, James R., 1953–
        ISBN 978-1-57542-493-4 (paperback) — ISBN 1-57542-493-2 (paperback) 1. Gifted children—Education—United States—Psychological aspects. 2. Classroom environment—United States. I. Delisle, James R., 1953– II. Title.
    LC3993.2.D36 2015
    371.95—dc23

                                                                2014037117

ISBN: 978-1-57542-493-4

Edited by Meg Bratsch, Pamela Espeland, and Alison Behnke
Cover and interior design by Michelle Lee Lagerroos
Cover photo © Getty Images; back cover photo © Serrnovik | Dreamstime.com.
For other photo credits, please see page 278.

10 9 8 7 6 5 4 3 2
Printed in the United States of America

Free Spirit Publishing Inc.
6325 Sandburg Road, Suite 100
Minneapolis, MN 55427-3674
(612) 338-2068
help4kids@freespirit.com
www.freespirit.com

SUSTAINABLE
FORESTRY
INITIATIVE
Certified Chain of Custody
Promoting Sustainable Forestry
www.sfiprogram.org
SFI-01268
SFI label applies to the text stock

Free Spirit offers competitive pricing.
Contact edsales@freespirit.com for pricing information on multiple quantity purchases.

Dedication

This book is dedicated to the devoted advocates of gifted youth whose efforts often go unnoticed or are undervalued. There may be days when you're not sure if your work is making any difference, and you may feel discouraged by a society that largely misunderstands the importance of what you do. I hope that, in some small way, this book encourages and helps you to carry on the good fight. Remember, your heart knows the truth: Gifted kids are worth your efforts. They need and appreciate your support, advocacy, challenge, and caring.

—Judy Galbraith

The first edition of this book was dedicated, wholly and completely, to my son, Matt, whose love and laughter I cherish. I see no reason to change that dedication, but simply to add someone to it: his wife, Jen, who completes him (and our family) in meaningful and beautiful ways.

—Jim Delisle

Acknowledgments

As we were preparing the final copy for this book, we were both struck by the number of letters, anecdotes, and personal reflections that are included in it. Some were written by colleagues we have known for years, others by students who were in our classes or who crossed our lives for only a brief moment, and still more by individuals close to our hearts due to the personal relationships we have shared with them. In all cases, their words and reflections have added immeasurably to our understanding of giftedness. Even more, though, these excerpts represent both the friendships and professional relationships that have been forged between us and so many generous others. To every individual who has helped make this book more complete, more "grounded," we thank you with much sincerity.

Contents

List of Reproducible Pages

*Download these forms at **www.freespirit.com/WGKDHA-forms**.*

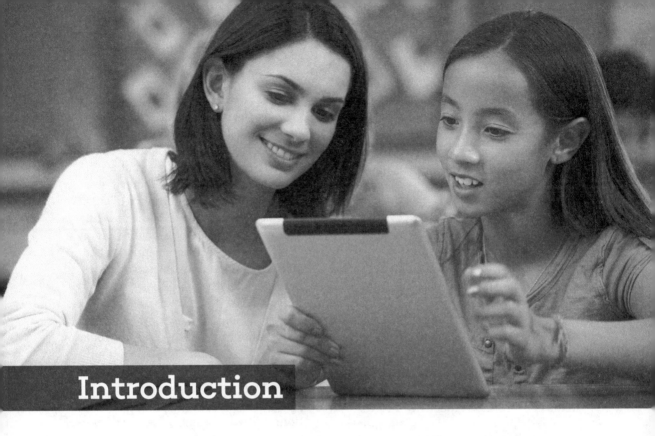

Introduction

Gifted kids are so much more than high grades and test scores. You probably know that already; that's why you're reading this book. But for teachers just starting out (or burning out, or overwhelmed with the day-to-day concerns of their job), it's sometimes difficult to see past all that achievement and potential to the child or adolescent who may be filled with anxiety, pressured to be perfect, lonely, alienated, confused, and unsure of what the future might bring.

We can both remember the specific incidents that first called our attention to gifted kids' social and emotional needs.

Judy: Early in my career as a gifted education specialist I worked with teens. One day, three boys hung around after class, and I overheard them talking. "Now I get to go be my family's identified patient,"

one said. Another asked, "Have you ever taken a Rorschach test?" The third said, "I'm seeing a psychiatrist." I suddenly realized that all three students had personal experience with mental health issues, and I wondered: What about the others? It was a wake-up call for me. Not long after, another of my students attempted suicide. When I looked at my program with new eyes, I saw that it was based entirely on meeting gifted kids' academic needs. It occurred to me that if a student's mental health is off-center significantly, or even a little, what point is there in trying to push academic challenge when that's usually the easy part of life for gifted kids? I made it my personal mission to educate myself about mental health, and to balance my academic program with life skills—learning about oneself and others.

Jim: Greg entered my life and my classroom at the same time. A fifth grader, he was fascinated by anything intellectual, and his sensitivity often caused him to see life from an altruistic angle seldom observed in boys his age. He drove his teachers nuts, though. He seldom finished anything he started, because once his fascination with a topic was sated, he felt it was time to move on. For two years, Greg was enrolled in my gifted program, and for two years, I had to fight to keep him there. He wasn't your stereotypical highachieving gifted child, but he was, indeed, a gifted child. I came to realize that the greatest needs he had were not in academics, but in the social and emotional realms of growing up gifted. Greg, and others like him, have guided my life ever since, and they have shown me the importance of looking beyond high achievement and glossy projects to find the gifted child beneath the academic veneer.

It's important to know that there isn't a big difference between addressing students' academic and emotional needs. You don't have to be a counselor with a degree. You don't have to have all the answers. We certainly don't! What we *do* have are years of experience working with gifted kids, studying gifted kids, reading about gifted kids, getting to know them, caring about them, and trying our best to help them.

We wrote this book to share what we've learned, to share what other experts say (including gifted kids themselves), and to give you some strategies, activities, and ideas you can start using right now to support the social and emotional needs of your own gifted students.

About This Book

- In **Chapter 1: What Is Giftedness?** we describe the general characteristics of gifted children and some problems associated with those characteristics. We present various definitions of giftedness and invite you to come up with your own definition. We spotlight many of the myths and misconceptions about giftedness (including the pervasive, pernicious myth that gifted education is "elitist"), and we consider the "gifted" label. This chapter includes two important information-gathering tools: a "Teacher Inventory" and a "Student Questionnaire." We strongly encourage you to complete the inventory and have your gifted students complete the questionnaire. Both will provide you with valuable insights.

- In **Chapter 2: Identifying Gifted Kids,** we wonder (as we're sure you do) why identification is so complex, suggest ways to improve the identification process, look at some questionable practices in current identification methods, and present common questions about identification—along with answers we hope you'll find helpful.

- In **Chapter 3: Emotional Dimensions of Giftedness,** we describe some of the challenges gifted kids face from within and without, including super-sensitivity and perfectionism. We talk about different ways of being gifted and focus on three categories of giftedness which may predict emotional needs: gifted girls, gifted students from ethnic and cultural minorities, and gifted children with physical and learning differences. We point out some trouble signs you can watch for, including symptoms indicating that a student may be deeply depressed or even suicidal.

■ In **Chapter 4: Being a Gifted Education Teacher,** we empathize with you and the challenges you face in your job. We understand; we've been there! We offer some ideas for explaining gifted education to parents, colleagues, administrators, and others who may not understand what you do or why it's necessary to do it ("Aren't all children gifted?"). We consider what makes a good gifted education teacher and suggest specific actions you might take to build your own strengths. Then we offer strategies you can use to create a supportive environment for your students, both as a group and one-on-one.

■ In **Chapter 5: Understanding Gifted Kids from the Inside Out,** we describe the difference between self-image and self-esteem and identify specific issues gifted children and adolescents face that set them apart. Then we present several activities related to those issues that help gifted kids explore their perceptions, consider their lives, learn more about themselves, be their own advocates, and like themselves more.

■ In **Chapter 6: Underachiever or Selective Consumer?**, we consider a label that's often applied to gifted kids who don't live up to others' expectations: "underachiever." We distinguish between underachievement and nonproduction, which we prefer to call "selective consumerism." We review the literature and research on what has historically been called "underachievement." Then we suggest strategies for

reversing patterns of underachieving and selective consumer behaviors through curricular and counseling interventions.

■ In **Chapter 7: The Eight Great Gripes of Gifted Kids**, we present a series of group discussions you can use to help students explore and understand the "Eight Great Gripes of Gifted Kids." The "Great Gripes" are problems and feelings that gifted kids have identified

as common to their experience: being bored in school; dealing with others' expectations; worrying about world problems and feeling helpless to do anything about them. The "Great Gripes" aren't new; in fact, gifted kids first told us about them more than thirty years ago. The specific gripes have changed somewhat in the decades since, but several core issues still loom large in kids' lives. Our discussions allow students to explore these issues in depth and feel more empowered to cope with them.

■ In **Chapter 8: Making It Safe to Be Smart: Creating the Gifted-Friendly Classroom,** we focus on ways to make gifted students feel welcome, wanted, and able to be themselves. We discuss the relationship between self-esteem and school achievement. We introduce the idea of "Invitational Education" and present specific strategies you can use to make your curriculum, grading procedures, student evaluations, classroom environment, and even your disciplinary procedures more supportive. We also talk about ways to feel better about yourself as a teacher.

At the end of some chapters, you'll also find reproducible forms to help you learn more about your students and support their academic, social, and emotional development. See page viii for how to access the digital versions of these forms through Free Spirit Publishing's website.

Our goals throughout this book are to call attention to gifted students' issues, problems, and feelings; to support your efforts on behalf of gifted kids; to answer some of the tough questions you may have (or that you may be asked by others); and

to provide you with concrete, easy-to-use strategies and activities for meeting students' social and emotional needs. The goals of the strategies and activities are to help gifted kids understand what giftedness means; to invite them to embrace giftedness as an asset in their lives; to inspire them to take more responsibility for their learning and their actions; and to help them build life skills for dealing with perfectionism, conflicts with others, self-esteem issues, and other mental-health concerns.

The strategies and activities you'll find here have been used in many classrooms, some for many years. We're confident that you'll have success with them, too. Watch what happens as your gifted students learn to understand and accept themselves, understand and accept others, and realize that being gifted is a blessing, not a burden.

A Few Words of Encouragement

Naturally, we don't know exactly what kind of gifted program you teach in—or even if you teach in a gifted program. Maybe you're one of the lucky ones, with a full-time program or even a gifted magnet school that's strongly supported, generally understood, and adequately funded (at least for now). Maybe you staff a resource room where gifted students spend part of each day. Perhaps you're a "pull-out" program teacher who travels from school to school, spending an hour or two each week with each group of gifted students (and you have many groups). Maybe you teach an enrichment class, AP (Advanced Placement) classes, or an after-school, weekend, or summer class for gifted students. Maybe you're a mentor to a gifted child.

Or maybe you're a "regular" classroom teacher, where your inclusive, mixed-abilities classroom may include students who range from highly gifted to gifted, to "average" students, those who have learning differences, kids at risk, students who have disabilities, homeless kids, and/or students for whom English is a new language. If so, you're probably being asked by your administration to differentiate the curriculum, or you will be at some point in the not-too-distant future.

Differentiation means changing the pace, level, or kind of instruction to meet each student's individual learning needs. In a time when gifted programs are being challenged or eliminated, differentiation is a way of ensuring that gifted students are given the learning opportunities they need. Depending on your situation, these opportunities may include curriculum compacting (compressing curriculum material into a shorter time frame, and allowing students to demonstrate mastery of content they already know); ability grouping (putting gifted students together for instruction in a particular subject area); flexible grouping (putting students together on an assignment-by-assignment basis); cluster grouping (putting all identified gifted students of the same grade level in the same classroom, usually one led by a teacher with training in gifted education); or individualized instruction (independent study projects).

Whatever your own situation might be, and however many gifted students you teach, we hope you know how truly essential you are. Over and over again, gifted

Relevant Research

As you read this book, you'll probably notice that some of the studies and research we cite aren't exactly new. In fact, some of them are relatively old. That's because—unfortunately—very little new, substantive research has been done about gifted kids and their needs. So when you do see references to older studies or research, we've included them because the results or information are still relevant—and also because there simply isn't newer information to offer.

students have told us about teachers who have made a tremendous difference in their lives. Gifted adults get misty-eyed when remembering grade-school teachers who took the time and made the effort to know them and guide them. Yes, you'll have bad days, maddening days, frustrating days, and days when you wish you'd followed a different career path altogether. Join the club! But please . . . keep teaching.

And please be willing to deal with the emotional lives of your students, not just their intellectual needs. Actually, working with students' affective needs may be (in the words of one teacher) "the best thing we can do for them." In an average busy day, with a tight schedule and loaded curriculum, it seems difficult to depart from the teacher's guide to deal with feelings. But as many people have pointed out, if students don't have good self-concepts and good interpersonal relationships, anything else positive comes to a screeching halt.

Affective education belongs in the teacher's guide. And that's what this book is.

Stay in Touch

We'd love to hear from you. Please let us know what's been helpful in this book, what works for you (and doesn't). Are there other strategies and activities you've discovered or developed that seem especially effective with gifted kids? We'd appreciate your sharing them with us. Are there stories from your own experience that make a point, illuminate a need, or support the importance of gifted education? Send them our way. We're always learning from "teachers in the trenches"—people like you. You may contact us by email or regular mail, and yes, we do respond:

Free Spirit Publishing Inc.
6325 Sandburg Road, Suite 100
Minneapolis, MN 55427-3674
help4kids@freespirit.com

We hope to hear from you. And we wish you continued success in your efforts to understand, teach, and encourage social and emotional growth among the gifted students in your care.

Judy Galbraith, M.A.
Jim Delisle, Ph.D.

CHAPTER 1

What Is Giftedness?

 Gifted can't really be defined, in my opinion. It means something slightly different to everyone, with gifted people being even more diverse in their definitions than anyone else.
—**Martin, 16**

When you hear the word "gifted," what's the first thing that comes to mind? Answer quickly. Don't spend a lot of time pondering or framing the "right" response. This is not a test!

Did you immediately think "genius," "prodigy," "Einstein," "exceptional," "talented," or "precocious"? Did you picture the child in your classroom who always seems to be one step ahead of you (or more)? Who never stops talking? Who's always the first to raise his or her hand? Who has a million questions? Or did you envision the child who spends hours staring out the window in apparent boredom, who seems to have few friends, who won't turn in an assignment until it's absolutely perfect? For you, is the word "gifted" positive—or negative?

Giftedness means many things. It means different things to different people, to society, and to gifted kids themselves. As a helpful starting point for understanding what giftedness is and means, consider the following list from the ERIC Clearinghouse on Disabilities and Gifted Education:

Some General Characteristics of Gifted Children[1]

These are typical factors stressed by educational authorities as being indicative of giftedness. Obviously, no child is outstanding in all characteristics.

1. Shows superior reasoning powers and marked ability to handle ideas; can generalize readily from specific facts and can see subtle relationships; has outstanding problem-solving ability.

2. Shows persistent intellectual curiosity; asks searching questions; shows exceptional interest in the nature of humankind and the universe.

3. Has a wide range of interests, often of an intellectual kind; develops one or more interests to considerable depth.

4. Is markedly superior in quality and quantity of written and/or spoken vocabulary; is interested in the subtleties of words and their uses.

5. Reads avidly and absorbs books well beyond his or her years.

6. Learns quickly and easily and retains what is learned; recalls important details, concepts and principles; comprehends readily.

7. Shows insight into arithmetical problems that require careful reasoning and grasps mathematical concepts readily.

Gifted Kids Speak Out

"Being gifted means I never stop asking questions!"
—Devorah, 9

"Giftedness means that I'm smart. It also means I wear my heart on my sleeve. Others see the former, but totally miss the latter. I don't just 'get over it.' It's who I am."
—Nadine, 16

"The best part of being gifted is being with intellectual peers who don't fret my endless questions and esoteric interests. The worst part of being gifted is living in a society whose focus is on making sure all the blades of grass measure up to level height and cutting off any that are higher than average."
—Annalee, 15

"It just means that I have a faster rate of computing things in my brain."
—Nori, 8

8. Shows creative ability or imaginative expression in such things as music, art, dance, drama; shows sensitivity and finesse in rhythm, movement, and bodily control.

9. Sustains concentration for lengthy periods and shows outstanding responsibility and independence in classroom work.

10. Sets realistically high standards for self; is self-critical in evaluating and correcting his or her own efforts.

11. Shows initiative and originality in intellectual work; shows flexibility in thinking and considers problems from a number of viewpoints.

12. Observes keenly and is responsive to new ideas.

13. Shows social poise and an ability to communicate with adults in a mature way.

14. Gets excitement and pleasure from intellectual challenge; shows an alert and subtle sense of humor.

In addition to these characteristics, gifted children can be extraordinarily sensitive. They often feel things more intensely than do other kids their age. They tend to develop empathy earlier than other children do. They often have a social conscience—and an intense awareness of the world's problems. They worry about the world, the environment, wars and conflicts, hunger and homelessness. Their emotions are raw and deep, yet close to the surface.

Along with these many fine qualities can come various problems related to them.

Just as not all gifted kids have every one of the characteristics shown in the chart on pages 10–11, not all gifted kids have each (or most, or even some) of the problems associated with these characteristics. In fact, many of the problems they do have aren't much different from those that other children and adolescents experience during the so-called "normal" process of growing up.

But many researchers, teachers, parents, and children themselves are realizing that gifted and talented kids may have special needs that come with being bright. Their view of the world, view of themselves, and other qualities (such as perfectionism and sensitivity) set them apart from peers and family—and at odds with their schools—just at a time in their lives when desire for conformity is greatest. Only in the last thirty years or so have we begun to address the cognitive needs of our brightest students, and many would argue that even this attention has been incomplete and spotty, as some schools offer much for gifted students and others do not. Still, to keep gifted children engaged in school and help them mature emotionally as well as intellectually, we must address their affective needs as vigorously as we address their cognitive ones.

What Does Giftedness Mean to You?

On pages 33–36, you'll find a "Teacher Inventory" we developed as a think piece—a way for you to focus on your attitudes about giftedness and your concerns about working with gifted students. Try filling it out like a diary or journal you'd want to read in another five years.

Dualities of Giftedness

The child who . . .	May also be the child who . . .
Shows superior reasoning powers and marked ability to handle ideas	Is impatient; seems stuck-up or arrogant; challenges your authority; has difficulty getting along with less able peers
Can solve problems quickly and easily	Wants to move on quickly to more challenging problems, despite what the rest of the class is doing; hates to "wait for the group"; gets bored and frustrated
Shows persistent intellectual curiosity and asks searching questions	Drives you crazy with questions; asks inappropriate or embarrassing questions; is perceived as "nosy"
Shows exceptional interest in the nature of humankind and the universe	Has difficulty focusing on ideas that are less grand and sweeping; feels that everyday class work is trivial and meaningless; can't connect with interests of age peers
Has a wide range of interests; develops one or more interests to considerable depth	Seems scattered and disorganized; takes on too many projects at once; gets obsessed with a particular interest; resists direction or interruption; rebels against conforming to group tasks; disrupts class routines; is perceived as stubborn or uncooperative
Has an advanced vocabulary	Talks too much; uses words to intimidate other people; finds it hard to communicate with age peers; seems pompous or conceited—a "show-off"; plays word games that others don't understand or appreciate; dominates discussions; has trouble listening
Is an avid reader	Buries himself or herself in books and avoids social interaction
Learns quickly; comprehends readily	Gets bored with the regular curriculum; gets impatient with peers for being "slow"; resists assignments that don't present opportunities for new learning; dislikes drill and practice; does inaccurate or sloppy work
Grasps mathematical concepts readily	Has little or no patience for regular math lessons or homework

The child who . . .	May also be the child who . . .
Is creative and imaginative	Goes too far; seems disruptive; lacks interest in mundane assignments or details; wanders off the subject
Sustains concentration for lengthy periods of time	Has tunnel vision; hates to be interrupted; neglects regular assignments or responsibilities; is stubborn
Shows outstanding responsibility and independence	Has difficulty working with others; resists following directions; seems bossy and disrespectful; is unable to accept help; is a nonconformist
Sets high standards for self; is self-critical	Sets unrealistically high goals; is perfectionistic; lacks tolerance for others' mistakes; fears failure; avoids taking risks or trying new things; becomes depressed
Shows initiative and originality	Resists going along with the crowd (or the class); is a loner
Shows flexibility in thinking; considers problems from a number of viewpoints	Has difficulty focusing on or finishing assignments; has trouble making decisions
Observes keenly; is responsive to new ideas	Sees too much; becomes impatient
Communicates easily with adults	Has difficulty communicating with age peers
Gets excitement and pleasure from intellectual challenge	Expects or demands intellectual challenge; resists sameness and routine tasks
Has a keen sense of humor	Uses humor inappropriately to gain attention or attack others; becomes the class clown; is disruptive
Is sensitive, empathetic, and emotional	Takes things personally; is easily hurt or upset; feels powerless to solve the world's problems; becomes fearful, anxious, and sad; has trouble handling criticism or rejection; is "too emotional," laughing one moment and crying the next; may seem immature

likely to emerge when the individual's talents coincide with what is valued by the culture."

—*David Sousa, from* How the Gifted Brain Learns (2009)

"Giftedness is natural ability in domains of life such as academics, athletics, the arts, spirituality, and many other areas. But it is far more than innate talent. It is commitment and dedication, diligence, respect for inquiry, and a near fanatical passion for excellence. There are a lot of bright people who clerk at convenience stores. The world-class sculptors, surgeons, and scientists are the bright people who know the secret to great accomplishment: hard work."

—*Jerry Flack, Ph.D., President's Teaching Scholar, University of Colorado*

"Giftedness is the manifestation of performance or production that is clearly at the upper end of the distribution in a talent domain even relative to that of other high-functioning individuals in that domain. Further, giftedness can be viewed as developmental, in that in the beginning stages, potential is the key variable; in later stages, achievement is the measure of giftedness; and in fully developed talents, eminence is the basis on which this label is granted."

—*Rena Subotnik, Paula Olszewski-Kubilius, and Frank Worrell, from "Rethinking Giftedness and Gifted Education: A Proposed Definition Based on Psychological Science" (2011)*

Write honestly what's on your mind. What do you know or believe to be true from your research and experiences? What do you know or believe on a gut level? What makes sense to you personally?

Even if you're feeling fairly comfortable with your perception of giftedness, your role as a teacher, and your relationship with the gifted students in your care, please don't skip this inventory. Your responses will help you prepare for the activities and strategies in the rest of this book.

What Other Gifted Educators Say

There are many views of giftedness, and even people who have studied the field for decades disagree on its definition. Here are a few examples showing the diversity of thought on the term "giftedness."

"Ask fifty people what is meant by giftedness and you will likely get fifty different definitions. Descriptions of giftedness also vary from one culture to another. For example, in a culture with no formal schooling, a skilled hunter might be the gifted one. Gifted abilities are more

"Sometimes it's easier to say what giftedness is not than what it is. My conceptualization of giftedness is changing all the time. The more I study and think about it, the more questions I ask, and the more I talk with people who know giftedness, the clearer it becomes. I used to think of giftedness as intelligence. Now I know that giftedness is more than intelligence. It's a way of being in the world. You can be smart and not be gifted. I think it's possible to have an IQ of 130 and not be gifted. I'm less sure about 145.

"Giftedness is a way of responding to what goes on around you and within you. There are affective as well as cognitive components. Some people say that giftedness is what you do. I say okay, but isn't who you are a big part of what you're capable of doing? I'm not sure you can separate the two. There seem to be common personality characteristics among people who achieve at very high levels, but you can have those personality characteristics and *not* achieve at very high levels, too. I'm saying that giftedness seems to require both—who you are and what you do. We do a lousy job in general education of paying attention to these psychosocial factors. There's too much emphasis on achievement without providing the psychological supports needed to get there. We tend to demand and abandon."
—*Maureen Neihart, Psy.D., National Institute of Education, Singapore*

"Men equate giftedness with achievement. After we tested his son, one dad said to us, 'He's only five. What could he have done in five years to be gifted?' Women, on the other hand, perceive giftedness as *developmental advancement*. If a mom sees that her daughter is asking names of objects at eleven months, and memorizing books at seventeen months . . . she gets very anxious. 'How will she *fit in* with the other children?' 'What will the teacher do with her if she's already reading in kindergarten?' Developing faster than other children makes a child vulnerable, and mothers are keenly aware of this vulnerability."
—*Dr. Linda Kreger Silverman, director, Gifted Development Center, Denver, CO*

What Does Giftedness Mean to Society?

An estimated three million children in the United States (or approximately 5.5 percent of the student population) are considered gifted. Of course, this figure varies widely depending on how individuals define giftedness and how students are identified.

Dueling Definitions

There is no one right, absolute, or generally accepted definition of giftedness. Instead, there are federal and state government definitions, school and district definitions, researchers' definitions, advocacy organizations' definitions, dictionary definitions, encyclopedia definitions, teachers' definitions, parents' definitions, students' definitions . . . and the list goes on. Here's a sampling of definitions currently in use, with our brief comments about each of them.

From *Encyclopedia Britannica Online*: [A gifted child is] any child who is naturally endowed with a high degree of general mental ability or extraordinary ability in a specific sphere of activity or knowledge. The designation of giftedness is largely a matter of administrative convenience. In most countries, the prevailing definition is an intelligence quotient (IQ) of 130 or above.

Authors' note: We appreciate the honesty here, calling the label of giftedness an "administrative convenience"—although there are probably those who see it more as an administrative *inconvenience*.

From the National Association for Gifted Children: Gifted individuals are those who demonstrate outstanding levels of aptitude (defined as exceptional ability to reason and learn) or competence (documented performance or achievement in top 10 percent or rarer) in one or more domains. Domains include any structured area of activity with its own symbol system (e.g., mathematics, music, language) and/or set of sensorimotor skills (e.g., painting, dance, sports).

Authors' note: The complete definition goes on for two more paragraphs. Its adoption by NAGC in 2010 created a maelstrom of controversy, as it was perceived by some as being both overly complex and focused too strongly on achievement.

From the U.S. Department of Education, *Marland Report* (1972): Gifted and talented children are those identified by professionally qualified persons who by virtue of outstanding abilities are capable of high performance. These are children who require differentiated educational programs and/or services beyond those normally provided by the regular school program in order to realize their contributions to self and society.

Children capable of high performance include those with demonstrated achievement and/or potential ability in any of the following areas:

1. General intellectual ability

2. Specific academic aptitude

3. Creative or productive thinking

4. Leadership ability

5. Visual and performing arts

6. Psychomotor ability

Authors' note: If your school or state has a published definition of giftedness, chances are it's based on this one.

From the *No Child Left Behind Act:* The term "gifted and talented," when used with respect to students, children, or youth, means students, children, or youth who give evidence of high achievement capability in areas such as intellectual, creative, artistic, or leadership capacity, or in specific academic fields, and who need services or activities not ordinarily provided by the school in order to fully develop those capabilities.

Authors' note: This is a less clunky federal U.S. definition than the one from the *Marland Report*.

From the State of Alaska: Gifted means exhibiting outstanding intellect, ability, or creative talent.

From the State of Nebraska: "Learner with high ability" means a student who gives evidence of high performance capability in such areas as intellectual, creative, or artistic capacity or in specific academic fields and who requires accelerated or differentiated curriculum programs in order to develop those capabilities fully.

Authors' note: Alaska's brevity distills giftedness down to its core elements, while Nebraska's eliminates the term "gifted" altogether in favor of the more school-based (or palatable) term "learner with high ability." But Nebraska's definition adds an important caveat: it states that highly able learners *require* special services to have their unique needs addressed. That's a key addition. (Three states—New Hampshire, Massachusetts, and South Dakota—have no definition of giftedness at all.)

From respected experts on giftedness: The following teachers, researchers, and others in the know about giftedness offer their own range of definitions.

Lewis Terman (1925): The top 1 percent level in general intelligence ability as measured by the Stanford-Binet Intelligence Scale or a comparable instrument.

Dr. Paul Witty (1940): There are children whose outstanding potentialities in art, in writing, or in social leadership can be recognized largely by their performance. Hence, we have recommended that the definition of giftedness be expanded and that we consider any child gifted whose performance in a potentially valuable line of human activity is consistently remarkable.

Dr. Joseph Renzulli (1978): Giftedness consists of an interaction among three basic clusters of human traits—these clusters being above average general abilities, high levels of task commitment, and high levels of creativity.

Dr. Francois Gagné (2003): Giftedness designates the possession and use of untrained and spontaneously expressed natural abilities (called aptitudes or gifts), in at least one ability domain, to a degree that places an individual among the top 10 percent of age peers. Talent designates the superior mastery of systematically developed abilities (or skills) and places an individual within the top 10 percent of age peers who are (or have been) active in that field.

Authors' note: Notice how we go from giftedness being the top 1 percent in 1925 to the top 10 percent in 2003. Witty's and Renzulli's definitions expand the pool of gifted candidates even further. No wonder people get so confused when asked to define a gifted child!

Annemarie Roeper (1982): Giftedness is a greater awareness, a greater sensitivity, and a greater ability to understand and transform perceptions into intellectual and emotional experiences.

The Columbus Group (1991): Giftedness is asynchronous development in which cognitive abilities and heightened intensity combine to create experiences and awareness that are qualitatively different from the norm. This asynchrony increases with higher intellectual

capacity. The uniqueness of the gifted renders them particularly vulnerable and requires modifications in parenting, teaching, and counseling in order to develop optimally.

Authors' note: The latter two definitions focus on a different view of giftedness: it is not *something you do* at an outstanding level of accomplishment, but rather *someone you are* as an intellectual and emotionally intense human being.

These dueling definitions make for very confusing conversations among advocates for the gifted, for it appears that even the domain experts can't agree on who should be identified, and hence served, in gifted programs.

We suggest that the main problem with any definition isn't what it says, but how it's used. When we use definitions of giftedness to develop criteria for identifying students who need more challenging educational opportunities, that's fine. When we use them to include people who really shouldn't be included, or exclude people who really shouldn't be excluded, that's not fine.

We're not sure that a universal definition of giftedness will ever be adopted. In fact, there are some who believe that we should follow the lead of South Dakota and not define giftedness at all. But as *Encyclopedia Britannica* points out, we often need labels like giftedness for administrative convenience. So, do definitions matter?

Do Definitions Matter?

Why do we need to define giftedness? Because in many schools, a definition serves as a foundation for developing and funding an appropriate educational program for gifted children. No definition, no program.

Many Ways to Be Gifted

Some experts speak about five "categories" of gifted children. There are those with **general intellectual ability**—in other words, they're smart at almost everything. These kids are quick learners who enjoy difficult problems and new ideas. Then there are those with **specific academic aptitude**, meaning they're exceptional in a particular subject or field. They tend to be well-read in the subjects that interest them and are typically motivated and self-directed. Other gifted kids shine in **creative or productive thinking**. These students are usually innovative learners and independent thinkers who don't mind standing apart from the crowd and who enjoy creative tasks. Some gifted kids **excel in leadership**. They are usually responsible, confident decision-makers, and are usually held in high esteem by their peers. Lastly, the gifts of some learners come out in the **visual or performing arts**. These students are expressive and artistically inclined, and tend to be discerning observers of artworks and performances.

By listing and describing certain abilities and talents, a definition helps teachers identify children who would benefit from a gifted program. That's why it's important for a definition to be broad yet specific, inclusive yet focused on particular qualities that set some children apart from their age peers and indicate the need for different types of educational opportunities.

Is your school working on a definition of giftedness? Is it reconsidering or revising an existing definition? If you're involved in this process, you might contribute the following suggestions from the ERIC Clearinghouse on Disabilities and Gifted Education:[2]

■ The concept of giftedness is not limited to high intellectual ability. It also comprises creativity, ability in specific academic areas, ability in visual or performing arts, social adeptness, and physical dexterity.

■ A program for gifted children should be based on the way in which the school system operationally defines giftedness. A definition should be the basis of decision regarding the selection of identification procedures as well as the provision of educational services for gifted children.

■ Definitions of giftedness are influenced by social, political, economic, and cultural factors.

■ Giftedness is found among all groups, including females and males, minorities, individuals with disabilities, persons with limited English-speaking proficiency, and migrants.

> "A person who is gifted sees the essential point and leaves the rest as surplus."
>
> —**Thomas Carlyle, historian and essayist**

Create Your Own Definition

You've taken our "Teacher Inventory." You've read many definitions of giftedness. Maybe you've worked with (or are working with) your school to create or improve its definition of giftedness. Now we suggest that you create your own personal definition.

Look around your classroom and consider your students. Not just the ones who have been identified as gifted or selected for the gifted program, but *all* of your students. Pay special attention to the following:

Girls. Many girls have learned to cover up or deny their abilities in order to be popular, fit in, or feel "normal." This is especially true in middle school/junior high.

Boys. Boys are more likely than girls to rebel and question authority. Also, boys are on a different developmental schedule than girls. In general, they mature more slowly, particularly in the verbal and reading areas. They may be designated hyperactive, distractible, or disorderly. Add to this the fact that most elementary school teachers are women who tend to value conformity and obedience, and you can probably see the need to look again at the "difficult" boys in your class.

Students with disabilities. Physical, emotional, or learning disabilities (we prefer the term "learning differences") may hinder students' capacity to demonstrate their giftedness in accepted, recognizable ways. The traditional methods used to identify gifted kids would have excluded, for example, people like Agatha Christie, Tom Cruise, and Cher, all of whom had or have dyslexia.

Gifted people with disabilities have been called an "unseen minority." Researcher Nicholas Colangelo has observed that when teacher and parent groups are asked to imagine a "gifted child," they rarely picture a gifted child with disabilities.

Students with behavioral challenges. Some teachers and administrators associate "good" behavior with being gifted and "bad" behavior with being unwilling or unable to learn. Look beyond these stereotypes to find the students whose acting out may be the direct result of boredom or frustration.

Students from minority or nonmainstream groups. Their gifts may not be measurable by standard IQ and achievement tests, which are often biased to majority (white middle- to upper-class) students. Also, their gifts may lie in areas that are not celebrated or valued by the mainstream society.

Even when minority students are identified for inclusion in gifted programs, they may not succeed. Their behavior may not fit with the teacher's beliefs about what giftedness means or how gifted students should behave.

Native American children are taught to value interdependence, not independence; in their culture, decisions are made collectively. Puerto Rican children learn to seek the advice of their family rather than act independently. Mexican-American children are taught to respect their elders, the law, and authority, not individual competition, initiative, and self-direction. African-American students may have mixed feelings about academic success. High-achieving black students may be accused of "acting white."

These are only a few examples of why minority students are often not identified for gifted programs—and why those who are may end up being mistaught, feeling frustrated, and either dropping out of the program or being asked to leave.

Students who perform poorly on tests. Some gifted kids aren't good test-takers. They may know the material backward and forward, but they find the test situation too stressful to perform at their best. Or they may have personal circumstances that prevent them from concentrating—for example, an empty belly or strife at home. Since test scores are one of the main methods used to identify gifted students, these situations clearly put them at a disadvantage.

Borderline cases. No matter what method(s) we use to identify and select gifted students, and regardless of how hard we try to be fair and inclusive, there are always some kids who fall through the cracks. If a student goes through your core curriculum faster than anyone else in the class; if he or she engages you in a conversation you don't have with most other students that age; if you think you recognize something special about him or her—a spark, a talent, raw potential—pay attention.

Is Everyone *Really* Gifted?

Of course, one way around the difficult decisions regarding the definition and identification of giftedness is to state—as

Giftedness in Brief

by Susan Winebrenner, M.S., consultant and author

People often ask for a short list of common characteristics of gifted children. Students who possess most or all of the following five characteristics may be gifted and may benefit from differentiated instruction and compacted curriculum.

1. They learn new material faster, and at an earlier age, than age peers.

2. They remember what they have learned for a very long time, making review unnecessary.

3. They are able to deal with concepts that are too complex and abstract for their age peers.

4. They have a passionate interest in one or more topics, and would spend all available time learning more about those topics if they could.

5. They do not need to watch the teacher to hear and understand what is being said, and they can process more than one task at a time.

When you observe students consistently exhibiting many of these behaviors, the possibility that they are gifted is very strong.

From *Teaching Gifted Kids in Today's Classroom: Strategies and Techniques Every Teacher Can Use* by Susan Winebrenner, M.S., with Dina Brulles, Ph.D. Minneapolis: Free Spirit Publishing, 2012), page 12. Used with permission.

many have—that "all children are gifted." This sounds like an idea that fits our culture's democratic ideals that anyone is capable of becoming whatever he or she works hard to become. People who believe it will tell you that IQ is less important than "I can." This all sounds well and good, until you realize the inherent absurdity in the notion that everyone could be *anything* when it comes to human development. If you believe that everyone is gifted, then logically you would also have to believe that everyone has a disability, everyone is musical, everyone is athletic, everyone is empathetic, and so on. To make giftedness a universal quality in people does a disservice to those children and adults who really do differ from their age peers in some recognizable intellectual and emotional ways.

One of the reasons that this "everyone is gifted" myth has circled our field for so long can be attributed to Harvard University researcher Howard Gardner, whose work in the 1980s on "multiple intelligences" (known as "MI") was interpreted by many to mean that giftedness was within reach of everyone. The idea was that you could be highly intelligent in a linguistic or mathematical sense, or your interpersonal or naturalistic intelligence could be off the charts. So if schools were simply designed to address each of these multiple intelligences, there would be no need for separate gifted programs. Granted, this is a misinterpretation of Gardner's work. Nevertheless, the juggernaut of MI was too strong for many school administrators to resist. As a result, some schools transformed themselves into "MI schools," with specific lessons developed to teach to one or more of the eight intelligences identified by Gardner.

There were several problems with applying the MI theory directly in classrooms. First, Gardner is a psychologist, not a classroom teacher, and he proposed his work as a *theory*, not a set of lesson plans. Second, where is the evidence that if I have a linguistic gift, that writing out my math facts will help me recall what nine times nine is? And third, educators were so entranced by the possibilities in MI that classroom practices were sometimes implemented without much forethought.

One of Gardner's loudest critics, Christopher Ferguson, contends that the MI theory is based more on philosophy than data. He also contends that plain old general intelligence still holds an important place in the development of children's minds. One of his quotes about the theory is especially incisive (and humorous): "Many people like to think that any child, with the proper nurturance, can blossom into some kind of academic oak tree, tall and proud. It's just not so. Multiple intelligences provides a kind of cover to preserve that fable. 'Okay, little Jimmie may not be a rocket scientist, but he can dance really well. Shouldn't that count equally in school and life?' No. The great dancers of the

Pleistocene era foxtrotted their way into the stomach of a saber-toothed tiger."[3]

MI theory gained traction because it was easy to understand and convenient to implement. It just also happened to be the wrong way to serve gifted children well.

Other Kinds of Intelligence

Are you ready for even more possibilities about what constitutes intelligence and giftedness? Here are some other ideas. Yale psychology professor Robert Sternberg has defined three types of intelligence. They are:

Contextual intelligence: the one you use when you adapt to your environment, change your environment, or choose a different environment that better suits your needs.

Experiential intelligence: the one you use whenever you build on your experience to solve problems in new situations.

Internal intelligence: the one you use to approach a problem, then evaluate the feedback to decide if you should change your approach.

Then there's **emotional intelligence,** which gained national attention when Harvard Ph.D. Daniel Goleman wrote a book about it in 1995. Goleman identified several qualities that add up to "a different way of being smart," including self-awareness, impulse control, persistence, zeal, self-motivation, empathy, and social deftness.

There's also **emotional giftedness.** This term was coined by Michael Piechowski, a former professor of education and psychology at Northland College in Ashland, Wisconsin, who studied and translated the work of Polish psychiatrist Kazimierz Dabrowski (1902–1980). When

Dabrowski studied a group of gifted children, he discovered that they displayed something he called "overexcitabilities." They perceived things more intensely and thought about them more deeply than their age peers. They lived life to the fullest and experienced emotional highs and lows, joys and sorrows to extreme degrees. They were extraordinarily, exquisitely sensitive to everything around them. Today, overexcitability—OE—is one of the signs of giftedness some teachers consistently look for.

Chapter 2 provides more ideas and suggestions for creating your own definition of giftedness.

Mixed Messages

We reward our gifted athletes with pep rallies, scholarships, and multimillion-dollar contracts and endorsements. We reward our gifted musicians with Grammys and our gifted actors with Oscars. What do we do for our intellectually and academically gifted students? We send them mixed messages.

It's good to be smart . . . as long as you're not *too* smart. *Too* smart makes you a nerd, an egghead, and a teacher-pleaser. It can even make you a target for suspicion, resentment, and open hostility. It's good to get high grades . . . as long as you

Gifted Kids Speak Out

"I'm kind of scared the word will get out (about my being gifted). I would like it to be kept a secret."
—**Basia, 10**

"When I met other family members, their first comment would be, 'So, this is the genius?'"
—**Adam, 15**

"It's okay to be called gifted. You get used to a lot of other worse names."
—**Mei, 10**

"Sometimes when I'm trying to fit in and have fun, I don't want to show people my differences. I don't push the fact that I'm gifted in other people's faces. That would just turn them off. I usually appear the same as them and wait for them to discover on their own that I might have a gift."
—**Ebony, 14**

"If an adult says that I'm gifted it feels fine. If it's a kid, it's different."
—**Suresh, 8**

don't talk about them. That's bragging, and besides, you might injure someone else's self-esteem. It's good to score high on tests . . . as long as you keep this fact to yourself, or within your small circle of similarly brainy friends.

We know that children are profoundly influenced by what they see on television, in the movies, and online. How are gifted children often portrayed? As solitary loners, loyal sidekicks, social misfits, outcasts, misunderstood rebels, geeks, weaklings, and geniuses in hiding, waiting to be discovered and saved from themselves.

Researchers Tracy L. Cross and Larry J. Coleman have studied the lives of gifted students in school since the mid-1980s. Their many published articles—including "Is Being Gifted a Social Handicap?" and "The Social Cognition of Gifted Adolescents in School: Managing the Stigma of Giftedness"—reveal a troubled and troubling world. One gifted adolescent Cross interviewed "perceived that gifted students are physically weak, socially inadequate, and not interesting

people. They are out of touch, unattractive, and have a high propensity for mental problems. While the student knew that many of these descriptors did not fit him, he had come to believe that to be gifted was somewhat limiting."[4]

In our own interviews and surveys with gifted children, many said that neither their parents nor their teachers talk much about giftedness. Many kids concluded that it was something secretive and therefore bad, which increased their fears of being different. We suspect that virtually all highly gifted kids know they are different by the time they are five or six years old. This awareness of difference can turn into feelings of being strange or "weird" if the differences are not acknowledged and appreciated.

Every gifted person we've ever taught, interviewed, talked with, worked with, or lived with admits to enjoying the benefits of being intelligent—knowing how to think deeply, think creatively, feel intensely, understand complex concepts, explore a variety of interests, make connections that others don't see, solve problems, come up with unique ideas, and so on. It's the mixed messages and skewed perceptions of giftedness that can make the label more of a burden than a blessing. It's the insensitive, uninformed comments from teachers, peers, and/or parents that make some gifted kids want to downplay, deny, or hide their giftedness.

Cross tells the story of a reporter for the *Chicago Tribune* who interviewed her about Theodore Kaczynski, the "Unabomber":[5]

The reporter had worked for weeks putting together a story about Kaczynski's history that emphasized the fact that he was a gifted student. Several leaders in the field of gifted education were interviewed. The reporter asked me, "Did Ted Kaczynski commit murder because he was allowed to skip two grades in school?" What an amazing assumption! Does accelerating gifted students cause them to become serial killers? My response was, "I hope not, because tens of thousands of students are grade-skipped each year." I was stunned to learn that such learned people could hold such foolish (and dangerous) misconceptions. Imagine what messages are sent to gifted students by less well-educated or academically oriented people. Also imagine how gifted students are actually treated if large numbers of adults, including well-educated adults, hold such wild misconceptions about them.

The Myth of Elitism

"Gifted education is elitist." We've heard this a million times (granted, that's probably a *slight* exaggeration), and chances are you have, too.

Ours is an allegedly egalitarian society. We're supposed to give all children the same opportunities to learn, grow, and realize their potential. We're not supposed to give some children special, better, extra opportunities. *That's not fair.*

In fact, gifted education is elitist only if that is the attitude of the staff. A quality program promotes a positive attitude about self-worth regardless of ability. And, as psychologist and giftedness expert Linda Kreger Silverman notes, "Contrary to popular public opinion, when the gifted are placed in classes together, they do not come to the conclusion that they are 'better than everyone else.' Rather, they are humbled by finding peers who know more than they do."[6]

Gifted children should not be asked to sacrifice an appropriate education to the needs of other children. If we make adjustments and provide for students who are having trouble performing to grade-level standards—which we do—then it stands to reason we should also accommodate those students whose abilities and knowledge exceed what's being taught in the regular classroom, and whose performance regularly surpasses those standards. As Thomas Jefferson noted, "there is nothing more unequal than the equal treatment of unequal people."

Yet the battle over elitism rages. One director of elementary education in a town in Massachusetts said, "I wouldn't want a gifted and talented program [here]. That's elitist. I think the very term 'gifted and talented' is elitist. I think that all children have different gifts and we should be trying to provide for them."[7] In contrast, an elementary school principal from Pennsylvania named Mr. Paluzzi grew tired of his school board's complaints that the school's gifted program was elitist—in fact, he believed it was not elitist enough!

Paluzzi then went on to detail how the gifted program should be modified:

1. There should be a statewide search for a teacher who has been involved in gifted programs while in school.

2. Once hired, this teacher will receive a salary supplement.

3. Additional teachers should then be hired to work with children who show a high level of promise.

4. Students will not qualify automatically for the gifted program; they will have to try out to gain entrance. If accepted, they will be allowed to work with other gifted students based on their level of competency, not their age.

5. Teachers will have the option of offering these students supplemental instruction after school, on weekends, and during school breaks.

6. School assemblies will be scheduled frequently so these gifted students can demonstrate their skills and discuss their dreams with the other students.

7. Community support for the gifted program will be enhanced by regularly reporting on the students' progress in newspaper articles.

8. Each gifted student will be outfitted with a jacket emblazoned with a large "G" so that everyone will know they are in the gifted program.

When the school board members heard of this plan, they grew even more enraged at how elitist it was. Then Mr. Paluzzi pointed out that they already had this program in place—through the district-sponsored football, baseball, and basketball teams.[8]

This just goes to show that elitism isn't such a bad thing after all, as it promotes a sense of excellence and pride sadly missing from many a school's day-to-day functioning.

Even schools that do have substantial gifted programs sometimes seem reluctant to acknowledge or promote them. They worry about the kids who aren't labeled "gifted," and they try to minimize the potential for bad feelings by calling their programs Quest or Explorer Clubs, SEARCH, SAGE, STAR, PEAK, REACH, or GATE, to give a few examples. Instead of "gifted students," these schools have "high flyers" or "high potentials." Other schools open up their gifted classes to all students capable of maintaining a B average; these students are given less threatening labels like "bright" or "high achievers."

As teachers, we've all met some overeager parents who lobby to get their children into the school's gifted program. In contrast, there are parents who feel unsettled by their kids' gifted status and would rather keep it quiet. Some children have refused to join a gifted program because they don't want the stigma or the threat of heavy new expectations. Some parents occasionally say, "I just wish my child was normal!"

What these wide discrepancies in attitude and behavior point to are the conflicts which come with thinking about a perhaps innately threatening concept: superior ability. Perhaps these conflicts arise because society is too quick to jump to the conclusion that superior intelligence, talent, or ability means superior *people*, which implies that the rest of humanity is inferior.

As a democratic society, we are still coming to terms with unequal distribution of "gifts" and "unfair" loadings of potential. "If 'superior' people get 'special' attention," the critics ask, "isn't that giving them unfair advantage?" Doesn't the existence of gifted education acknowledge that individual students do not have equal chances to get a piece of the pie?

As an educational community, we are still very much in the process of defining giftedness, of measuring it, and of accepting the gifted student as a legitimate target for differentiated instruction. Part of the challenge of gifted education stems from working in a young discipline still busy discovering its necessary "truths" and appropriate methods of practice. As Neil Daniel wrote in 1985, "The simple truth is ... we don't know what intelligence is. We are unable to define giftedness. And we can't say, really, how anybody thinks." A generation after Daniel penned this observation, his thoughts still ring true.[9]

Meanwhile, gifted students keep turning up in our classrooms, their eyes sparkling with eagerness and challenge, their worries pouring out—or being locked up within. And highly gifted but underachieving students continue to drop out of school—if not physically, then mentally and emotionally. In some tragic instances, our brightest young adults commit suicide or turn to the destructive, self-numbing forces of drugs or alcohol. These gifted students have a right to an education designed for their levels of ability, which is what *every* student in our schools deserves. With few exceptions, as gifted as some of our students may be,

they cannot and do not find their way on their own.

More Myths and Misconceptions

"Gifted education is elitist" is just one of several myths and misconceptions about giftedness. Noted gifted advocate Carolyn Coil has a few more that she'd like to dispel.[10]

Myth #1: Intelligence is inherited and does not change. Gifted students, therefore, do not need any special services.

Truth: All of us do inherit certain traits, intelligences, and talents. But these need to be developed and nurtured throughout life for them to grow and reach their full potential. For example, a flower inherits certain traits, but if it is not watered and fed and if it does not get the right amount of sunlight, it will not develop as it could. The same is true for gifted children.

Myth #2: Giftedness can be easily measured by intelligence tests and tests of achievement.

Truth: Giftedness is difficult to measure. This is why schools and school districts try so many different ways to identify gifted students. Tests are often culturally biased and may reflect ethnicity, socioeconomic status, exposure, and experiences rather than true giftedness. Other children may simply not be good at taking tests. They may not score well on standardized tests but may be gifted, especially in creative and productive thinking.

Myth #3: There is no need to identify gifted students in the early grades.

Truth: Many school districts do not begin identifying gifted and talented students until third grade. There is a belief among some educators that giftedness cannot be properly identified in the early grades. However, the *National Association for Gifted Children* programming standards start with prekindergarten. The group's early childhood network position paper says that "providing engaging, responsive learning environments . . . benefits all children, including young gifted children."

Myth #4: Gifted students read all the time, wear glasses, and/or are physically and socially awkward.

Truth: From Jason, the cartoon character in the *Foxtrot* comic strip, to Sheldon on the TV show *The Big Bang Theory*, we can see this stereotype in action. But like all other kids, gifted children come in many varieties. Some are successful in sports or music, and some are physically attractive. Some have many friends, while others have only a few. Some are extreme extroverts, while others are introverts. There is no one type of person or personality we can pinpoint as gifted.

Myth #5: Gifted kids are (or should be) well-behaved model students who get good grades.

Truth: Some gifted children are model students. They are compliant, follow directions, never misbehave, and make straight A's. But many others challenge teachers, do their own thing instead of the assigned work, procrastinate until the last minute, get low grades, are disorganized, and have poor study skills.

Myth #6: Gifted students work up to their potential.

Truth: Most schools have their share of gifted underachievers. These students have the potential for excellence but, for a variety of reasons, do not fulfill that potential. Gifted underachievers may decide they will only do the minimum requirements and choose the easy work instead of the more challenging tasks. They often lack study and organizational skills because in the early grades they don't need to develop them. Some get discouraged when the work doesn't come easily, and others don't want to achieve because it isn't "cool."

Myth #7: Teaching gifted students is easy.

Truth: Some believe that a good teacher can easily teach any student. If this were the case, good teaching with no special training would be all that is needed to teach gifted students. However, good teachers add to their skills and learn new strategies and techniques targeted particularly to meeting the needs of the gifted. Most teachers of the gifted claim it is the most challenging, most exhausting, and most rewarding teaching they have ever done.

Myth #8: Gifted students will get by on their own without any special help from the school.

Truth: Some people claim that gifted students often come from well-to-do families who should be able to meet their children's special needs outside of school. Others assert that the expense of providing gifted programs cannot be justified. In general, the assumption is that gifted students will succeed regardless of the quality of the education they receive. In truth, gifted students come from a wide variety of family circumstances, including differing levels of parental support and involvement. Like all children, they rely on their school to meet their educational needs and also, in part, to help guide their social and emotional growth.

Myth #9: It benefits everyone to have gifted students teach the material they already know to other kids.

Truth: This is faulty logic. It assumes that teaching other kids, let alone struggling students, is something gifted kids innately know how or want to do. Most gifted students do not know how to tutor others. They often are frustrated that struggling students don't understand what they perceive as easy. Requiring gifted students to be peer tutors also takes away time they should be using for more advanced work, more rigor, and higher-level thinking.

Myth #10: All children are gifted.

Truth: All children have distinctive and unique qualities that make them valuable. However, as discussed earlier, this does not mean that all children are gifted. Identifying some students as gifted simply means they have needs that are different from those of most others at their age and grade level. All gifted students need programs and services to ensure their growth and prevent the loss of their advanced abilities. Gifted students learn at a rate and range that is significantly different from the norm.

What About the Label?

That "gifted" is a controversial label you know well enough, probably through personal experience. Think back to your first introduction to the term. What did you assume it meant? Think back to your first parent or staff meeting on the topic of gifted education. Can you remember what people's reactions were?

One mother we know had a 5-year-old child who scored above 150 on the Stanford-Binet Intelligence Scale. Both she and the school had suspected that the boy was gifted. When she called her relatives to tell them the news, their response was, "Oh, boy, I bet you're going to have trouble with him now!" Compare this reaction to telling a friend that you had just inherited a million dollars or won the lottery. Imagine your friend saying, "Oh, boy, I bet you'll have to pay a lot of taxes on that load!" How likely is that?

"In general, I don't tell many people," this mother said. "I get the feeling they'd be a whole lot more supportive if I said my son had a learning disability."

The language people use to describe gifted students indicates how comfortable they are with the concept of exceptional intellect or talent. For some reason, it's easier for society to name, praise, and financially reward the outstanding athlete or entertainer than the brilliant mathematician or poet. The teasing that "brainy kids" endure in junior and senior high school contrasts sharply with the celebration that "jocks" enjoy.

To some people, giftedness suggests elitism in the racial or class sense. They assume that kids selected for gifted programs are well behaved, upper-middle-class, and white. They fear that the inherent cliquishness of ability grouping will invite the "good test-takers" to assume the mantle of moral and intellectual superiority. Both of these concerns are probably true in what we fervently hope are isolated occurrences. Whenever gifted programs do drift toward biased selection processes, or confer undue privilege on certain students, they do real damage to the credibility of gifted education. Nonetheless, it's important to realize that resentments inevitably come with the selection process itself. By identifying one group as gifted, does that make all other children "ungifted"? Aren't we all equal, and all special? Well, yes, but . . .

Parents whose children are not selected for the program may question whether gifted students are getting *different kinds* of instruction, or whether they're simply getting *better* instruction. Wouldn't gifted education programs benefit the average child, too? These parents worry that student performance in "regular" classrooms will go down once the top-level students are pulled out. In

fact, the opposite is true. Able children may suddenly find themselves blossoming without the presence of clearly advanced students. It's as though the way has been cleared for them to perform at higher levels.

Disagreement over the term extends to education professionals as well. Some experts promote more generalized labels and advise against calling any group of students "the gifted." They recommend that schools broaden their assessment processes by testing all students and relaxing cut-off scores. They favor "throwing a wide net in early childhood and later allowing the educational programming to select those students with unusual talent and motivation."[11] Others believe that to water down the definition is to lose whatever momentum the movement has gained; the end result would (again) be inadequate education for children at the highest levels of ability.

> "Some degree of 'labeling' is essential if gifted children are to grow up understanding how and why they experience the world differently from others."
> —**Draper Kauffman**

Like it or not, the label "gifted" is here today, and we need to get used to it. In our view, all labels are equally bad, and calling kids "high flyers" as opposed to "gifted" fools no one and imparts a sense of secrecy (shame? false modesty?) as well. Intelligence is a good thing. So is athletic ability. We don't go out of our way to call the football team something other than the football team, or the marching band anything other than the marching band. Why must we call our brightest

Gifted Teachers (and Kids) Speak Out

When we piloted our "Teacher Inventory" on gifted education teachers, we asked them whether or not they use the label "gifted." Here are some of the responses we received:

- "I use it because it is good to get it into the vocabulary and to become used to it. It shouldn't be a word to avoid."

- "I try not to use it because it is so misunderstood and misused."

- "I haven't felt qualified to use this label."

- "A gift is something you've been given and you shouldn't have to apologize for that."

- "It is appropriate, although it often means different things to each person hearing it."

- "I do not use it all the time because of the problems it creates for kids. I do use it in specific sessions to help them know how to deal with the label."

- "I use it for lack of anything better, but I don't like labeling any student, whether they are slow or advanced. Teachers do need to categorize students, but I don't think students need to hear the labels we place on them."

- "What's wrong with the word 'gifted'? Everyone knows what it means."

When we asked kids how they feel about being called "gifted," here's what they said:

- "It depends on how it is being used. If someone is giving me a compliment, I like it. But if someone is making fun of me, I don't."

- "Sometimes I don't like it because it makes me feel different."

- "I feel proud."

- "I don't like being called gifted that much. I just like being called my regular name."

- "I feel great, but I don't like to show it."

- "I feel happy because my parents are proud of me, but other times I feel embarrassed."

students something other than bright, talented, or gifted? Parents who try to protect their child from the label may end up doing more harm than good. Kids will hear the label anyway, yet have no skills for making sense of it.

One teacher commented, "I don't think any of us in the field can give up the term [gifted] because we've finally been able to get it accepted and recognized on a national level." This is an important point, because designing curriculum to serve newly identified needs or populations is definitely a political act. As another teacher said, "Politics is right up there next to direct service. You're constantly involved with politics." And a political movement or group cannot survive without a name.

How students feel about their abilities and the label "gifted" (or whatever group name is used) will depend a great deal on how their parents and teachers feel about them, and how parents and teachers use the term. Therefore, assessing your own attitudes about giftedness is critical.

What Does Giftedness Mean to Kids?

When you ask a dozen gifted kids what giftedness means to them, you're likely to get a dozen (or more) different answers. Some won't want to talk about it. Some will toss a succinct phrase or two your way. And some will go into detail because giftedness—being gifted—is at the core of who they are. It affects their school experience, their relationships with friends, families, and teachers, their self-esteem, their future plans, their expectations, their goals, and almost everything else about their lives.

If you want to know what your gifted students think about giftedness—and themselves and their lives—invite them to complete the "Student Questionnaire" on pages 37–43. The purpose of the questionnaire is twofold:

1. It will give you a reading on how your students feel about themselves and others, on what they think being gifted and being in a gifted class means, and how seriously affected they are by problems known to surface among gifted students.

2. It will stimulate kids to think about these conflicts, their areas of strength and need, and their feelings.

The questionnaire is a good first strategy for discussing these issues because students have the option to remain anonymous. As such, it won't give you answers from specific individuals (although some students may choose to give their names, and you may know the identities of others by their answers). It *will* give you overall insight into the following:

1. Why do students think they are in your class?

2. What do students think the class is all about?

3. What do students think gifted (or whatever label is used) means?

4. In what ways do students feel different from most other peers?

5. In what ways do students feel the same?

6. What emotional issues and challenges do they have in their lives right now?

7. Who are the people in their support systems?

8. What do they do to feel good about themselves?

The questionnaire is designed for all gifted and talented students, but you may wish to modify it in some way for your students. Younger children may need a shortened form and slightly different lists under certain items. Older students may need differently worded instructions.

We've found that the more time we spend introducing the questionnaire and our purposes, the better data we receive. High school students in our pilot group took about fifteen minutes to complete the survey, junior high students slightly longer.

We suggest that you *don't* assign the questionnaire as homework (you won't get many back), and that you *don't* give

Students Surveyed on School Engagement

The results of the 2010 High School Survey of Student Engagement by the Center for Evaluation and Educational Policy in Bloomington, Indiana, which surveyed 43,000 students in twenty-seven states, found many intriguing results, including these:

■ 66 percent of respondents reported being bored in school every day.

■ 81 percent attributed the boredom to "uninteresting material."

■ 33 percent reported finding "no challenge" in school.

■ 63 percent reported having to work hard in either "none" or "one or two" of their classes.

■ 35 percent reported having no meaningful interactions with their teachers.

In 2012, when the Center for American Progress examined three years of data from the U.S. Department of Education's "National Assessment of Educational Progress" (NAEP), they found the following:

■ 37 percent of fourth graders stated math was "often" or "always" easy.

■ 57 percent of eighth graders reported history classes were "often" or "always" easy.

■ 38 percent of twelfth graders reported that they "rarely" wrote about what they had read in class.

These data come from the general population of students. Imagine if the respondents were identified gifted students? The picture would likely be even bleaker.

students only five minutes at the end of the day to complete it. Rather, we recommend using this tool as a learning activity and allowing students ample time to fill it out. You might have your students complete the questionnaire at the beginning and the end of the year for comparison, or use a variation as a course or program evaluation form.

Section D of the questionnaire asks students to indicate how often they experience a series of feelings or problems. These feelings or problems are common among gifted kids, as indicated by our own surveys. In fact, they're so common that we call them the "Great Gripes of Gifted Kids." In Chapter 7: The Eight Great Gripes of Gifted Kids, you'll find in-depth discussions of all eight topics that you can use with your students.

Teacher Inventory

1. Personally, I think giftedness means _____
   _____
   _____
   _____

2. I do/do not use the "gifted" label because _____
   _____
   _____
   _____

3. I appreciate and value my gifted students in these ways: _____
   _____
   _____
   _____

4. I'm different from my gifted students in these ways: _____
   _____
   _____
   _____

5. When I tell other people that I work with gifted students, I feel . . .
   (Check all that apply, and/or add your own descriptions.)

   _____ Proud   _____ Compelled to explain/justify what I do

   _____ Embarrassed   _____ Eager to talk about it

   _____ Guilty   _____ Nothing in particular

   _____ _____   _____ _____

   _____ _____   _____ _____

   →

Teacher Inventory, continued

6. To minimize any hard feelings between students in my gifted class/group and their

   peers (or between my class and other classes), I try to _____

   _____

   _____

   _____

7. When I think about my gifted students,

they seem *similar to* other children their age in these ways:	they seem *different from* other children their age in these ways:
_____	_____
_____	_____
_____	_____
_____	_____

8. This is what I expect of my gifted students as a group and individually:

   _____

   _____

   _____

9. The gifted kids I have the easiest time with are those who are: _____

   _____

   _____

   _____

   or do: _____

   _____

   or are good at: _____

   _____

→

Teacher Inventory, continued

10. The gifted kids I have the most challenging time with are those who are: _____

_____

_____

_____

or do: _____

_____

or lack skills in: _____

_____

11. When I can't answer a student's question, or I feel that I'm "losing control" of the

class, these are the things I do: _____

_____

_____

_____

12. The best thing(s) I have to offer my gifted students is/are my: _____

_____

_____

_____

_____

13. I think I could improve my teaching by: _____

_____

_____

_____

_____

→

Teacher Inventory, continued

14. I think that we, as an education community, need to change or improve gifted education programs in the following ways: _____

_____

_____

_____

_____

15. One thing I'd like to change or do differently in the gifted program at my school is:

_____

_____

_____

_____

Student Questionnaire

This questionnaire is about you. I'd like you to fill it out so I can be a better teacher for you and this class. There are no right or wrong answers. The most important thing is for you to think honestly about the questions. You may remain anonymous if you wish, and you may choose to skip some of the questions. But I hope you'll try answering them all—you'll get more out of the questionnaire if you do. All answers will be kept strictly confidential, although we'll talk about some of the questions later on as a group.

A. Basic Information

Your age: _____

Your gender *(circle one):*   M   F

The number of years you've spent in a gifted class or program (circle one):

0   1   2   3   4   5   6   more

B. Questions You May Already Be Asking Yourself

1. What does "gifted" mean to you? _____

   _____

   _____

   _____

   _____

2. How do you feel about the "gifted" label? _____

   _____

   _____

   _____

   _____

→

Student Questionnaire, continued

3. How were you selected for this class or program? _____
_____
_____
_____

4. How do you feel about the selection process? _____
_____
_____
_____

5. What do you think the purpose of this class/program is? *(Check all that apply. Add your own ideas, if you want.)*

_____ I don't know   _____ Harder work than other classes

_____ More work than other classes   _____ More challenging or interesting work

_____ Friendships with people like me _____ Place where I'm not considered weird

_____ Place to have fun   _____ Be stimulated to try new things

_____ Learn something new   _____ Nothing different from other classes

_____ _____   _____ _____

_____ _____   _____ _____

C. Feelings About Yourself

6. In what ways are you the same as most other kids your age? What things do you have in common? _____

_____
_____
_____

Student Questionnaire, continued

7. In what ways are you different from most other kids your age? What makes you unique?

_____

_____

_____

8. In terms of your popularity . . . *(check one)*:

_____ I have tons of close friends and am liked by almost everybody.

_____ I have a lot of close friends.

_____ I have several (four or five) close friends.

_____ I have one or two close friends.

_____ I have no close friends.

9. In terms of how you feel about yourself . . . *(check one)*:

_____ I don't like myself much.

_____ I like parts of myself but dislike other parts.

_____ I feel okay about myself.

_____ Most of the time, I like myself a lot.

_____ I've always liked myself a lot.

10. If you could change one thing about yourself, it would be:

_____

_____

_____

_____

_____

➡

Student Questionnaire, continued

11. The best thing about you, as far as you're concerned, is:

_____

_____

_____

_____

D. Conflicts

12. How often do you experience the following feelings, concerns, or problems?
For each, circle 1 (not at all), 2 (hardly ever), 3 (sometimes), 4 (a lot), or 5 (all the time).

Feeling or Problem	How Frequently Felt
I miss out on activities other kids get to do while I'm in my gifted and talented class.	1 2 3 4 5
I have to do extra work in school.	1 2 3 4 5
Other kids ask me for too much help.	1 2 3 4 5
The stuff I do in school is too easy and it's boring.	1 2 3 4 5
When I finish my schoolwork early, I often am not allowed to work ahead.	1 2 3 4 5
My friends and classmates don't always understand me, and they don't see all of my different sides.	1 2 3 4 5
Parents, teachers, and even my friends expect too much of me. I'm supposed to get A's and do my best all the time.	1 2 3 4 5
Tests, tests, and more tests!	1 2 3 4 5

→

Student Questionnaire, continued

13. What's your biggest challenge or difficulty in life right now?

_____

_____

_____

_____

14. Generally, how do you feel about your life? *(Make a slash somewhere along this continuum.)*

Feel really great,
confident, happy

Feel extremely bad,
upset, worried; think
about dying

E. Support Systems

15. Who do you share your feelings or problems with when you're wondering what life is about, or who you are? Who do you go to—or like to be around—when things aren't so great? *(Check all that apply.)*

_____ Friend

_____ Mother

_____ Father

_____ Sister

_____ Brother

_____ Other relative

_____ Pet (dog, cat)

_____ Coach

_____ Clergy (minister, rabbi, priest, spiritual leader, etc.)

_____ School counselor

_____ Camp counselor

_____ Psychologist or doctor

_____ Official Big Brother or Sister

_____ Other adult (*example:* neighbor)

_____ Teacher

_____ I prefer just being alone

_____ I don't think about that kind of stuff

→

Student Questionnaire, continued

16. What do you do to feel good about yourself? *(Check all that apply. Add your own ideas, if you want.)*

_____ Think or study harder

_____ Get some exercise (get on my bike, go for a run, head for the gym, dance, etc.)

_____ Call or text a friend

_____ Communicate with a friend online (via social media, a chat room, email, instant messaging)

_____ Write in a journal

_____ Paint or do other artwork or crafts

_____ Play a musical instrument

_____ Work on a project (club, play, newspaper, etc.)

_____ Play harder in sports

_____ Earn money

_____ Go somewhere (mall, park, a friend's house, place of worship, etc.)

_____ Watch TV

_____ Talk to my parent(s)

_____ Talk to my teacher

_____ Volunteer

_____ Listen to music

_____ Go to a party

_____ Cook or eat

_____ Use relaxation techniques (yoga, meditation, deep breathing, etc.)

_____ Surf the Web

_____ _____

_____ _____

_____ _____

_____ _____

_____ _____

→

Student Questionnaire, continued

17. If you could get this class or program to do or provide one thing for you, what would it be? _____

_____

_____

_____

_____

Your name (optional): _____

Identifying Gifted Kids

 I know I wouldn't be where I am today
without my fourth-grade teacher, Mrs. Duncan.
She so believed in me, and for the first time,
she made me embrace the idea of learning.
—Oprah Winfrey

Even if you're not old enough to remember watching *American Bandstand,* the TV show hosted by Dick Clark that highlighted pop singers from the 1950s and 60s, it's such a vivid icon of our culture that the mere mention of its name conjures up images of poodle skirts, white sport coats, and pink carnations. A memorable feature of every show was the debut of a song by an up-and-coming rock and roller. The assembled masses would dance, applaud at the end . . . and then came the drama: Dick Clark, microphone in hand, would approach several teenagers and ask for a vote.

"Well, it's got a catchy beat, and I like his voice," an articulate 17-year-old would say. "I'd give it an 8." More applause, a brief reprise of the new song, then break to commercial.

That was how *American Bandstand* made stars out of singers: a quick vote by a renowned authority—a radio-addicted teen—who knew a catchy tune when she heard one.

If only identifying gifted kids followed this model: Reveal evidence of the gifts, recognize them as extraordinary, defend the reasons behind the decision, applaud, and move on to the next child. But identifying giftedness is not as easy as deciding that "My Girl" deserves to be a #1 hit. The complications are many, and we as teachers are often caught in a place where we may not want to be.

Why Is Identification So Complex?

Long ago, when a high IQ score was all one needed to be identified as gifted, few people questioned why. If your IQ was 140 or above, you were gifted. If it was 139 or below, you weren't.* It was as simple as that.

This single-score determination of giftedness was as wrong in 1940 as it is today, but almost no one back then voiced strong opposition. So the IQ score reigned supreme, and placement in gifted programs—the few that existed—was based solely on that magic number.

As times changed and schools became more diverse, educators and others began to challenge the wisdom behind any one number determining a child's school placement—and, often, the child's eventual success in life. Teachers (and some parents) started asking:

■ What if my student doesn't test well or gets test anxiety that clouds his or her true abilities?

■ What if some of the questions on the IQ test are biased in favor of certain ethnic, cultural, or socioeconomic groups and against others?

■ What if my student speaks a language other than English at home?

■ What if my student is shy and doesn't respond well to a stranger asking odd questions?

■ What if my student has a reading or writing disability or difference? How does an IQ test compensate for that?

These questions made educators and test-makers squirm. They were good questions, but no one had any answers—at least, not yet. Meanwhile, admitting to the flaws of the esteemed IQ standard left gaping holes in both the theory and the practice of testing.

It was about then, in the 1960s, that the *American Bandstand* form of identification began to be instituted more widely. Teachers—who actually knew children and how they learned—were asked, "Which kids in your classroom do you think are gifted, and why?" This epiphany of common sense—letting experienced observers of children attest to their high intelligence—was disparaged by some in higher education who alleged that teachers:

■ were biased

■ were ignorant of the traits of a "real" gifted child

■ tended to identify kids whose talents most resembled their own

■ tended to identify "teacher pleasers" as gifted, instead of those children who were highly intelligent but undermotivated in school

*In some versions of the IQ scale, the break between gifted and not gifted is 140. In others, it's 130. Furthermore, different school districts have different cutoff points for acceptance into gifted programs. For some, it's 145. For others, it's 125. These variations from scale to scale and school to school are reason enough not to use IQ tests alone to determine giftedness (or the lack thereof).

More Possible Meanings for the Acronym IQ

I Quit
Some people believe that an average IQ predicts a life of menial jobs and dreary relationships. Wrong! IQ is only one way to measure intelligence, and it's by no means the last word. No one should be labeled anything based solely on a test score.

Individual Quirks
One IQ test asked students to find the "best, most sensible" word to complete this sentence: "The foundation of all science is _____." The choices are "observation," "invention," "knowledge," "theory," and "art." Which fits best? The test developers had a particular word in mind. If your opinion differs, no points for you.

Insufficient Quantity
Some IQ tests last only twenty minutes, which doesn't leave much time for revealing specific strengths and weaknesses. If kids are going to be selected for (or barred from) gifted programs on the basis of IQ, they deserve more time to show what they know.

Intense Queasiness
Tests have been known to make people anxious. The typical IQ test is administered in a situation that is stressful and constrained by time limits. "Brain drain" isn't uncommon. Students may forget everything they've ever learned—only to recall it all five minutes after the test ends.

Impressive Quality
Although IQ tests are criticized, the fact remains that people with high IQs often do very well in life. The tests appear to do an adequate job of identifying overall intelligence; a score of 150 usually isn't an accident or a fluke. But do the tests fail to identify some smart people who just don't perform well on tests? The evidence points to "yes."

I Question
Even amid all the controversy, many gifted kids still question what their IQ is and want access to their scores. If your students bring this up, ask them this: "If your score is lower than you thought it would be, will you be disappointed? Disillusioned? If the number is higher than you estimated, will you feel pressured to live up to that number?" Help kids see that there are pros and cons to knowing their scores.

Of course, some of these observations were true. Identifying gifted kids based on personal opinion and interpretation is as flawed in its own way as identifying them by test scores alone.

Sounds like a stalemate, doesn't it? The old-guard IQ advocates on one side, the proponents of teacher-directed identification on the other. In truth, there hasn't been a lot of movement by either faction since the 1960s. IQ tests are rarely used as the sole way to identify gifted children, although virtually every school district we know of uses some type of aptitude assessment as a piece of its gifted identification plan. But teacher nominations are still dismissed by some as being inaccurate, invalid, and inconclusive

evidence of high intelligence, especially if not accompanied by high test scores.

> "I know from my own experience that there is much more to 'intelligence' than an IQ number. In fact, I hesitate to believe that any system could really reflect the complexity and uniqueness of one person's mind, or meaningfully describe the nature of his or her potential."
>
> **—Daniel Tammet, autistic savant, synesthete, and best-selling author of** *Born on a Blue Day*

How It Should Be

It's unlikely that an identification plan (some districts call it an "identification scheme") that satisfies everyone will be developed in our lifetimes. But if teachers and psychologists are ready to admit their own fallibility, identification doesn't have to be an onerous task. Consider the following example.

A growing Southern school district is changing from a blue-collar and agricultural enclave to a more diverse suburb filled with homes ranging from $80,000 to $600,000. Kids are everywhere—and they come from everywhere—including the nearby urban metropolis, the neighboring towns where apartment dwellers seek their first houses, and neighborhoods where McMansion buyers have gobs of money to spend. Also, the district has experienced a large influx of new immigrants, and the school corridors are filled with the colors and languages of the world. Teachers call it "the U.N. in miniature."

Gifted identification in that district, as required by the state, is as test-score-dependent as any: two standard deviations above the norm on an aptitude measure, and the 95th percentile or above on various standardized achievement tests. However, for students whose first language is not English, or for those whose cultural or economic backgrounds may have limited their exposure to the middle-class values and ideas common on IQ tests, the verbal IQ test requirement is lowered to one standard deviation above the norm—an IQ of approximately 115 to 120.

Other corroborating evidence from teachers, a gifted education consultant's observations, or examples of the student's work are accepted as evidence of a child's giftedness. When searching for creativity, paper-and-pencil tests (which are never very accurate in measuring creativity) may be replaced by real-world evidence of that creative spark that a teacher, parent, or peer might see in a 3D printing project or a Google Science Fair submission.

When kids move into this district from another town where they were in a gifted program, their gifted program acceptance is automatic, with a reevaluation (if deemed necessary) occurring within six months to check the placement's "goodness of fit." The program also allows for identification of children with learning disabilities or differences. If they have slightly above-average test scores, these are combined with an interview conducted by the gifted education teacher, who looks for evidence of complex and abstract thinking.

In other words, although criteria are established by the state to locate gifted children in the typical ways (by using test

Three Tips for Successful Gifted Placement

1. All placements in a gifted program should be considered *tentative*, with the fit between the child's needs and the program's offerings being the bottom-line criterion for continued placement. Bad match? Look for something that better matches the child's strengths within the school's curriculum.

2. All placements in a gifted program should be considered *voluntary*. No one should have to be in a gifted program if they sincerely don't want to be.

3. The names of students selected for a gifted program should be *shared with the students' teachers*, who should also be asked if they know of any other children who might be considered for placement whose names didn't appear on the "qualified" list. However, teachers cannot *remove* a student's name from this list, since this creates an opportunity to unfairly eliminate perceived underachievers and so-called troublemakers.

scores), gifts and talents are also sought and identified in children whose life circumstances would otherwise make them ineligible for gifted services.

The result? A gifted program that resembles the ethnic, cultural, and racial makeup of the school district as a whole. It's an even *more* miniature U.N. This is gifted identification done right, for although the process is multi-tiered and, in part, subjective, it offers many gateways for program admission.

What You Can Do Right

Classroom teachers are the key players in the eventual success or failure of a child's gifted program placement. It all begins with proper identification, as outlined previously. But without your keen eyes and ears, it's likely that many gifts will go unnoticed, and many gifted kids will never have the support, encouragement, and opportunities they need to reach their intellectual and creative peaks. Here are some ways you can help.

Be a Talent Identifier

As a classroom teacher, it's possible that you interact with your students more than anyone else in the school. When you notice a child with gifted characteristics (see pages 8–9), run, don't walk, to your school's or district's gifted education specialist to document your observations and get the identification ball rolling.

Be a Student Advocate

If you suspect that one of your students is gifted, nominate him or her for the gifted program—and follow up to make sure that your nomination is acted upon. If you're told that "the test scores or grades just aren't there," ask about alternative paths for identification. If such paths don't exist, pave one yourself. Offer evidence of the child's work and thinking that made you suspect giftedness in the first place.

For example, we know one student who spoke six languages and was taking a high school geometry class in eighth grade—but never qualified as gifted because the verbal IQ test he took was administered during his first year of learning English. This is a perfect example of an unfortunate and unnecessary oversight!

You may be your student's strongest advocate. Don't give up without good cause.

Be Supportive and Flexible

If one or more of your students is selected for gifted services, it's likely that this will require some out-of-classroom time with the gifted education specialist. Our experience tells us that if you pile on the makeup work, some gifted students will begin to resent you, your classroom, and the gifted class. After all, if they are gifted, they are probably well versed in some aspects of the grade-level curriculum.

What can you eliminate so your gifted students don't experience the "double whammy" of needing to do all the gifted program work and assignments on top of your own? The simplest suggestion we can offer—and it works—is to have students complete *one-half* of the week's work or assignments. Their performance will indicate whether they have already mastered a particular skill or need additional practice. You might also consider changing the timing of your assessment, allowing gifted students to take your tests or quizzes at or near the *beginning* of your instructional unit. If they score to your satisfaction (we suggest 85 percent or higher), they are excused from homework and classwork that covers these topics.

Some of your students—and colleagues—might spout off that this isn't fair and that you are giving this student special privileges others aren't getting. Your response? "I take every student's individual learning needs into account and then plan accordingly." Also, you can invite other students to take a pretest and if they do well enough, then they, too, may be excused from certain assignments or tasks.

Be a Treasure Hunter

Some kids are hard to like. They may announce that "this work is boring" (while you're being observed by the principal, of course). They may refuse to do their homework, declaring that "it's easy and stupid." They may wear old, holey, sweat-stained T-shirts printed with Bart Simpson and his favorite expression: "Underachiever, and proud of it, man!"

Even kids like this might be gifted. You will need—and this is often difficult—to look beyond their rebelliousness or nonchalance about schoolwork. Notice, instead, when these students do well. Thoroughly check their school records to see if previous years' teachers noted "a fine mind going to waste" or made other comments ripe with possibilities about the student's giftedness. Get to know them as people, not just students, so you'll be in a position to identify and support talents that might show up primarily in hobbies or extracurricular activities. These are important steps toward an academic turnaround in which you can play a part.

> "Make the most of yourself by fanning the tiny, inner sparks of possibility into flames of achievement."
>
> **—Golda Meir, former prime minister of Israel**

What We Sometimes Do Wrong

Nobody's perfect—not even experienced teachers with the best intentions and most comprehensive approach to identifying students as gifted. We all make mistakes and errors in judgment. Let's not forget that our decisions influence our students' futures. With that in mind, here are three mistakes we should all work hard to avoid.

We Assume That "Once Identified, Always Identified"

Giftedness is a lifetime quality. If *properly* identified in childhood, the phenomenon of giftedness will continue to be as immutable a part of one's life as eye color. Proper identification is essential—but it is rare.

For example: Using a group IQ test of suspicious reliability and validity, a second grader is noted as having an IQ of 133, identified as gifted, and placed in a gifted class. All seems well. Subsequent years' testing shows a pattern of widely discrepant scores—110, 121, 108, 113. Is this a problem? Yes and no.

Yes if the child struggles through daily work that provides too much challenge, causing you, the teacher, to lower the level of work expected to be completed by this child. *Yes* again if your gifted program has only a limited number of "slots" and this

Ten Traits and Behaviors That May Prevent Identification

1. Students may get easily bored with routine classwork. Some may say so, often and loudly. Others may tune out and say nothing.

2. Students may work intently on one area or subject, neglecting homework and classwork in other areas of study.

3. Students may use their advanced vocabularies to "retaliate" against those who are not as verbally adept.

4. Students may get so excited about a discussion or topic that interests them that they monopolize the conversation or begin "preaching" about it, even to the teacher.

5. Students may get excited about a particular topic but, once initial interest is satisfied, resist doing additional work that relates to the topic. They've learned what they wanted to learn and are ready for something new.

6. Students may dislike or resent having to work with others who do not have equally high abilities, and they may express this dissatisfaction through words, loud sighs, or rolled eyes.

7. Students may possess vast knowledge of many topics, and they may correct adults (and peers) they perceive as giving incorrect or incomplete information.

8. Students may use their advanced senses of humor and cunning to intimidate, manipulate, or humiliate others.

9. Students may be self-assured and passionate about particular political, social, or moral issues and state their views openly, distancing themselves from classmates and educators who don't share (or care about) their views on these issues.

10. Students may prefer working independently and resent any adult who wants them to toe the line by following a specific procedure with which they disagree.

Some of these negative behaviors may be due to the gifted child having intellectual or emotional needs that are not being met at home or in school. While arrogant behavior should not be tolerated, and academic nonchalance should not be ignored, it's good to know that the source of these issues might be intellectual frustration, not emotional disorder.

child, whose placement may be inappropriate, is retained while a more highly gifted child waits in the wings.

Of course, it's uncomfortable to call parents and say, "We're sorry, but it appears that your child is no longer gifted." In fact, you should *never* say that. *Never even allude to that possibility!* Instead, focus on the reality that the child's needs—intellectual and emotional—will be better met in a setting that's challenging, but not to the point of frustration and discouragement.

When are wild fluctuations in test scores not a problem? When the child's behaviors, interactions, and accomplishments make it obvious that the level of high challenge is on par with his or her level of intellect. In this case, the proverbial match made in heaven is taking place, and test scores should no longer be the prime consideration in the child's gifted program placement.

We Accept That "Once Not Identified, Never Identified"

This is the equivalent of the Gifted Olympics. A child takes part in the tryouts (group IQ testing) for his particular grade level and, for whatever reason, doesn't make the cut. He's out of the game for life—with no second chances, no opportunity to clear the bar on a second push of his intellectual muscles. He had his chance, and he blew it.

Some people in charge of identifying gifted children see themselves as blockers for kids who "don't belong." What can you do to help a child who deserves another chance? Keep records of potential indicators of giftedness, as you have seen it expressed. For example:

Reliability and Validity

Reliability is the likelihood that a test, given once, will produce similar results the next time it (or a comparable instrument) is administered. For instance, if you have a group IQ test that gives you a 110 result for a child in October and a 145 in April, that test would not be considered very reliable—statistically or practically.

Validity can have various facets, but the overall concept refers to whether you're measuring what you think you're measuring. *Content validity* concerns whether a test adequately covers enough breadth of information about a subject to make the score a good indicator of one's ability within that subject. For example, if you use a math achievement test that only contains fraction problems, it's not a very valid measure of your students' abilities across the spectrum of mathematics.

- Save copies of papers or projects that clearly show evidence of the child's advanced abilities or complex thought processes.

- Ask the parents to provide examples of precocious performance or question-asking from early in the child's life. We know one parent whose four-year-old daughter asked, "Do people feel the same way right before they're born as they do right after they die?" And she demanded an answer. We're not sure what answer her parents gave her, but we do know that this is not a typical question from a four-year-old.

■ Record your own examples or vivid memories of times when this child far exceeded the bounds of the usual in terms of journal-writing, question-asking, or the ability to juggle complex thoughts. A young man we're acquainted with was three years old when he announced to his mother, "I know that numbers and letters are different." "And how do you know?" his mother asked. "Because," he replied, "when you count, you never get to the end." At thirty-six months, he had grasped the concept of infinity.

Your role in properly identifying gifted students is essential, so don't be content with filling out a numerical checklist (a common identification method) about a child you suspect is truly gifted. Add depth and substance. After all, who knows a gifted child better than an

Grade Equivalent (G.E.) Scores

There is much confusion about the meaning of G.E. scores obtained by children on standardized tests. For example, if a sixth grader takes a math test and performs at the G.E. level of 9.3, does this mean that the student is ready to be placed in a ninth-grade math class? Probably not. Here's the truth about G.E. scores:

■ A student who has scores above grade level on a standardized test is, indeed, showing superior performance relative to other classmates. However, since many of the items that make up this test are at or below grade level (and are therefore easier), it could be that this student did very well on these easier items while missing several of the more difficult ones. Placing the student in ninth grade based on a 9.3 G.E. is an easy solution, but likely not the best one.

■ G.E. scores can vary widely in a given year. If a third grader has a 6.4 G.E. on a reading test in September and a 5.2 on the same or a similar test in May, it does not mean that the student's intelligence decreased during the school year. Even missing one or two extra items in retaking the test can cause a dramatic shift in G.E. scores.

Even more than teachers, parents are confused about these G.E. scores. Share the above information with them and, in some cases, seek out enrichment or acceleration options that may be a better fit than a multiple-year grade jump.

informed teacher who has spent 185 days out of a year observing and interacting with that child?

We Treat Identification as an "April Event" Instead of an Ongoing Process

Although it's common to identify children near the end of one school year so the next can begin with an intact class of gifted students, there's no reason why a child who comes to your attention at another time should not enter a gifted program during other months. This situation can occur if a child moves into your classroom midyear from another town or school, or when you have a gifted child whose abilities are not initially observable— perhaps the child is shy, quiet, or not screaming out "This is boring!" at the start of each lesson.

Be sure to know the process for nominating a child for your school's gifted program. And if you are told, "We don't identify children until April," state politely (but firmly), "I don't think that

when I call Sara's parents about my nomination, they're going to want to wait that long. Sara has intellectual needs *now*, and she deserves to have them met as soon as possible." That should help speed up the process.

Questions and Answers About Identification

"Can giftedness coexist with disabilities?"

Yes, which means that the child might benefit from both the gifted and the special education programs, with appropriate modifications made in each setting. Gifted children may have learning disabilities, emotional or behavioral difficulties, dyslexia, sensory impairments, or behaviors that fit on the autism spectrum. Don't discount the importance of locating and serving these "twice-exceptional" children.

"If a child moves from a gifted program in one town, should he or she be automatically included in the gifted program in another town?"

Yes, provided the programs offered focus on similar content areas. If you are gifted in St. Paul, you should also be gifted in Minneapolis (after all, they are Twin Cities). If, after an appropriate trial period—perhaps one school quarter—it becomes obvious that the placement is not working well for the child, adjustments can be made. But let's proceed on the basis of optimism, not pessimism, and give the St. Paul gifted child the benefit of the doubt. Denying access to gifted services to a child who qualified elsewhere creates confusion for both the child and the parents.

A Wise Voice from the Past

Long before identification became a hot topic, a pioneering psychologist named Leta Stetter Hollingworth was wondering how to help gifted children. She started researching them in the early 1920s. At that time, most other educators believed (as some still do) that bright kids could simply take care of themselves. Here are a few of Hollingworth's observations.

- "When we hear repeatedly, from various people, that a given child is 'old for his age,' 'so reliable,' 'very old-fashioned,' 'quick to see a joke,' 'youngest in his class,' or that he has 'an old head on young shoulders' or 'such a long memory,' we usually find him to be highly intelligent, by test."

- "Teachers may judge as 'most intelligent' very dull, over-age children doing good work in lower grades. Thus, for instance, they may not realize that being 'youngest in the class' is an important symptom of superior ability."

- "Teachers rate bright children higher in all respects so far reported than their parents do. This is because teachers know a great variety of children, including the incompetent; whereas parents know well only their own children and those of their friends, constituting usually a very restricted range of competency."

- "Schools cannot equalize children; schools can only equalize opportunity. It may well be thought to be highly undemocratic to provide full opportunity for the exercise of their capacities to some, while to others the same offering means only partial exercise of their powers. It is hard for a psychologist to define democracy, but perhaps one acceptable definition might be that it is a condition of affairs, in which every human being has opportunity to live and work in accordance with inborn capacity for achievement."

We have long believed that some of the best advice about understanding gifted children comes from authors and researchers who studied them generations ago. If Hollingworth's quotes here have meaning for you, look up her other texts and articles. You may be surprised how something written in the 1920s can seem so current and so relevant to your classroom and students today.

From "Provisions for Intellectually Superior Children," by Leta S. Hollingsworth in *The Child, His Nature and His Needs*, edited by M.V. O'Shea (New York: Arno Press, 1975, 1923).

"Should classroom teachers be a part of a gifted selection committee?"

Of course! The perspectives you can offer on typical behaviors and academic expectations of kids in a certain grade level will add valuable insights to placement decisions. This is especially true if the bulk of your school's gifted identification comes near the end of the school year, as you will have taught the children in question for multiple months. Your insights could cause others to see a child from a new or different perspective.

What if your district doesn't have a selection committee and all decisions are made by one or two people crunching test scores on kids they don't know? For the sake of your program and the students eligible for it, it's time to insist (or firmly suggest) that such a committee be formed.

"How can I make sure that atypical gifted kids are found?"

Gifted programs are often accused of being academic options for middle- to upper-class white kids. In many cases, this accusation is accurate.

Don't confuse gifted children with "teacher pleasers"—those kids who get straight A's, have good behavior and manners, finish their work on time and ask for more, and always wear the latest styles. Some gifted kids do have these attributes (and clothes), but many don't. Instead, look for kids who:

- Are easily bored by routine tasks
- Can play and work independently
- Prefer complex tasks and open-ended activities
- Rebel against conformity

- Creatively make toys or tools out of anything
- Ask probing questions
- Make connections between ideas that classmates "don't get" (but you do)
- Have an "adult" sense of humor; understand irony and puns

There are many more characteristics, behaviors, and traits that can be used to informally identify gifted children. You read about many of them in Chapter 1: What Is Giftedness? *Whichever ones you look for, make sure to compare them against the characteristics, behaviors, and traits of other kids the same age.* If you keep this caveat in mind, finding gifted children need not be the arduous process that some make it out to be.

Is It a Cheetah?

by Stephanie S. Tolan

The child who does well in school, gets good grades, wins awards, and "performs" beyond the norms for his or her age, is considered talented. The child who does not, no matter what his innate intellectual capacities or developmental level, is less and less likely to be identified, less and less likely to be served.

A cheetah metaphor can help us see the problem with achievement-oriented thinking. The cheetah is the fastest animal on earth. When we think of cheetahs we are likely to think first of their speed. It's flashy. It is impressive. It's unique. And it makes identification incredibly easy. Since cheetahs are the only animals that can run 70 mph, if you clock an animal running 70 mph, IT'S A CHEETAH!

Certain conditions are necessary if it is to attain its famous 70 mph top speed. It must be healthy, fit, and rested. It must have plenty of room to run. Besides that, it is best motivated to run all out when it is hungry and there are antelope to chase.

If a cheetah is confined to a 10- by 12-foot cage, though it may pace or fling itself against the bars in restless frustration, it won't run 70 mph. IS IT STILL A CHEETAH?

If a cheetah has only 20 mph rabbits to chase for food, it won't run 70 mph while hunting. If it did, it would flash past its prey and go hungry! Though it might well run on its own for exercise, recreation, fulfillment of its internal drive, when given only rabbits to eat, the hunting cheetah will run only fast enough to catch a rabbit. IS IT STILL A CHEETAH?

If a cheetah is fed Zoo Chow it may not run at all. IS IT STILL A CHEETAH?

If a cheetah is sick or if its legs have been broken, it won't even walk. IS IT STILL A CHEETAH?

And finally, if the cheetah is only six weeks old, it can't yet run 70 mph. IS IT, THEN, ONLY A "POTENTIAL" CHEETAH?

A school system that defines giftedness (or talent) as behavior, achievement, and performance is as compromised in its ability to recognize its highly gifted students and to give them what they need as a zoo would be to recognize and provide for its cheetahs if it looked only for speed.

Stephanie S. Tolan is a writer, an educator, and a passionate advocate for gifted students.

A Few Final Thoughts

> "The dream begins with a teacher who believes in you, who tugs and pushes and leads you to the next plateau."
>
> **—Dan Rather**

Identifying one child and not another as gifted, seeing past negative attitudes and behaviors, advocating for the child who doesn't test well—these aren't easy choices to make. Ultimately, identification is not a game of numbers, but a judgment call based on your own beliefs and preferences. What can you do when seeking to identify gifted children? Your best, while acknowledging that no choice will be perfect or completely agreed upon by others.

Of all the issues in gifted education, identification may well be the most vexing, complex, and frustrating. Once we find the kids, we generally know how to channel their talents with curriculum and creative experiences. It's the process of selecting the "right kids" that causes gifted education specialists to toss and turn in bed.

It doesn't have to be that difficult. If we see identification as a way to get highly able kids the kinds of education they deserve; if we allow enough flexibility in our identification systems to select children based on test scores *and* on the professional judgments of well-informed educators; and if we realize that identification is as much an art as it is a science, then we will do right by those gifted young people who are just waiting to show us the glow of their fine minds.

Gifted? You Decide.

Noah wrote this journal entry on his first day of first grade:

School is so difficult for a kid like me. I wish I were a grown-up NOW! (Because grown-ups are allowed to drive cars, which I like.) But, I'm lost in thought. How am I going to afford a car and a house? How am I? How am I? How am I? How am I going to get money? How am I going to get a job? It looks hopeless. Help me, help me, HELP ME! How am I going to pay my financial tax? AHA. Why didn't I think of this before? I'll let my mom and dad help me. The End.

Sara wrote this poem in seventh grade:

NOWHERE
(To the people with nothing inside them)

Where will it take you?
Your shallow pleasure
In making others cry . . .

At their imperfections
And disabilities
Suddenly magnified
For the world to see and laugh?
Where do you expect to get to?
Living off the tears they shed . . .
Life isn't always
That grand.
Screwing up
In front of everyone.
Being tripped
In the halls.
You laugh and point now
"What losers."
I don't see you
In the spotlight
Trying your hardest
Failing, just to be
Laughed at again
By the people with nothing inside them
Who think they'll
Survive?
Us, the legs they stand on.
Us, standing tall above them.
Them, the losers in the back row.
They won't last long.
They're on the road
To nowhere.

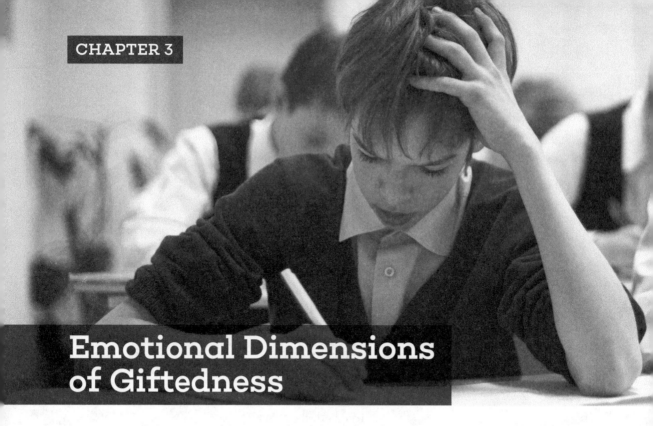

CHAPTER 3

Emotional Dimensions of Giftedness

 A child is a total entity, a combination of many characteristics. Emotions cannot be treated separately from intellectual awareness or physical development. All three intertwine and influence each other. A gifted five-year-old does not function or think like an average ten-year-old. He does not feel like an average ten-year-old, nor does he feel like an average four- or five-year-old. Gifted children's thoughts and emotions differ from those of other children, and as a result they perceive and react to their world differently.

—Annemarie Roeper

How gifted kids feel on an emotional level doesn't always match logically with their intellectual capabilities. Brighter doesn't necessarily mean happier, healthier, more successful, more socially adept, or more secure. Neither does brighter necessarily mean hyper, difficult, overly sensitive, or neurotic. In terms of emotional and social characteristics, brighter may not mean anything "different" at all. But while gifted kids don't all have the exact same personality traits, they *do* face common concerns.

Like members of any minority, gifted students may feel insecure just because they're different from the norm. Teenagers and preteens in particular desperately want to be like everyone else, and any difference, whether positive or negative, can be a cause for anxiety. But sometimes gifted kids are very different; they may feel isolated, alienated, or alone, and as a result, may become anxious. "They have so many problems connecting with other people their age," one teacher told us. "There's a sense of isolation that gets bigger and bigger as years go by, unless some interventions are made."

The educational community has been quick to dismiss the emotional lives of gifted people for many of the same reasons we have dismissed their educational needs. Perhaps we have too many other kids whose problems seem worse. Perhaps we think that smart kids don't need our help because "if they're smart, they'll figure things out." Many of us may not realize that some of our brighter students are, in fact, in quite a bit of trouble. They don't necessarily look needy; they seem to have it all together. Except sometimes, they don't.

Accustomed to conquering intellectual problems logically, gifted students themselves may deny their emotional concerns by saying, "I'm supposed to be smart. I should be able to think my way out of this." Or, because they are smart, they can successfully delude themselves, rationalize their behavior, or talk themselves into believing that burying their true feelings is a legitimate option.

Finally, many of us may realize that some gifted students suffer emotionally, but we aren't sure how to handle it.

"Anywhere I go, no matter if it is school or home, there is always a little block that separates me from everyone else. The signs of it are subtle, like people not understanding a word I use, or everybody jumping to work with me in group projects, but there they are, isolating me from them, making it hard to make friends. Some people would laugh at this, saying it's nothing, but the thing they don't realize is that *it isn't nothing*. The barrier is there, and not being able to get past it is sometimes painful . . . The distance between me and other people is hidden, but still there if you know where to look. That block hurts me, and there is only one way to make it stop, and that is to spend time with a person who also has to deal with this barrier, this wall."[1]

—**D.J. Gallenberger, 14**

Challenges from Within and Without

Kazimierz Dabrowski was a Polish psychiatrist who experienced the brutalities of World Wars I and II from his own backyard. He helped Jews hide from the Nazis and suffered imprisonment by both the Nazis and Communists for his beliefs that people should decide their fates, not governments. After becoming a clinician and counseling many talented artists, writers, actors, and members of the clergy, Dabrowski was struck by their intensity and sensitivity, as well as their tendency to experience emotional extremes. While many others saw these traits as abnormal and excessive, Dabrowski saw them as merely aspects of growing up talented, creative, and gifted. Much of his career was spent helping those individuals realize that they were not sick, just intense—a career path that people in the gifted child education field, including Michael Piechowski and Susan Daniels, have continued to tread.

We provided this bit of history as part of the increasing evidence that certain challenges to emotional balance may come automatically with exceptional intellectual ability or talent. Challenges may come both from within the person and from without. Challenges from *within* include being, by nature, highly perceptive, highly involved, super-sensitive, and perfectionistic. Challenges from *without* come from conflict with parents, peers, or educators who are either clueless

about the inner workings of gifted people or choose to dismiss or dispute their importance.

Of course, not all students experience all of the issues described here. Some have few adjustment problems generally and feel fine about life. Others experience difficulty in one or more areas—friendship, school, expectations, or hopelessness. A student's needs will depend on his or her maturity level, degree of intelligence, environment, and a whole host of other personality characteristics that make each gifted individual unique. Let's examine a few of these emotional aspects of growing up gifted.

Overexcitabilities

Consider the effect that being highly perceptive to stimuli (sounds, sights, smells, touches, tastes, movements, words, patterns, numbers, physical phenomena, people) would have on one's daily life. While other people might agree, "These two colors match," the artist says, "No, they don't." The musician hears the difference between a note played perfectly and one played slightly off-key. Howard Gardner speaks of the poet as someone who is "superlatively sensitive to the shades of meanings . . . to the sound of words . . . to the order among words."[2] Whether their medium is one of language, art, social action, or physics, gifted persons are profoundly sensitive to small differences—and those differences make all the difference. Michael Piechowski named these heightened levels of experiencing the world "overexcitabilities" (or OEs), and he categorized them into five dimensions: psychomotor, sensual, intellectual, imaginational, and emotional. With tongue firmly in cheek, Piechowski

also noted the OE could stand for "original equipment," as gifted children have some or all of these OEs from birth.

High Involvement

While most other children seem comfortable letting thoughts come and go and are relatively unbothered by unsolved problems and inexact answers, gifted students dream repetitively of treasured problems, pictures, patterns, or concerns. They are obsessed with the intricacy or beauty of phenomena at hand. The creative composer constantly hears tones in his head. The mathematician dreams of her favorite proofs; the writer carries precious fragments of verse in his memory. Gifted individuals perceive greater levels of complexity in the world around them, and they find this complexity interesting and meaningful. They can also be quite bewildered that many other people don't share this need to explore everything in great depth.

Super-Sensitivity

In addition to being exquisitely perceptive of and receptive to stimuli, sensitivity in the gifted can also mean moral or emotional sensitivity. Many gifted students are super-sensitive to ethical issues and concerns that are considered unimportant by their peers. Even as young children, they may try to "make things right" at recess and try to ensure that everyone who wants to play a game gets the chance to do so. However, these efforts at fairness might be rebuffed by classmates. In addition, gifted children may be highly moralistic. They can be quick to judge others and slow to forgive those whose moral standards don't match their own. While they may be intellectually precocious,

The Creative Mind
by Pearl S. Buck

The truly creative mind in any field is no more than this: A human creature born abnormally, inhumanly sensitive. To him, a touch is a blow, a sound is a noise, a misfortune is a tragedy, a joy is an ecstasy, a friend is a lover, a lover is a god, and failure is death.

Add to this cruelly delicate organism the overpowering necessity to create, create, create—so that without the creating of music or poetry or books or buildings or something of meaning, his very breath is cut off from him. He must create, must pour out creation. By some strange, unknown, inward urgency, he is not really alive unless he is creating.

these children are not always emotionally mature for their age. In many cases, gifted kids are both emotionally immature and intellectually advanced at the same time.

Perfectionism

The pursuit of excellence in accomplishing something personally important is a valued trait in an individual. However, when students strive for perfection (not just excellence) and experience anything less than a perfect outcome, negative consequences typically ensue. To some gifted students, simply "doing well" is unacceptable. Putting forth effort or trying something new regardless of the outcome is unacceptable.

"Failure is simply the opportunity to begin again, this time more intelligently."

—Henry Ford

"It's not that I'm so smart, it's just that I stay with problems longer."

—Albert Einstein

Perfectionism means that you can *never* fail, you *always* need approval to feel good about yourself, and if you come in second, you're a loser. The pursuit of excellence means taking risks, trying new things, growing, changing—and sometimes failing. Perfectionism is *not* about doing your best or striving for high goals. Instead, it can actually block your ability to do well. And it can take a heavy toll on your self-esteem, relationships, creativity, health, and capacity to enjoy life. Because perfection isn't possible, deciding that's

The Plight of the Silver Medalist

Cornell University's Thomas Gilovich studied the facial expressions of Olympic medalists and found something intriguing: the gold medal winners almost universally beamed as they were awarded their medals, and the bronze medalists weren't far behind in smiles. However, the silver medalists—second bests in the world in their event—were "consistently and significantly" less happy with their performance, as evidenced by their facial expressions.

what you want—and that you won't be satisfied with anything less—is a recipe for disappointment, stress, and anxiety.

Gifted people of all ages seem especially prone to perfectionism. This may be rooted in the awareness of quality. They know the difference between the mediocre and the superior. Once they see how something "ought to be done" (ought to sound, ought to look), they may naturally want to do it that way. And they may drive themselves (and others!) crazy in the process. This is why gifted students need support to persist despite their constant awareness and fear of "failure."

Many of the problems gifted students have with high expectations are reinforced by their environment, particularly if they have had a string of early successes (and a history of lavish praise and encouragement to keep up the stellar work). As Ruth Duskin Feldman, a former Quiz Kid (the Quiz Kids were gifted kids who appeared on a popular radio and TV series in the 1940s and 1950s), explains: "Whatever I accomplished, it never seemed enough. I had the nagging feeling I should be up there at the top, as I had been in my youth." She also speaks of intelligence as a trap. When exceptionally bright and capable children (like the Quiz Kids) are "accustomed to easy success and . . . are praised for work requiring modest effort [they] may not develop discrimination or learn to meet a challenge. When these children grow up, they seek applause constantly without knowing how to get it. Children held to impossibly high standards and deprived of praise may get caught in a cycle of hopeless, misdirected perfectionism, trying to please parents, teachers, or bosses who never can be satisfied."[3]

Perfectionism at a Glance

How a Perfectionist Acts

- Overcommits himself
- Rarely delegates work to others
- Has a hard time making choices
- Always has to be in control
- Competes fiercely
- Arrives late because one more thing had to be done
- Always does last-minute cramming
- Gets carried away with the details
- Never seems satisfied with his work
- Constantly busies himself with something or other
- Frequently criticizes others
- Refuses to hear criticism of himself
- Pays more attention to negative than positive comments
- Checks up on other people's work
- Calls himself "stupid" when he does something imperfectly
- Procrastinates

What a Perfectionist Thinks

- If I can't do it perfectly, what's the point?
- I should excel at everything I do.
- I always have to stay ahead of others.
- I should finish a job before doing anything else.
- Every detail of a job should be perfect.
- Things should be done right the first time.
- There is only one right way to do things.
- I'm a wonderful person if I do well; I'm a lousy person if I do poorly.
- I'm never good enough.
- I'm stupid.
- I can't do anything right.
- I'm unlikable.
- I'd better not make a mistake here, or people will think I'm not very [smart, good, capable].
- If I goof up, something's wrong with me.
- People shouldn't criticize me.
- Everything should be clearly black or white. Grays are a sign of confused thinking.

➡

How a Perfectionist Feels

- Deeply embarrassed about mistakes she makes
- Disgusted or angry with herself when she is criticized
- Anxious when stating her opinion to others
- Extremely worried about details
- Angry if her routine is interrupted
- Nervous when things around her are messy

- Fearful or anxious a lot of the time
- Exhausted and unable to relax
- Plagued by self-hatred
- Afraid of appearing stupid
- Afraid of appearing incompetent
- Afraid of being rejected
- Ashamed of having fears
- Discouraged
- Guilty about letting others down

Adapted from "Perfectionism at a Glance" in *Moving Past Perfect* by Thomas S. Greenspon, Ph.D. (Minneapolis: Free Spirit Publishing Inc., 2012), pp. 9–10. Used with permission.

Uneven Integration

Challenges to emotional peace can also come from within when a student's intellectual abilities are out of sync. For example, a student who has strong conceptual and verbal skills but a reading disability may feel quite frustrated. Someone with strong spatial ability but weak drawing skills is likely to be similarly stymied. A person may be talented athletically, but too shy to compete in team sports. Within each of us, certain abilities may or may not combine gracefully or productively into a cohesive, balanced whole.

Although in the past we've tended to stereotype gifted students as exceptional across the board, few are actually good at everything they do. This type of integrated ability is both rare and exciting. More typical is the student with demonstrated ability in one academic area, or who can transfer one process skill into a number of different content areas. This same student may be a lousy speller or average in math, have terrible handwriting or poor study skills.

Wait . . . poor study skills among gifted kids? Really? Yes—really. For many gifted learners, gliding through elementary and middle school without ever having to study or prepare for a test is very common. So, when a gifted student reaches a point—often in high school or college— where real studying and planning is needed, they have no idea how to go about it. As a teacher, you'll need to watch for this and offer help as needed. Regardless of how smart they are, some gifted kids may be clueless about how to allocate their time, organize their learning environments, keep track of daily and long-range assignments, take good notes, and more. There are many resources available on how to develop strong study skills (we especially like *Becoming a Master Student* by David Ellis), including many written for students. You might want to build a classroom library and hand out books as appropriate. At times, you may need to offer one-on-one instruction, or ask some of your students who have mastered the organizing and studying routine to share their techniques with your floundering gifted students. You might also share websites that focus on study skills, such as studygs.net and howtostudy.org.

> "I have one sheet of paper called '50 Things.' It's a list of all the important initiatives, tasks, and projects at the company. It's just a piece of paper. It sounds very 1980s, but it folds nicely; you can put it in any kind of pocket! Ninety-nine percent of my life is digital, but this is my low-tech way of staying focused."
>
> **—Aaron Levie, CEO and entrepreneur**

Different Ways of Being Gifted, Different Emotional Needs

With gifted kids so unique, is it possible to generalize about their emotional needs? The answer is yes—with caution. Based on the work of countless researchers and practitioners who have studied and worked with gifted children across the decades, we can make some generalizations about who is gifted and what their affective needs may be. Moreover, as practitioners, you'll *have* to make some generalizations to get the ball rolling in designing and using classroom-based activities to address these needs.

A good place to start is knowing your school's gifted identification process and program options. What kinds of gifted students are you working with? Kids with high verbal or math skills? Those who score in the exceptionally gifted range (150–180) on the Stanford-Binet Intelligence Scale? Students whose abilities tend to require enrichment opportunities as opposed to accelerated opportunities (or vice versa)? The types of cognitive strengths your students demonstrate may determine, to some extent, the kind of emotional needs they'll have. Keep in mind, however, that our foremost concern should be for what young people say they need help with. Don't deny a child a reaction, an emotion, or assistance because he or she doesn't fit the "right" category.

There are several frameworks for categorizing students that seem useful to us for predicting emotional needs. The first has simply to do with the degree of intelligence and the type of intelligence involved.

Quantity and Quality of Intelligence

The degree of difference between the gifted and average student (whether in IQ score, music, language, or chess playing) influences, by itself, the gifted student's self-concept. The young adolescent with a very high IQ (above 150) is likely to feel more different and isolated than kids with IQ scores of 130, simply because he or she is that much more different from the norm. Both are gifted, but because the number of kids in the top 1 to 2 percent of the population is so small, these students are dramatically limited in terms of same-age peer groups.

In addition to quantity or degree of ability, giftedness has obvious qualitative differences. Creativity in the visual arts is different than logical-mathematical ability. The interpersonal skills of leadership are different than the linguistic skills of a poet. These areas are equally important, although the degree to which schools actively address them will vary.

For the most part, schools are more likely to offer advanced options for kids whose talents are expressed in traditional academic subjects. This is more true as students progress through school, as it would be rare to find a high school that did not offer Advanced Placement, honors-level courses, or dual enrollment in high school and college. Elementary and middle schools, though, are more of a mixed bag when it comes to serving gifted students in separate or advanced classes. Due to qualms about labeling children too soon, kids in the early grades are likely to be grouped more heterogeneously than by ability. This is less true in the middle grades, but still a concern for those educators who believe that all students should be given the chance to take any class they feel equipped to take.

This is not to say that services for gifted students are less common in kindergarten through eighth grade, but they may take on more of an enrichment focus—perhaps a one-day-per-week pull-out program, or a "cluster" of several gifted students housed in particular teachers' classrooms. Rarely do you find self-contained gifted programs in elementary and middle schools, where students are taught all day/every day alongside other gifted students. Even though this can be a great option, the potential political fallout from such a program offering often finds school administrators shying away from this provision.

What if your talents as a gifted kid are expressed most strongly outside of the core subject areas? In this case, the route often taken is the extracurricular one: theater or drama clubs, orchestra and band, chess clubs or poetry slams. The problem with this is that these activities take place after school or as electives, leaving the gifted child's school day untouched by any enrichment options. Of course, individual teachers may see the spark in the eye of the creative child and offer in-class options to take advantage of these abilities and interests, but this is more a luck-of-the-draw scenario than an organized approach to serving gifted kids whose lights shine in areas outside of traditional subject areas.

Accelerated Students and Passionate Learners

One way to think about the needs of gifted students is in terms of two types of learning styles: that of the accelerated student, and that of the passionate learner. As is the case whenever so-called "categories" are defined, you're very likely to have students who blend qualities of each type. Nevertheless, taking time to consider these learning styles will help you meet students' needs by providing more targeted challenges and support.

Accelerated students are interested in mastering and integrating increasingly complex material. They have the ability to quickly learn and recall large amounts of information. They are highly efficient information-processors. They crave new information and harder problems. Their sense of fulfillment comes from mastering higher and higher levels of material and applying it to solve problems of increasing difficulty.

An image of the mathematician solving a difficult problem comes to mind, as does a historian who remembers and interprets long, complex sequences of events; the poet or writer who quotes passages verbatim with ease; the doctor who generates four hypotheses and cites ten particular cases bearing on her diagnosis—these are adult examples of individuals who process, retain, and apply large quantities of knowledge well.

Often, adolescents and preadolescents with this type of ability simply "do well" in school. They are high achievers in a well-defined discipline such as science or literature, and they succeed in curricular systems which stress knowledge acquisition, linear skill-building, and logical analysis. They may also be wholly indifferent to certain academic subject areas, but suddenly need to know "everything there is to know" about the Civil War, plate tectonics, or Tolkien's *Lord of the Rings* trilogy.

Passionate learners, by comparison, are gifted students with the ability and the desire to become wholly involved or immersed in a problem, to "form a relationship" with a topic and study it until their need to know is satisfied. These students may bounce from one topic to another, eager to explore in depth anything that attracts their interests. Often, they are more generalists than those who prefer acceleration, and their explorations often involve multiple subject areas simultaneously. For example, not only will they examine the evidence for and against climate change, they will also explore how weather extremes affect animals, the economy, and people's preferences for vacation spots.

Passionate learners may also be highly emotional, imaginative, internally motivated, curious, and driven to explore and experiment. They tend to be reflective and emotionally mature. Frequently, they have a keen sense of humor. The enriched student becomes passionate about a subject, a project, or a cause, often pursuing it with fierce energy.

Artists, musicians, dancers, writers, and actors tend to fall into this category, although research scientists, political activists, religious leaders, lawyers, and educators are other adult examples. The child who writes, directs, and stars in a play is demonstrating the characteristics of a passionate learner, as is the student who designs and constructs a futuristic model city, and students who "live and breathe" dinosaurs, computers, or entrepreneurial businesses. These students thrive on discovery and experience.

In terms of counseling or emotional need, accelerated learners are most frustrated by lockstep learning. They need to move on and master more material, not do endless drill-and-practice exercises (sometimes referred to as "drill and kill" exercises). Because these students have high achievement expectations (for example, they must score 100 percent on every test), they may need help setting realistic (or at least humane) goals for themselves. Teachers and parents can drive achievers in this category too hard, which then reinforces the students' fear of failing.

Passionate learners, in contrast, may not be especially concerned with achievement (and may never be the top academic performers in a content area), but they invest a significant amount of emotional energy in what they are striving to learn. In return, they require teachers who are sensitive to their intense feelings of frustration, passion, enthusiasm, idealism, anger, and despair. Passionate learners may also need adult support to persist with a single task, to narrow their topic to something manageable (for example, it's tough to study *all* of World War II!), or to use their time efficiently.

Other Categories of Gifted Kids

Other groups of gifted kids that may have special emotional needs include those from low socioeconomic classes, ethnic and cultural minorities, and gifted children with physical and learning differences. Generally, the needs of these children are related to being simultaneously bright and members of one or more underachieving minorities. They reflect the isolation and challenges of their

respective situations. Gifted boys and gifted girls also have some special needs that have to be addressed if we're to help them achieve their full potential.

All of these students would especially benefit from more role models, which can be offered in the form of teachers or presenters, graphic displays, verbal examples, biographies, special reports, or projects. When teachers are systematic about being diverse and inclusive, attitudes and expectations can change.

Gifted Girls and Boys

Gifted girls and boys face special conflicts in resolving society's expectations of them in terms of gender stereotypes and biases about what it means to be female or male. Especially in junior and senior high school, girls and boys may be exposed to many deep-seated cultural taboos that make it difficult for them to comfortably display their intelligence and pursue their interests as aggressively as they could. The result of this inhibition can be underachievement, discouragement, long-term depression, and low self-esteem.

For gifted girls who do display their abilities, further conflicts can result. Bright girls may hear messages to develop their talents and be driven in the pursuit of their goals. And they are often active, exploring, and assertive by nature. On the other hand, women in our society are widely expected to be selfless, nurturing, and supportive of others. Likewise, a gifted female today has stronger role models than ever before, but women's careers typically place second to men's in dual-career marriages. Women generally earn less income and (when children are involved) are expected to perform most parenting duties. When males in high school or college talk about their career plans, no one asks what they're going to do about childcare if they have children someday.

In addition, for adolescent girls busy with the work of establishing a sexual identity, confusion may result. The question is how to be feminine and talented at

Ways to Support Gifted Girls—and Boys

- Support their exploration of a wide variety of interests and activities without creating pressure for students to be good at all of them or pursue all of them long-term.

- Encourage them to take high-level courses in subject areas that might not be traditional for their gender (math and science for girls; arts, literature, and humanities for boys).

- Use multiple measures of ability and achievement. Some standardized tests underpredict female performance and overpredict male performance, while other measures can be ill-suited to boys who might think and learn in creative, nontraditional, and unconventional ways.

- Encourage them to recognize their unique talents and be as proud of their *attempts* as they are of their *successes*.

- Provide a wide range of material (fiction and nonfiction) highlighting the accomplishments and lives of men and women in many fields. Encourage them to form friendships with gifted peers, especially those who share similar interests.

- Foster mentorships with adult experts in fields of interest.

- Provide a diverse array of male and female role models who have successfully integrated multiple aspects of their careers and lives, including those who might hold non-gender-traditional jobs or family roles. Invite them to visit your class to talk about their backgrounds and fields of interest.

- Discuss biased depictions of girls *and* boys (and women and men) in the media, and talk about students' experiences with being sex-role stereotyped themselves.

- Encourage independence and risk-taking.

- Avoid having different academic, social, and emotional expectations for girls than for boys.

Adapted from "Many Gifted Girls, Few Eminent Women: Why?" by Anita Gurian, Ph.D. (New York University Child Study Center, 2000), www.aboutourkids.org, and "Being a Gifted Boy: What We Have Learned" by F. Richard Olenchak, Ph.D., in *Digest of Gifted Research*, 2006, tip.duke.edu.

world onto their radar. Also, reading about career options, bringing guests into the classroom to talk about their fields, and sharing news stories are all good ways to achieve career awareness.

With respect to gifted boys specifically, it's been said that the least popular students in America are gifted, non-athletic boys—even with the influence of "cool nerd" icons like Steve Jobs and Harry Potter. Also, boys are falling behind girls in terms of college attendance and academic achievement. Gifted boys may feel pressured if they hear messages about the importance of participating in competitive sports, even when they're not interested in those pursuits. They are also more likely than girls to rebel against meager curriculums and choose not to play the school "game." As a result they may get lower grades and even be discouraged about the prospect of going to college. Although attending college doesn't guarantee success in the workplace, without a degree (much less advanced degrees), certain professions simply won't be options.

Ethnic and Cultural Minorities

A similar dilemma develops for gifted minority students who have to resolve being black (or Hispanic or Native American) and succeeding in a white classroom at the same time. In trying to develop their talents or interests, these students can get caught between two worlds. To illustrate: In one workshop with gifted Native American teenagers, a fifteen-year-old boy remarked, "Some of the people in the Indian community think I've sold out because I go to a challenging private school."

the same time. In the words of one bright woman, "When I was 10 years old and entered seventh grade . . . one of the popular girls took me aside and said, 'Don't raise your hand so much, the boys don't like it.'"[4] As adults, some gifted and motivated women have to consider whether they want to have children if they want to achieve in particularly demanding fields such as engineering, law, or medicine. Meanwhile, gifted girls have to deal with the biases of some school counselors who are slow to identify them as bright, or who counsel them into sex-stereotyped fields.

Of course, whether we're working with gifted boys or girls, it's our job to introduce them to broad ranges of careers that exist now, and into the future. We also need to educate them about what types of education are needed to succeed in those careers so they have ideas about how to prepare. Exposing them to mentorships or job shadowing opportunities is a great way to bring the real

Ways to Support Gifted Minority Students

- Communicate high expectations.

- Be sensitive to the experiences and beliefs of people from different cultural groups. Get to know all students and their cultures. Consider the challenges that students may face in school.

- Continuously and firmly encourage students to continue their education, whether that means college, technical training, or equivalent experience in a particular field of interest. Discuss the necessary coursework, tests, and other preparations with students and parents.

- Create a multicultural learning environment and make sure the curriculum reflects a variety of cultures.

- Help students connect with role models and mentors. Organize peer support groups for students with similar interests and abilities.

- Reach out to parents and family members. Enlist their support in providing encouragement and high expectations.

- Provide students with a variety of learning options. Select or create activities that are engaging, active, and grounded in reality.

- Listen to students' concerns, fears, and beliefs about their experiences and education.

Adapted from *The Inclusive Classroom: Meeting the Needs of Gifted Students: Differentiating Mathematics and Science Instruction* by Jennifer Stepanek (Portland, OR: Northwest Regional Educational Laboratory, 2000), p. 20. Used with permission. Also available online at educationnorthwest.org.

Sometimes the conflict stems from peer pressure to resist white authority figures or the white "system" in general. Other times, just being different from one's parents, family, and ethnic or cultural community causes anxiety or guilt. Like children of immigrants to this country, gifted minority students may feel conflicted about being more successful in the white majority culture than their parents. The adjustments and other conflicts may be less painful for many Asian-American students, however, for a disproportionately high number of them are identified as gifted, and many learn quite successfully in American school systems.

Gifted minority students may not be recognized as talented or able because their gifts lie in areas that are celebrated by their ethnic group but not usually by Western society. For instance, a study found that teachers in the United States tend to nominate children for gifted programs on the basis of "individual, competitive, conspicuous achievement."

However, in some minority cultures, standing out from the crowd is discouraged, so those gifted children might learn to show their ability in less conspicuous ways.[5] Further, when cognitive skills are assessed via achievement tests and English is not their native language, gifted minority students may test below their ability level and be inappropriately labeled and counseled. Intelligence is, as Howard Gardner notes, a culturally defined and conditioned capability.[6] A society that values navigational skills, for instance, shapes children from an early age to direct a canoe at night by the stars, and views its best navigators as its wisest members. The spatial ability required by this feat is less prized in the wider culture.

Because the abilities we value in human beings are very much tied to the products our society needs or cherishes, we can't help but define intelligence in terms of cultural priorities. Western academic traditions tend to mirror Western concepts of intelligence: rational thought and the cognitive domain (normally measured by IQ and achievement tests) are the rule and not the exception. Both in conception and in fact, these notions and these instruments impart a cultural bias.

Minority students may, of course, be talented in areas and ways similar to majority students. But, in many cases, cultural heritage continues to influence how minority gifted students develop and express their talents.

Children with Physical and Learning Differences

Research finds high-ability individuals in all segments of society, but traditional identification procedures remain largely inadequate for those with physical and learning differences. As a result, this may indicate a small but highly underserved population.

In thinking of Helen Keller, we're reminded of how difficult it was for her to find people and programs to educate and treat her. We consider her intense struggle to communicate with the world, and her emotional isolation before Anne Sullivan became her teacher. We also reflect on how extraordinarily gifted she must have been to learn concepts—the whole meaning and flow of language—through the medium of hand signals alone. For those of us with sight and hearing, it's difficult to separate our knowledge from our visual and auditory perception of the world. Keller's learning, in contrast, was independent of such experiences and relied heavily on sensory, linguistic (in the abstract, not vocal, sense), and spatial intelligence.

Today, gifted children with learning differences are often labeled "twice exceptional" ("2E" for short), or sometimes "students with dual exceptionalities." Like all labels, this one has its shortcomings, but at least it calls attention to students whose giftedness might otherwise be overlooked. For example, a student who is easily distracted and has difficulty completing assignments or concentrating on tests may be passed over when teachers are identifying students for gifted programs. Since school success is often based on graded assignments and test scores, students who don't perform well on these tasks may not be seen as "smart," even though they are, in fact, intellectually, creatively, or otherwise gifted.

Twice-exceptional students may have uneven academic skills and may appear

Ways to Support Gifted Children with Learning Differences

Identification

- Include students with disabilities in the initial screening phase.

- Be willing to accept nonconventional indicators of intellectual talent, such as nonverbal or creative abilities.

- Look beyond test scores.

- When applying cutoffs, bear in mind the depression of scores that may occur due to the disability.

- Do *not* aggregate subtest scores into a composite score.

- Weight more heavily characteristics that enable the child to effectively compensate for the disability.

- Weight more heavily areas of performance unaffected by the disability.

- If the data collected provide a mixed message in terms of giftedness, allow the child to participate in gifted programs on a trial basis.

Instruction

- Be aware of the powerful role of language; reduce communication limitations and develop alternative modes for thinking and communicating.

- Emphasize high-level abstract thinking, creativity, and a problem-solving approach.

- Have great expectations: These children often become successful as adults in fields requiring advanced education.

- Provide for individual pacing in areas of giftedness and disability.

- Provide challenging activities at an advanced level in the child's noted areas of strength and interest.

- Promote active inquiry, experimentation, and discussion.

- Promote self-direction, giving the child the choice of what and how to learn.

- Use intellectual strengths to develop coping strategies.

- Assist in strengthening the student's self-concept through honest self-appraisal.

Classroom Dynamics

- Discuss disabilities/capabilities and their implications with the class.

- Expect participation in all activities; strive for normal peer interactions.

- Facilitate acceptance; model and demand respect for all.

- Candidly answer peers' questions.

- Treat a child with a disability the same way a child without a disability is treated.

- Model celebration of individual differences.

Colleen Willard-Holt, "Dual Exceptionalities," *ERIC EC Digest* #E574 (Reston, VA: ERIC Clearinghouse on Disabilities and Gifted Education, 1999).

unmotivated. They may have "processing problems" with the way they see and hear, causing them to seem "slow." They may have motor skills problems that affect their handwriting. Because they are often frustrated with school, they may act out and have low self-esteem.

On the other hand, many gifted students with learning differences score in the gifted range on ability, achievement, and creativity tests. They may have a wide range of knowledge about a variety of topics, as well as fertile imaginations. They may have superior vocabularies and sophisticated ideas.

How common is twice exceptionality? Data on the numbers of 2E students as a percentage of the total and/or gifted student population varies widely depending on which source you check. We found numbers as low as 120,000 and as high as 3,800,000![7] The real number is almost surely somewhere in between

these extremes. Clearly, this is a group that merits our attention and flexibility in terms of identification, programming, and social-emotional support.

Like all students, those who are twice exceptional benefit most when we focus on their strengths, not their perceived weaknesses or deficiencies. These children also need more opportunities to learn and to show what they know in ways that are natural, comfortable, and effective for them.

Recognizing Problems

Now that we've described some of the emotional dimensions of being gifted, the challenges gifted students face from within and without, and the specific issues particular categories of gifted students might encounter, how would you describe your students? What kinds of problems and needs would you say they have?

A Perspective on Twice Exceptionality

Marcie Booth is the founder and director of Twice Exceptional/2E Network LA, which provides advocacy and resources for twice exceptional individuals. Here she shares her thoughts on 2E education, based on her research, her knowledge of her own twice-exceptional children, and her experience mentoring other parents.

Working with twice exceptional kids isn't always easy. Some of these students have challenges with social skills, making them seem less "likable." They may have sensory processing issues which make it difficult for them to pay attention or to join in activities. They may have physical or motor differences that impede their ability to write, or language challenges that impede their ability to communicate what they know. At times they may get on your nerves by talking too much about subjects that interest them. Yet these bright kids need and deserve the same support, encouragement, and quality instruction as any other learners. Teachers of 2E students need to have strong problem-solving skills, good verbal communication, creativity, and plenty of patience.

One note: In general, the term "gifted" is a label that shows that a child has been tested and has reached a certain level of proficiency. I prefer to use the terms "bright," "high ability," and "talented" to include children who have not yet been assessed.

Following are some ideas for helping these students thrive.

■ Give all children access to enrichment opportunities. Enrichment activities not only facilitate learning but also help stimulate brain pathway growth and intellectual development.

■ Provide students with opportunities to cooperate, not compete. Encourage team building and social skills for all. Use service learning projects to build community and cohesiveness, and to teach acceptance of differences.

■ Use multisensory modes of instruction, so students can receive information through different senses at the same time.

■ Offer options that enable students to use strengths and preferred ways of learning and expressing, such as writing, typing, kinesthetic, and visual or performing arts.

■ Recognize that some 2E students may need to learn in a different way or at a slower pace than other bright and high ability kids, and be patient with those differences.

■ Look for talents in areas that are non-academic, such as sports or the performing arts.

■ Focus on the *whole child*, not just test scores.

■ Seek areas of interest or talent where the student may already have an accumulation of knowledge. Use these areas to prompt further investigation or to ignite a spark of confidence.

■ Keep tabs on your own attitudes and behaviors. If and when you grow frustrated (or even exasperated) because of a child's challenges, never be negative or critical in the presence of students. Always model patience and positive attitudes. Students will take note of your positive attitudes and behaviors, and become more accepting of their peers.

■ Treat parents with honesty and respect. They are your students' primary guardians, caregivers, and teachers, and they must be included in giving and receiving information about the child's progress and behaviors at school. Parents who are treated this way are likely to become more cooperative and less adversarial.

If you haven't already asked your students to complete the "Student Questionnaire" (see pages 37–43), we encourage you to do so. Put this information together with what you've just read in this chapter. Then look around your classroom.

Signs of Trouble

It's believed that half of gifted children underachieve in school. (For more on this topic, see Chapter 6: Underachiever or Selective Consumer?) Poor school performance, dropping out, and not completing college are three ways gifted students can go awry. There are more. As one teacher commented to us about her gifted classes (K–12), "I've always got a kid in trouble." Her examples of trouble included everything from the inability to concentrate to the need for attention, physical closeness, and affection; from poor schoolwork and attendance to disruptions in class.

In terms of everyday sorts of dysfunction, unhappy gifted kids display the same patterns and symptoms that other unhappy children do. They may brag, tease, put others down, avoid responsibility, develop a negative attitude, confront adults relentlessly, stop working, stop trying, withdraw. A seriously troubled student is one who seems isolated, who stops participating in and outside of school and at home, whose lack of interest seems to pervade every conceivable subject or endeavor. Students trapped in this sort of inertia cause some teachers and parents to feel hopeless themselves: "I'm just not getting through to him, no matter what I try." When we asked teachers which types of gifted kids they had the hardest time working with, they frequently answered, "The underachievers, the unmotivated, the apathetic, those full of grudges, the snobs, the ones who have given up on the system."

Frequently, teachers can recognize low self-esteem or depression most clearly in students' body language. Chin-on-chest posture, a low or inaudibly pitched voice, habitual mumbling, lack of eye contact, self-deprecating comments, and a lethargic attitude are all signs of poor self-concept.

Similarly, the student who is demonstrably angry, who loses control easily, underachieves, and has no close friends but plenty of "associates in class crime," is also a troubled kid. A sense of powerlessness and rage came through in the words of one teenage boy we observed during a group discussion about school: "What's the point of confronting teachers on how boring the damn school is? The teachers aren't going to change!" As the boy continued to blast away at "the system" and everything else in sight, we noticed how difficult it was for him to use the pronoun

"I." Other people were at fault, and other people projected his sentiments. Yet he wasn't able to say what he was feeling. Anger? Fear? Frustration? When asked to use the word "I" so the group could recognize who he was talking about and what he was feeling, the student could not (would not) comply. Inability to own feelings and opinions is a sign of emotional conflict and lack of insight. Symptoms of the seriously depressed or suicidal teenager have been well-documented. Depressed gifted students may, because of their sensitivity, become "hostages of their own special insights," and need immediate support and help in coping with reality. Some danger signs to watch for are:

- Sudden changes in personality or behavior

- Severe depression that lasts a week or longer

- Concealed or direct suicide threats

- Talking about suicide, either jokingly or seriously

- Giving away prized possessions

- Self-imposed isolation from family and peers; avoiding all social occasions and invitations

- Narcissism (total preoccupation with self and with fantasy)

- Unusual fascination with violence, or preoccupation with death and death-related themes

- Indications of alcohol or other drug abuse, or an eating disorder

- Any other rigidly compulsive behaviors—even excessive studying and running marathons (ask yourself, "Have I ever seen this kid relax?")

There is no firm evidence that gifted teenagers are more likely to attempt or commit suicide than less able adolescents. That said, they are no less likely, either. In any case, while it would be inappropriate to approach every gifted student as a potential suicide, some aspects of being gifted can, in some cases, contribute to suicidal behavior. For example:[8]

- A perception of failure that differs from others' perceptions of failure (for example, feeling that a B is equivalent to an F if your personal standard of success calls for an A)

- External pressures to always be number one and a life orientation that identifies one as a future leader or a "mover and shaker of the next generation"

- The frustration that comes when one's intellectual talents outpace his or her social or physical development ("for being so smart, I'm awfully dumb at making friends," or "Starting school early and skipping second grade was fine, but now I'm the freak of the locker room—I'm so puny!")

- The ability to understand adult situations and world events while feeling powerless to effect positive change

Teachers (and other caring adults) should take all talk of death seriously. Never assume that gifted adolescents are "too smart" to even consider ending their own lives. Some do consider it—and some go beyond considering it to attempting it. If you observe any of the previously mentioned signs of a teen in trouble, get help. Contact your school counselor, school psychologist, or principal for advice about what to do. *Don't wait.*

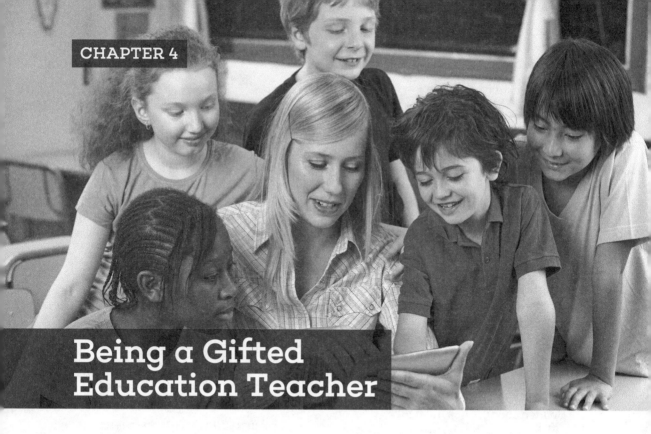

Being a Gifted Education Teacher

 This is definitely not a 'cushy' job.
—Gifted education teacher

Have you noticed that teachers of the gifted suffer many of the same stereotypes that gifted students themselves do? Somehow, parents, colleagues, and administrators seem to think gifted education teachers should know all the answers; that life for them is probably easier than it is for the rest of us; that gifted education teachers probably think they're better teachers. Like gifted students, gifted education teachers may also lack supportive peers, either because they are physically the only person in the building (or district!) working in their field, or because they are subtly ostracized. As one teacher managing 120 gifted kids from twelve grade levels told us, "No one wants to hear about my problems."

Contrary to these misconceptions, teaching gifted students is an extremely demanding job. These kids have tremendous physical and psychic energy, and they are "on to you" in a minute—they know if you're unprepared. Yet gifted education teachers are capable of making mistakes, just like any other human being. Furthermore, it's not possible to know all the answers when working with young "content experts." By training and experience, you may be better prepared to work in certain subject matter areas than with others. But no matter what your training, a tremendous amount of preparation is necessary before each class. And although there are a variety of curricular materials in the marketplace to help you, finding the truly high quality resources that meet your needs and those of your students takes time and money. As for feeling like gifted education teachers are "better teachers," the comparison is irrelevant. One hopes that we are good teachers, and that we have chosen to work with gifted students because we feel most successful with or drawn to this group. One also hopes that teachers working with other populations will be best for their assignments. We all have the potential to fail with particular assignments in which we're simply not interested, or for which we're unprepared.

Roadblocks to Gifted Education

As a gifted education teacher, it's likely that you have more challenges to deal with than misconceptions about your program and your role. Chances are your job is threatened with each new administration (federal, state, and local) and each new budget cycle. When cuts must be made—and increasingly, that's the case—legislators and administrators tend to look first at gifted programs.

We've often heard from colleagues whose jobs are in jeopardy and whose programs have been eliminated (in one case, after twenty years). Others face larger classes (of thirty students or more) and are told to differentiate the curriculum to meet everyone's needs.

Over the years, gifted educators have faced these and many other roadblocks. There have also been some tentative steps forward. The *Jacob K. Javits Gifted and Talented Students Education Act* received $5 million in funding for fiscal year 2014—good news, indeed. Less encouraging news, however, is the fact that this was the first time the Javits program had received any funding at all since fiscal year 2011, and the future financial health of the program remains uncertain. (By way of comparison, the federal budget in 2013 for children with disabilities approached $13 billion.)

Various education initiatives also bring various ups and downs. The *No Child Left Behind Act*, which President George W. Bush signed into law in 2002, focuses—as its name implies—on children who need help learning. One of its main goals is to close the achievement gap between disadvantaged and minority students and their peers. We agree that no child should be left behind. We also believe that no child should be *kept behind* because his or her learning needs aren't being met.

More recently, in 2010, the Common Core State Standards initiative began to be implemented across the United States. As of this writing, the standards have been adopted by 45 states and the District of Columbia. The CCSS have the potential to affect gifted education in positive ways—and not-so-positive

→

ways. For example, the standards place an emphasis on critical thinking, rigor, and depth for all kids. These areas of focus align with many of the needs (and strengths) of gifted learners, and reflect longstanding tenets of gifted education. On the other hand, the danger exists that some teachers, administrators, or observers may come to believe that with these high-level standards in place, gifted kids no longer need special help.

You are also, no doubt, well aware of the pushback to the CCSS on many levels and from many quarters. And as is the case with any educational initiative (as you'll know if you've spent any time as a teacher), it's impossible to know whether or not the CCSS are here for the long haul, or how the standards may change with time.

In the meantime, even as we wait to learn if and how the CCSS will evolve, we know for certain that—unfortunately—gifted education continues to be up against many challenges. And we know that, overall, the national effort to serve gifted children remains disjointed, to say the least. These statistics from a 2013 report by the National Association for Gifted Children paint a clear but worrying picture:[1]

- Fourteen states provide no funding to local school districts to serve gifted children.

- Although most states have policies and laws requiring school districts to identify and serve gifted children, only four states fully fund these obligations.

- Only three states require preservice teachers to have any training in how to teach gifted students.

- Only nine states have written policies permitting acceleration of students; twenty-two states leave these decisions to local school districts.

- Sixteen states prohibit children from entering kindergarten early and three states disallow middle school students to be dually enrolled in high school courses.

- Only nine states report on the academic performance of gifted students as a separate group on their state report cards.

This mishmash of state policies and implementation leaves gifted children vulnerable to spotty or nonexistent academic services. And it leaves many gifted educators without sufficient resources, support, or stability.

Are You Gifted?

Suppose we were to ask you this question: "Are you gifted?" How would you answer it?

You may not know whether you're "officially" gifted. There may not even have been programs for gifted kids when you were in school. As an education descriptor, this term wasn't coined until the federal guidelines appeared in 1976. But suppose you do know that you're not "officially" gifted. Your IQ score is below 130; you were an average student and developed no outstanding abilities; you didn't get into an Ivy League college; you didn't complete four years of college ahead of your time. Does that mean you have nothing to offer gifted students? Of course not!

Many important jobs in the world don't require genius-level intelligence, and they may require attributes that other people have in abundance. According to one theory,[2] the optimum range of intelligence runs from 125–145 on the Stanford-Binet Intelligence Scale. People who score in this range are able to master most tasks, work in any occupation they choose, and may function more easily in the world than people with profoundly high IQ scores. And let us not forget that high intelligence is also only one set of personal characteristics that we value. Leadership, loyalty, creativity, empathy, tenacity, honesty, humor, joy, and enthusiasm are some of the most important, useful qualities.

But suppose you are—or think you may be—in the upper 3 percent of the population in intellectual ability. Would you stand up in a meeting with school colleagues (everyone from the principal and secretaries to teachers, coaches, and luncheon staff) to be identified? Would you want your name in the paper? How would you tell your friends or relatives . . . or would you? Would telling them help explain what you're all about, or merely intimidate them? Are you comfortable with your abilities, or anxious about them? If you're ambivalent or confused about it, imagine how confused young students are.

Perhaps, you say, recognition for a job well done is okay. What's not okay is the effect of the "gifted" label—the calling-to-attention of an abstract quality that people can't really define but resent or envy anyway. On the other hand, it may be the "packaging" of your personal abilities you resist. "What am I," you ask, "a commodity for others to trade on?" And then there's your sense of justice (and injustice): Perhaps you know plenty of people who have been labeled "gifted," but for the life of you, you can't see why.

These are some common reactions you (or others) may have when thinking about the "gifted" label. Because many of us haven't lived through this ability grouping, we can only guess what it is like to be told in second, fifth, or tenth grade that one's abilities are extraordinary and require special instruction. We do know that it is a label students will live with for the rest of their lives. If they can't talk about it with their gifted education teacher, who *can* they talk about it with?

Explaining Gifted Education

As a gifted education teacher, you'll need to become comfortable with the "gifted" label sooner or later. (You may want to read or review "What About the Label?" on pages 27–30.) You'll first have to define it for yourself, because you can count on having to explain it to parents, students, other teachers, possibly a coordinator, and other administrators as well. You'll have to be able to explain to students how they were identified for the program ("How come I'm in this class and Johnny isn't?"), why their needs can't be met through traditional instruction, and how your class is different than other classes. You'll want to make sure for yourself that the school's selection process identifies students for programs that are targeted for particular abilities, and that your strengths as a teacher match what you are assigned to teach.

On pages 103–113, we'll outline some tactics for discussing the label with small groups of students. They have a right to know why they are in the program they're in, yet they need help putting the label in perspective and making neither more nor less out of it than is appropriate. Having students complete the "Student Questionnaire" on pages 37–43 will prepare them to approach this issue.

Questions and Answers About Gifted Education

Following are some of the "tough questions" you may be asked by kids, parents, your colleagues, and others who are curious about gifted education, along with some possible answers you can try.

"What does 'gifted' really mean?"

- "'Gifted and talented' are words used to describe kids who are exceptionally capable in some way. Usually this means they are more advanced than other kids their age in terms of intellect, creativity, artistic ability, leadership, or a specific academic subject, like math or science."

- "'Gifted' means that a student learns very differently than most other children. A gifted student is capable of learning more and faster at school, and can usually perform at a really outstanding level in some area."

- "Actually, there are five so-called 'categories' of gifted children. These categories are: general intellectual ability, specific academic aptitude, creative or productive thinking, leadership, and visual or performing arts." (See page 16 for more on this topic.)

For other ideas, you might also review the definitions of giftedness in Chapter 1: What Is Giftedness? If you created your own definition, you might respond with that and also use other definitions that exist.

"How are children selected for the gifted program?"

- "At this school, we include children in the gifted program if (choose the appropriate response): they score in the top 3 to 5 percent on the Stanford-Binet Intelligence Scale; they score in the 95th percentile or above on achievement tests; they are recommended because of artistic, creative, or leadership skills; or . . . (a combination of the above, or whatever method your school uses)."

- "We select students for this program when they have unusual academic or creative potential, and they need learning opportunities that aren't usually available in the regular classroom. We use a combination of teacher and parent recommendations along with achievement and ability tests."

"How come Joey (Janey's brother) didn't get picked for the program?"

- ▪ "I don't know Joey, so I can't tell you why he isn't in the program. I do know Janey, and she's in the program because . . ."

- ▪ "Joey may do well on classroom tests, and that's really good. This program, however, was developed for kids with high overall learning potential, as measured by intellectual ability tests. The difference between achievement and ability is that achievement tests measure what you have learned—what you have been taught. Ability tests measure what you are capable of learning in certain areas. If Joey is working up to his potential and scoring well on classroom tests, he's probably in the right place."

- ▪ "It's probably because Janey scored higher on some tests of general ability, or on tests of creativity or achievement. Although no test is perfect, and we're still learning a lot about how to identify children with special talents, these tests are the best tools we have to work with today."

- ▪ "After one of Janey's teachers nominated her for the program, a review of her work and her potential showed that the program would be a good fit for her abilities. Perhaps Joey's teachers feel that his needs are already being met."

- ▪ "Janey's unique portfolio of work showed that she would probably benefit from the program's added challenge and

support. Joey may already be thriving where he is, however."

"What's the best way to teach students with high ability? Isn't it better for them to stay in the regular classroom?"

- "Depending on the child, her age, maturity, and type of ability, it may be best to move her ahead in a particular subject, or even a whole grade. Or she may need enrichment classes that go beyond the regular curriculum. What's best for her will depend on the type and degree of ability she has and what we as a school have to offer."

- "A 'pull-out' or 'cluster' class for only gifted kids may be best if a student is ready to move on and work more deeply, at higher levels, for longer periods of time. Gifted students who stay in regular classes often don't get enough of a workout. They get bored, frustrated, and can suffer emotionally as well as intellectually. Some develop behavior problems. Others actually fail school,

Why Even Have Gifted Education?

You may be asked this question by people who are confrontational (as in "Aren't all kids gifted?" and "Isn't gifted education elitist?") or merely curious ("What is gifted education all about, and why do we need it?"). You may be challenged to defend gifted education in a time of budget cutbacks, when anything considered "nonessential" is at risk. Following are some reasons why we think gifted education is necessary—today, tomorrow, and always.

- Gifted kids need a place where they can be themselves and feel accepted for who they are. That can mean almost anything: brainy, impatient, show-offy, moody, obsessed with a particular interest, off in a mysterious direction. Our society has traditionally valued equality. Often that translates into favoring conformity and people who don't stand out from the crowd. This way of thinking is at odds with what's in the best interests of gifted kids.

- Gifted kids need a place where they can feel safe and supported. Some high-ability students actually hide what they know or cover up what they can do to improve their chances of being accepted or to win popularity with their age peers.

- Like all kids, gifted kids have the right to the best education for them. They need opportunities to learn at their own speed, opt out of work they already know and understand, study things that interest them, go beyond the basics, work with abstract concepts that require more than simple thinking, work with peers who share their interests and abilities, and participate in options that connect their learning to the "real world."

- By the time they reach their senior year of high school, gifted kids will have spent more than 12,000 hours in school. Shouldn't at least some of those hours be challenging, rewarding, stimulating, meaningful, and enjoyable?

or they fail to make connections with meaningful work and friends."

■ "Kids at this level of ability simply learn faster and have different learning needs than other students. They need different materials, different kinds of supervision, and different goals set for them. They are also ready to work more on process skills, such as critical thinking and higher-order learning skills. Finally, it's important for them to be with other students like themselves—kids who share their interests, who are closer to their intellectual age than their actual peers. For these reasons, it's best to provide a separate opportunity for them."

"What will my child be learning or doing differently in this gifted program?"

■ "Depending on the options chosen for your child, he may work in an advanced class or with advanced materials. Or he may work on projects demanding higher-level thinking skills. Or he may work on special creative, musical, or problem-solving skills."

■ "In addition to more challenging courses or a broader curriculum— meaning more courses to choose from— students in this program are expected to take more responsibility for their learning. They are expected to help set goals, monitor their own learning, and manage independent time."

■ "The work in this class is demanding. We cover more complex concepts in greater depth, and we require students to do several kinds of assignments. We encourage them to work in a range of media or presentation modes, such as writing, speaking, music, a staged or filmed documentary, audiovisuals, social media platforms, or websites that students can use to learn and also to present what they know."

"Should I tell my child that he or she is gifted?"

■ "Yes. Depending on the student's age, you might explain that she did very well on a particular test, or that she's been recommended for the program because of her work (performance or whatever) in a certain area. Show that you're happy or pleased for her. And even though it's tempting to look ahead to a glorious future, try to limit your expectations to the present. For example, instead of telling your child, 'You should really be able to make something of yourself now,' you might say, 'This program sounds like a good opportunity for you. I hope you like it.'"

■ "Yes. Tell her that the class is designed for kids who learn especially well in math (or English, science, or whatever), and that you're really proud of her for qualifying."

■ "Yes. Tell your child how he was selected for the program, and explain that some kids need extra enrichment classes to think about subjects more deeply or explore projects in a number of different ways. Reassure him that he may also find other students with similar interests in the class."

"How do I cope with the feelings (such as jealousy) of other siblings in our family (or other children in my child's class) who aren't selected for the gifted program?"

- "Focus on the individual differences and achievements of both (all) children."

- "Show each child that he or she is valued. Show by your words and actions that many different qualities are important to have, including humor, commitment to learning, honesty, creativity, loyalty, and caring."

- "Reinforce all children equally in public. Save some of your praise for the gifted child to deliver in private."

- "Make sure that you give each child as much one-on-one time as possible. Don't let the gifted child's talent take up all your time."

"Are YOU gifted?"

- "Yes."

- "No."

- "I don't really know, but I suspect that I may be in some areas."

- "I would probably come out very close to the top in math, but I'm only average in other subjects."

- "I'd like to think I'm a gifted teacher, but they haven't come up with a test to measure that yet!"

- "Children weren't tested in exactly this way when I was growing up. But somehow I've always known (or people have always told me) that I was very smart, unusually talented, or bright."

- "I've always been a high academic achiever, but my IQ is not in the gifted range, so it's hard to say. I think I'm gifted in some ways."

"It must be nice having all the smart kids in your class."

- "I really do like these kids. They are a challenge, however."

- (Depending on how the remark is said): "To be honest, it kind of upsets me to hear you say that. I wonder if you think I don't work as hard as you, when in fact I work very hard."

- "I do have some unusual kids in my class, but I'm sure I don't have all the smart ones—there are plenty in other classes, too! Besides, all kids have something to offer."

- "It's very different working with gifted students. They can be extremely demanding, and they don't automatically succeed at everything they do."

"Shaundra isn't doing very well in my math class this year. Are you sure she belongs in your gifted program?"

- "Have you talked to Shaundra about her performance in your class?"

- "Gifted students aren't usually exceptional in everything they do, and math has never been Shaundra's strong point."

- "Would you like to sit down with me and Shaundra and discuss this?"

- "Are you sure that Shaundra needs to do all of the work you're assigning her? Is it something she could test out of, or do an independent study on? Some gifted kids have a hard time doing assignments for things they've already mastered. Could this be the case here?"

You may want to think through and reflect on some of these issues in more depth and detail. Write down the

Gifted Kids Speak Out

Do you sometimes dumb yourself down to get along or fit in?

"No. If being dumb or acting dumb makes you fit in better, then I'd rather not fit in at all."
—**Cole, 13**

"No. I know that being smart is just part of me, as much as my eye color, hair color, name, and so on. There is no reason for me to hide my intelligence."
—**Megan, 15**

"Yes. I don't usually tell my friends I'm in the gifted program. Sometimes I also act stupid, or I usually try my best on all my work, but sometimes if a friend says they got a bad grade and I got a good grade, I might not say my score."
—**Kendal, 13**

"Yes. I purposely act as if I don't know the material, so people won't make fun of me. I don't want to have the pressure of everybody expecting me to know the answer."
—**Sam, 17**

questions you most frequently hear and experiment with different answers. Imagine all the parents who have ever confronted you. What were they asking you? What were they worried about? What did they really want to know or be told? Consider the questions and comments you've heard from teachers and administrators over the years. Do they understand what you do every day? Do they grasp the special challenges you face? (And are you sympathetic to the special challenges they face?) Think back to the questions you've heard from students. What do they ask you in the hall? Before school? After school? Between classes? In notes or emails?

What Makes a Good Gifted Education Teacher?

"Outstanding teachers of the gifted, as identified by their colleagues, agree that the most important characteristic of a successful educator is to like gifted children."
—**Laurie Croft**

Contrary to what you might expect, veteran teachers of the gifted tell us that what is needed most of all to survive in gifted education is a sense of humor. Humor—plus a strong self-concept, a high energy level, and a sincere liking for gifted students. Rather than in-depth content knowledge or terrific analytical powers, an underlying commitment to students and a positive attitude about learning seem to be most essential. In the words of one elementary-school gifted education teacher, "I'm not an expert in anything. What I have to offer is an attitude of life-long learning. I like to learn anything."

For the elementary classroom or enrichment teacher, the ability to learn along with the students is probably more important than standing up in front of the class and disseminating knowledge. As another teacher observes, "In gifted education, you have second-, third-, and fourth-graders who are content-area specialists. They may already know more facts than you." What they don't know, necessarily, is how to put things in perspective, how to organize their learning, and how to chart where they want to go.

Requirements for successful teaching change somewhat when the classes are subject-specific and designed for accelerated students. A high school course in Chinese must be taught by someone competent in that language, and advanced calculus needs a well-versed mathematician. But even here, teachers can expect to be challenged by students. That's where that sense of humor and strong self-concept we mentioned come into play. These qualities, along with a positive attitude about their own continued learning, enable teachers to handle challenges gracefully. Teachers should have a solid mastery over their material, but also know their limitations, and be willing (we would hope eager) to continuously expand their knowledge.

Aside from the personal qualities already mentioned, several didactic

This Magic World
by Carol Ann Tomlinson

"Is it important to know math well in order to be a great math teacher, to know science deeply in order to be a great science teacher, to have a passion for music in order to be a great orchestra teacher? I absolutely think so! But I have no evidence it's enough. I think a great teacher constructs durable and trustworthy bridges between herself and her students (often using subject matter as part of the construction material), then issues the irresistible invitation, 'Come see this magic world I love. I care for you so much that I must share it with you.'"

Carol Ann Tomlinson, "What Is the Teacher's Role in a High Quality Classroom?" *Gifted Education Communicator* (Summer 2001).

talents may be particularly useful to gifted education teachers. Primary among these is versatility with a range of teaching strategies. If you heavily favor one mode of teaching, such as lecture-discussion, you may find yourself in trouble. To work with gifted students, you need to be very flexible, capable of individualizing and differentiating instruction, and adept at managing small- and large-group activities as well. Gifted students particularly thrive on student-centered instruction, yet they need variety in their daily instructional diet. You can't assign them to independent study all year long. You'll therefore need to be capable of designing small-group discussions, large-group projects, tutorials, and other learning activities to foster either content knowledge or process skills. Also, there are an increasing number of online options for independent study. See pages 228–229 for recommendations.

Prior to writing *The Gifted Teen Survival Guide: Smart, Sharp and Ready for (Almost) Anything*, we surveyed 1,400 gifted students, asking them a broad range of questions about growing up gifted. When it came to their teachers, the one thing 50 percent of our survey respondents said they wanted most from them was flexibility. Good gifted education teachers also need considerable communication skills. By this we mean a whole cluster of "people skills" including:

- Observation skills: listening, watching, picking up verbal and nonverbal cues
- Intuition: sensing needs or issues
- Empathy: communicating concern and interest

- Role-modeling: demonstrating positive attitudes, appropriate behaviors
- Verbal presentation skills
- Writing skills
- Group leadership and counseling skills

When two teachers asked students in a special project for gifted and highly able learners (ages six to sixteen) to describe their concept of a gifted teacher,[3] over 50 percent of the responses listed someone who:

- understands them
- has a sense of humor
- can make learning fun
- is cheerful

Thirty percent listed someone who:

- supports and respects them
- is intelligent
- is patient
- is firm with them
- is flexible

Only 5 to 10 percent listed someone who:

- knows the subject
- explains things carefully
- is skilled in group processes

It may be that the most relaxed, cheerful, and confident teacher is also most knowledgeable (and can therefore afford to be relaxed and cheerful!), but it's interesting that students pick up on these affective qualities as more important than expertise.

The Qualities of a Successful Gifted Education Teacher

by Susan Winebrenner

Do teachers have to be gifted themselves in order to teach gifted students? Rest assured that you don't have to have a superior IQ to teach gifted students. The truth is that many teachers who pursue training in gifted education have some personal connection to gifted students. They may have children who have been identified as gifted, or perhaps they went through gifted programs themselves. In the interest of being able to handle any issue in their class, many teachers seek training in gifted education. Of course, it sure helps to be a wonderful teacher who welcomes the challenge of facilitating academic progress for all students.

Teachers who are successful with gifted kids often possess certain qualities that gifted children respond to positively. They tend to:

- Be enthusiastic about teaching and the joy of lifelong learning.

- Have confidence and competency in teaching their content area(s).

- Have flexible teaching styles and be comfortable with situations in which students are flexibly grouped for learning and some students are doing different activities than others.

- Possess strong skills in listening, leading discussions, and using inquiry-based instruction.

- Be knowledgeable about the unique characteristics and needs of gifted students and willing to accommodate them.

- Be willing and able to create and nurture a learning environment where it's safe to take risks and make mistakes.

- Know how to praise effort more than products.

- Respect students' strengths and weaknesses and have the ability to encourage students to accept both without embarrassment.

- Be eager and willing to expose students to new ideas and provide opportunities for exploring those ideas.

- Have a free-flowing sense of humor and a level of comfort with their personal strengths and weaknesses.

- Be comfortable connecting the curriculum to students' learning profiles, interests, and questions and are good at empowering students to follow their passions.

- Be well organized—though not necessarily neat!

- Be able to multitask and effectively manage their time.

- Provide a wide range of learning materials, including those that are appropriate for older students.

- Network with organizations and local experts who can help gifted kids.

- Be aware that gifted students need less time with practice and more time with complex and abstract learning tasks.

- Understand the importance of communicating with students and their parents about their individual progress.

- Be willing to advocate for what gifted students need.

Adapted from *Teaching Gifted Kids in Today's Classroom: Strategies and Techniques Every Teacher Can Use* by Susan Winebrenner, M.S., with contributing author Dina Brulles, Ph.D. (Minneapolis: Free Spirit Publishing, 2012), p. 34. Used with permission.

Seven Tips for Gifted Education Teachers

The focus of this chapter thus far has been on you, the gifted education teacher. Your attitudes about yourself, about giftedness, and about your gifted students are fundamental to the strategies and activities that follow in this book. If you're uncomfortable with gifted students, or unsure of what the label does and doesn't mean, your students will pick up on that discomfort.

Before we proceed, we'd like to suggest some specific actions you might take to strengthen your own abilities as a gifted education teacher, build support for gifted education, and take care of yourself. We have found them helpful, other teachers we know have found them helpful, and we think that you will, too.

1. **If you don't have specific training in gifted education, get it—any way you can.** If you're able to take the time and can afford to enter a master's program, do it. If not, try to get whatever in-service training is available. Meanwhile, read as much as you can, observe other classrooms or programs, and learn all you can about your students.

2. **Advocate that all staff at your school take at least basic in-service training on the gifted.** Everyone should understand more about these students, even if they're working with them for only a few hours a week. (Gifted kids are, after all, gifted twenty-four hours a day.) You set yourself up for a lot of problems if you allow yourself to become the only "expert" in the house. You'll find that other teachers become more cooperative once they learn more about gifted students and what you're doing with them.

3. **Get a support group going for yourself.** Don't expect "regular" classroom teachers to provide all the support

you may need in teaching gifted kids; many of your problems and issues are different. (You may actually have more in common with teachers in special education services.) But isolation is not good. Join a network at the district or state level. Form your own professional learning community, or find a few other gifted education teachers to talk with routinely, in person or online.

4. **Keep parents informed of your program's goals.** Particularly if the program is new, parents will need a certain amount of education. Try to build a strong parent group in the first years, but don't "take over." Let them become responsible for the ongoing management of the group. You may find parents can be effective advocates and important sources of support if budget cuts or other political issues threaten your program.

5. **If you're new to gifted education, give yourself time to grow into your job.** Gifted education teachers have been known to burn out quickly. Many of us suffer from the same need for perfection as our students do, and we set unrealistic goals and unreasonable deadlines for ourselves. Take care of yourself by limiting the number of hours you work overtime. Realize that you won't turn underachieving kids around overnight, that you can't guarantee each kid will reach her or his potential, and that you'll stumble in many of the same ways other teachers have. Don't expect miracles from your students, and don't expect them from yourself.

6. **Give yourself permission to assert yourself and defend your students' rights.** Becoming an advocate is not easy. You may feel at odds with a lot of people. Use your support group and the parents of your students to help you keep your balance.

7. **Enjoy your students.** Enjoy the subject you're teaching. Learn right along with your students, and remember the valuable and important job you're doing working on their behalf. They need you!

Creating a Supportive Environment

Picture the following scene: a special class of young teenagers in a large urban public school.

First there's Tomas, who is sitting on the edge of his seat, with his lank hair falling in front of his eyes. His foot taps the floor in a nonstop staccato rhythm. His eyes are shining; he is busy explaining the proof he wrote on the board for an advanced calculus class. Several people are talking at once.

Most audible is Janine, who is loudly groaning for help. "Ms. Petroff, I'm totally lost! If you want to know why we're not asking questions, it's because we don't know enough to ask questions!"

Another student goes to the board, demonstrating her method for solving last night's homework. Does Janine get this? "Heck, no! I'm drowning! Send in a life preserver!"

A young boy with braces and thin arms, well under five feet tall, confers with his neighbor—a muscular giant whose face is in full hormonal flower. The small boy grins wickedly as he whispers, "I actually did number 21! I'm so proud! As a matter of fact, I have this incredible desire to write it on the board."

"Well, go for it!" his friend replies, tossing a crumpled ball of paper in the corner wastepaper basket.

Across the room, various conversations overlap as students review their answers, question the teacher and each other vigorously, and recalculate their figures.

"You call that a life preserver?" Janine says to Tomas, whose proof has still left her in the dark.

"Try saying that in English," another kid suggests. (Tomas is new to the country but extremely well spoken.)

"Who understands this now?" the teacher asks, as she demonstrates a critical step in notation on the board. Silence lasts but a second.

"Hey! That's slick! That's so slick I'm going to write it down!" "I'm gonna write home about it!"

"I'd say there's a *real lack of life preservers* here! They all have holes in them!"

The three-ring circus begins again, with kids teaching other kids, multiple kids working at the board, the teacher questioning students, checking for comprehension. Students appear to be capable of attending each of the "three rings" simultaneously, integrating the information without much trouble and moving on. Their questions are answered once, they understand, and they want more.

All eyes return to the teacher as she writes a new problem on the board. She says very little about it, mentioning only which theorems might come into play. Once the problem is posed, students pounce on it like lions on raw meat. Immediately, arguments and questions break out. Just when they seem to reach an impasse, Janine asks—and then answers—her own question (the teacher silences Tomas in time with a "Shhh, Tomas, let's see if she can figure it out"). Janine does get the right answer, and the class applauds her with high-fives.

When the class is over, we ask the teacher to talk about two of her students: Tomas, who (as the youngest of the class) seems so obviously precocious, and Janine, who struggles dramatically to keep up with the group. The teacher responds that Tomas certainly is bright; he already knows all the material she hopes to cover in the coming year and is enrolled in her university math class. But Janine . . . Janine is probably the next brightest student in the room.

This example comes from but one class in the country for gifted and talented students. It was an exceptional class in all respects. The students were intelligent, highly motivated, well behaved, gregarious, and supportive of one another. The teacher was impressive both in terms of math knowledge and pedagogy; she knew how to teach bright students, knew how to guide and support their learning as well as how to stimulate them. Yet even within this small, homogeneous, well-defined, and apparently well-adjusted group of kids, interesting differences in ability and affect could be seen.

Tomas's obvious facility with terms, computation, and problem-solving enabled him to perform years ahead of his chronological peers. Janine's math intelligence, on the other hand, may have been the product of intuition, originality, or intense interest. Some educators distinguish between academically gifted and socially gifted; between highly gifted and normally gifted; and between highly creative and highly talented students. As we noted in Chapter 3: Emotional Dimensions of Giftedness, many breakdowns and categories exist.

Ms. Petroff not only noticed and addressed her students' academic and intellectual needs. She was also alert and responsive to their social and emotional needs. For example, she perceived that Tomas sometimes got impatient with Janine, who couldn't keep up with his lightning-fast thought processes. And she was aware that Janine, despite her abilities, was something of a perfectionist who rarely risked giving an answer of which she was not 100 percent sure. Ms. Petroff's other students included those who were occasionally rebellious, sometimes obsessed with projects that weren't part of the curriculum, overly sensitive, and not always receptive to criticism. In many ways, they kept her on her toes.

How Supportive Are You?

You may feel like there's not enough time in the day to add an entirely new component (affective education) into your curriculum, but it's already there anyway. You may not be addressing emotional issues directly, but indirectly you're already sending messages that guide or impede students' search for self-knowledge—messages that broaden students' understanding of themselves and others (or not).

We've provided you with background information on giftedness, and we've asked you to take the "Teacher Inventory" (pages 33–36) and give your students the "Student Questionnaire" (pages 37–43) because knowledge of yourself and your students is vital in determining how you behave in the classroom. A supportive attitude is built into (or not built into) the many small things you do every day—the gestures and remarks you make, the amount and type of physical and eye contact you have with your students, the comments you write on paper, the verbal instructions you give. To communicate expectations clearly, to give honest and supportive feedback, to reward learning processes as well as products, to involve students in decisions, to take time to listen, to see yourself as facilitator and not just "knowledge disseminator"—all of these attitudes and techniques affect your students' emotional well-being as much as (or more than) any single group discussion about thoughts, feelings, and attitudes. Certainly, they go together.

Creating a supportive environment begins the first moment of the first day when students walk into your classroom, and runs concurrently with every instructional task you undertake.

Gifted Program Standards from the National Association for Gifted Children

The National Association for Gifted Children (NAGC) has defined a set of preK–grade 12 standards for gifted education programming. As you work to create a supportive environment that addresses your students' needs—including their social and emotional needs—you may wish to consult these standards from time to time. Excerpts follow. You can see the full standards at nagc.org/information-publications.

From **Standard 1: Learning and Development**

1.1. Self-Understanding. Students with gifts and talents demonstrate self-knowledge with respect to their interests, strengths, identities, and needs in socio-emotional development and in intellectual, academic, creative, leadership, and artistic domains.

1.1.1. Educators engage students with gifts and talents in identifying interests, strengths, and gifts.

1.1.2. Educators assist students with gifts and talents in developing identities supportive of achievement.

From **Standard 3: Curriculum Planning and Instruction**

3.2. Talent Development. Students with gifts and talents become more competent in multiple talent areas and across dimensions of learning.

3.2.1. Educators design curricula in cognitive, affective, aesthetic, social, and leadership domains that are challenging and effective for students with gifts and talents.

3.2.2. Educators use metacognitive models to meet the needs of students with gifts and talents.

From **Standard 4: Learning Environments**

4.2. Social Competence. Students with gifts and talents develop social competence manifested in positive peer relationships and social interactions.

4.2.1. Educators understand the needs of students with gifts and talents for both solitude and social interaction.

4.2.2. Educators provide opportunities for interaction with intellectual and artistic/creative peers as well as with chronological-age peers.

4.2.3. Educators assess and provide instruction on social skills needed for school, community, and the world of work.

National Association for Gifted Children, *Pre-K to Grade 12 Gifted Programming Standards*, NAGC: Resources. nagc.org/resources-publications/resources/national-standards-gifted-and-talented-education/pre-k-grade-12 (2010).

Support stems from truly liking and enjoying your gifted students. But support involves more than smiling, showing enthusiasm, and offering words of encouragement, although these are requisite ingredients. Support is also conveyed by setting clear expectations; giving constructive criticism; being honest; being flexible; and providing your students with structure, tangible rewards, comfortable classrooms, accommodating schedules, and routine times for sharing or relaxing.

Some of the strategies we suggest may seem obvious to you. If that's your initial response, take a moment to consider how often you put them into practice. Do you periodically check out how well you're coming across in these areas? Some of the simplest strategies are also the best.

For more strategies and activities that will help you create a supportive environment for your gifted students, see Chapter 8: Making It Safe to Be Smart: Creating the Gifted-Friendly Classroom.

STRATEGY Clarify Your Role as Teacher and Your Students' Roles as Learners

Read your students this famous saying: *Give a man a fish, he eats for a day; teach a man how to fish, he eats for a lifetime.* *

Invite them to talk about this in terms of knowledge and learning. Is it more important for teachers to tell students the facts and answers ("knowledge"), or to teach them how to learn facts and answers for themselves? Generally, we know that knowledge is "exploding" so fast that much of the information we learn today will be out of date before

long. Many specific jobs and careers will require different sets of knowledge and even different skills by the time students are ready to enter the workforce. We also know that people's memories are limited, and learning itself can be a pleasurable process. These are arguments for "learning how to learn."

Ask your students if they can think of other arguments—both pro and con. Ask them if they have already experienced learning something only to find it has gone out of date. Or perhaps they've seen this happen in the lives of their parents, who may have changed jobs, gone back to school, or been retrained by their employers.

Reinforce that while human beings need fish (or other food) to satisfy their immediate hunger, they also need to learn how to fish to survive beyond the day. Similarly, students need to know certain facts, concepts, and procedures, but they also need to learn how to learn and think on their own.

Ask your students what they think your job as teacher entails, and what their job as learners is. Are you to give them the information they need in order to progress, but also to teach (or encourage) them to learn on their own? Should students learn how to ask questions, analyze problems, research topics, evaluate their own work and the thinking of others? Should they try to just memorize what the teacher says is important? Talk about how teachers can communicate information and function as resources and coaches at the same time.

At some point during this discussion, try to articulate whatever role you define for yourself. You may wish to let students know your limits by saying something

---

*Although the original author refers to "man," we interpret his meaning to include all human beings.

like, "I make mistakes, too. I have strengths in these particular areas [give examples], but I don't know everything, as I'm sure each of you has come to realize!"

STRATEGY Clarify Expectations—Yours and Theirs

What do you expect students do to in your class? You'll want to state this as clearly as possible. At the start of the year (or semester, or week), prepare a handout explaining what you want from your students and what you hope to accomplish. State your expectations in terms of the following:

- **Learning objectives** (*examples:* understand the components of a research paper; master the procedures for completing a particular science experiment; communicate ideas and feelings about one's own ethnic background in a creative project; compare autocratic and democratic decision-making

- **Content** (*examples:* reading assignments—including titles and page numbers; films or websites to review; bloggers with a particular expertise to check out)

- **Products** (what's due when)

- **Process** (*examples:* how students are supposed to proceed; an overall schedule with a list of activities)

- **Assessments** (*examples:* the type of assessment—self-assessment, teacher comments, tests; purpose of measures; policies such as those regarding retests)

- **Intangible outcomes** (*examples:* to start from wherever you are and make progress; to make work personally meaningful; to feel pride in oneself and

one's group; to compete in the state spelling competition)

Go over the handout with your students and allow time for questions. If possible, indicate options they may have under content, products, process and assessments. For instance, they may choose to work with different content or materials, or pick from three suggested final projects: prepare a photo essay, stage a debate, write a paper, or some other project. Indicate how you want students to negotiate with you for different options, and at what point.

When addressing intangible outcomes, try to express what signs of learning are really most meaningful to you—what you would be most pleased to see in your students, as well as what you believe you can realistically expect. This is where understanding your own

expectations of gifted students comes into play. Be as fair and honest in your expectations as you can.

Also check out expectations students may have of you or the class. See if there are other topics they'd like to cover, other processes or materials they'd prefer to use.

Explicitly stating objectives and expectations has a known impact on students' learning. Given an overview of where they're going and what they're responsible for, they can better focus their learning energy and evaluate their own progress.

Even when assignments are "open" and assessment consists of measures other than grades or tests, teachers (and other adults) still have expectations. Often we just take them for granted or assume kids automatically understand them. Making your expectations known may cause concern at first, but in the long run, making goals known causes less anxiety than hidden or ambiguous goals will.

Alleviating the concerns students have about assignments, grades, grading criteria, team assignments, books, and other resources helps build a supportive atmosphere. Checking for these concerns should be done periodically, if not almost every session.

STRATEGY Set Ground Rules

> "A successful teacher doesn't get down to the students' levels, but raises them up to his."
> **—Frank Davies**

All students need help learning and understanding how to behave in a group. They need help improving their social skills and developing trust for each other and in their learning environment.

Every classroom has rules, whether stated or implied. Often, these rules suggest (or dictate) how students should behave, what supplies students should bring to class, or what the consequences are of misbehavior or late work. But rules don't have to be punitive. Instead, they can be inviting and affirming. Some can even be "disguised" as indirect ways of perceiving the class as a functioning assembly of good people.

Discuss the "Class Rules" on page 101. You may want to list the appropriate rules on a chart and post them ahead of time, or use a group discussion and student input to develop a unique set of rules.

Whatever rules you decide to use, talk with your students about what they mean. Talk about how they will be reinforced in your classroom. Look for opportunities to role-model ways to respond to or offer criticism, to respect someone's privacy, or to follow other class rules.

STRATEGY Decide What to Reward and How

What kinds of student behavior (other than compliance, good test scores, and complete homework) do you want to reinforce? How will you reinforce that behavior?

Observe your students for several days. Note the behaviors you'd like to encourage and those you'd like to discourage. Write them down so you don't forget them. Include any other behaviors you can think of which may not have surfaced during your observations.

Think about this collection of behaviors. If you wish, share it with a colleague and get his or her feedback.

Class Rules (Grades K–12)

There are no dumb questions or dumb answers.

It's okay to say "I don't know."

Keep asking until you really understand.

No one is perfect.

You can TRY NEW THINGS here.

This is the place to TAKE RISKS and learn from mistakes.

If you don't agree, say so, and explain your thoughts.

Teasing, bullying, and put-downs are NOT allowed.

Don't criticize people—agree or disagree with their ideas.

During discussions, sometimes it's okay to listen and not talk.

It's good to have a MIND OF YOUR OWN.

Here are examples of positive behaviors to look for (or include in your written list):

- Following through on tasks
- Sharing something personally meaningful
- Supporting a friend
- Spending time on-task
- Asking high-quality questions
- Taking initiative
- Demonstrating patience or self-control
- Exploring something new
- Using humor appropriately

Now come up with specific ways to acknowledge students who demonstrate positive behaviors. Here are some suggestions to consider:

- Praise (and be specific about what you're praising)
- Public recognition
- Formal awards
- Permission to do other things
- Class celebrations
- Opportunity to present work at a parent night or in a variety show
- Free time
- Individual attention
- Special class events (speakers, films, field trips)
- Opportunity to collaborate with you or another mentor
- Roster of "stars"
- Progress charts
- Thank-you notes (public or private)

Never underestimate the power of positive verbal messages. Here are several you may want to try:

- "This looks like you've learned a lot. How do you feel about these grades?"
- "I'm glad you're helping your friend."
- "You tried something new today. That took courage."
- "Congratulations on finishing this."
- "I think this group is ready for the state spelling championships."

- "You did a good job of standing up for yourself in that discussion."

- "I'm glad you asked that question, because I'll bet there are ten other people who want to know the same thing."

- "I believe you can do it."

- "I think it's great how you took the initiative to . . ."

- "You showed a lot of patience (or compassion, or self-control) today."

Gifted students need straightforward feedback on their accomplishments, but they also need lots of reinforcement

Gifted Kids Speak Out

When we asked gifted kids, "How can teachers help gifted kids?" here's what they said:

"Remember that gifted kids are not sleepless, working machines."
—Danny, 12

"Gifted kids like being creative and thinking outside the box. Offer us creative activities instead of always giving things like reports. There are a lot of projects that are more fun than reports."
—Stephanie, 12

"Accept that some students may know more than you do and do not feel intimidated by this. If they know something, let them teach it to you. You can't challenge us if you are afraid of us."
—Ted, 13

When we asked gifted students, "What makes the difference between a good teacher and a great teacher?" here's what they said:

"Teaching is all about relationships. Great teachers will go out of their way to truly get to know all of their students personally."
—Simone, 17

"A great teacher understands that just because someone isn't great in one area, it doesn't mean that they can't still be gifted."
—Asad, 11

"They should have the time to talk with you and help you out when you need it, but they should also be able to let you do things yourself."
—Heidi, 16

for simply being—for relating well to one another, for relaxing, showing compassion, following through, or taking criticism well. They need encouragement when they demonstrate positive social behaviors and emotional maturity (or progress).

One additional point you may want to check on immediately: Some gifted classes don't "count" in terms of credit. Depending on the type of class you have, the number of hours and types of work accomplished, this may be very inappropriate and discriminatory. Gifted students should not have to complete all required coursework and activities in the regular education classes, on top of their gifted class work, for no additional credit. Participation in advanced or enriched classes should be noted in school records and rewarded. Otherwise, some kids may regard gifted education opportunities as a punishment for being bright.

Supporting Gifted Kids One-on-One

The four preceding strategies, and those found in Chapter 8, will help you establish a supportive classroom environment for your gifted students. But what if you need or choose to work with students individually on social or emotional issues? You may have a mixed-abilities classroom with only a few gifted students. Or you may have students with unique or challenging needs, or students who don't respond well in large groups.

The following strategies are ideal for working with students one-on-one or in smaller groups. Of course, you can also adapt them for use with larger groups.

🏹 **STRATEGY** **Use Questionnaires and Surveys**

When you ask students to complete the "Student Questionnaire" on pages 37–43, the answers you get may not seem all that significant, especially the first time around. What *is* significant is that you asked the questions in the first place. You've opened the door for kids to tell you something about themselves, and you've let them know it's okay to communicate with you on a personal level.

On most days, in most schools, students aren't encouraged to express or clarify their feelings. They're probably not used to identifying conflicts, sources of stress, and sources of support in their lives. Some kids who feel uncomfortable with this process at first may ridicule the questionnaire as "silly" or "a waste of time." Yet for students to mature emotionally, they need to examine their perceptions, even when it's awkward or painful. Posing the questions via the questionnaire is a good first step. It stimulates thinking in a relatively safe way and requires no public response.

Surveying students is, in general, a good strategy for getting individuals to address sensitive questions. Unlike open-class voting (which is a useful group strategy), surveys demand anonymous (though some students readily include their names) yet personal answers, and they can be much more explicit. You may wish to implement very brief weekly surveys on questions concerning academic pressures, career or hobby interests, or social pressures, and post the results on a board, class website, or other spot. For example: "In answer to last week's survey on choosing a career, 78 percent of the girls anticipate having a full-time job outside the home as adults, compared to 99 percent of the boys." Again, surveys can engage students individually to reflect on personal traits, values, and attitudes.

A variation on the idea of surveys is found in *100 Ways to Enhance Self-Concept in the Classroom* by Jack Canfield and Harold Clive Wells.[4] Their strategy "Weekly Reaction Sheets" consists of quick, ten-item inventories that help students examine how they are using their time. Some sample questions: "What was the high point of the week?" "What did you procrastinate about?" "What unfinished personal business do you have left?" After six weeks of recording their weekly reactions, students are ready for a discussion on what they've learned. By changing the focus of the content, you can use weekly reaction sheets to address a broad range of growth issues.

STRATEGY Use Journaling

> "I write entirely to find out what I'm thinking, what I'm looking at, what I see and what it means. What I want and what I fear."
>
> **—Joan Didion**

The possibilities for personal growth are almost unlimited when journal writing is approached as creative self-examination. Frequent, private writing has both therapeutic and technical value (in terms of language skills development—although journals shouldn't be assigned for this reason). Journals have become commonplace in classrooms, but their real benefits aren't always tapped.

Often, students are given inadequate direction ("Write something down every day"; "Write about anything, just make it at least three lines long"). Lacking the drama and gravity of Anne Frank's story, students quickly become bored with the tedium of their lives and of their writing. Fortunately, there are several concrete journaling techniques which give enough form and direction to the process to make the writing revelatory—even without the drama. (More about this in a minute.)

An effective way to use journals as a way to get to know your students better is to invite them to share their journals with you. You can then provide a personal response, either within their journal or verbally. Teachers reading student journals should respond to each entry with a simple statement which acknowledges the student's feeling without judging it. In spoken counseling, the equivalent is, "Yes, I hear you. It sounds like . . ." You may wish to provide comments, suggestions, words of encouragement, or drawings.

Because responding individually to student journals takes time, you may need to limit how often you assign journals, or assign them only to students who seem to enjoy them the most. Journals may work best for students who already like to write or seem inclined to introspection. A shy student who tends to observe rather than participate may flower with this type of individual assignment.

We don't believe that journals should be graded. Nor should they be required if, after a mandatory trial period, they seem unnecessary, duplicative, or unproductive for the writer.

Although many forms and styles of journaling would be useful to any student, some may be particularly provocative for gifted students trying to come to terms with their differences. For example, you might ask a gifted student to:

- Write an entry from the point of view of someone not in the gifted program.

- List your favorites—books, songs, food, clothes, hobbies, whatever.

- Describe the traits of an imaginary friend.

- Compose a portrait of yourself as you are now and as you expect to be in ten years.

- Describe a tranquil, beautiful, or particularly stimulating place to be; invent an episode which could take place there.

- Reconstruct an angry dialogue you had with a friend or relative.

- Write an imaginary conversation with a favorite (talking) pet.

Journal assignments can be supplemented by readings from other famous diarists such as Franz Kafka, Anaïs Nin, Anne Frank, and Zlata Filipovic. Some autobiographies and memoirs provide excellent models of journal-style approaches. Students benefit from learning about the authors' lives, and they also gain permission to examine their own lives more deeply and thoughtfully. Certain authors can also function as positive role models for students.

Ask your local librarians or media-center specialists to help you identify diaries and autobiographies you might recommend to your students. In addition, books on journaling that we like include *Journal to the Self* by Kathleen Adams and *Journal Keeping: How to Use Reflective Writing for Learning, Teaching, Professional Insight and Positive Change* by Dannelle D. Stevens and Joanne E. Cooper.

STRATEGY Use Bibliotherapy

"Why are we reading, if not in hope of beauty laid bare, life heightened and its deepest mystery probed?"

—**Annie Dillard**

Bibliotherapy, simply defined, is the use of books to help people solve problems. Through guided reading, students learn to understand themselves and their environment, build self-esteem, meet the developmental challenges of adolescence, and form coping skills. Bibliotherapy is not about sending kids off on their own to read books and think about them (or not). It's a structured interaction between

Featured Films

Along with the use of books through bibliotherapy, the guided viewing of films can be a way to build and support gifted kids' social and emotional development. As educational psychology scholars Thomas P. Hébert and Daniel R. Hammond write, "Using movies to guide gifted students toward self-understanding provides them with numerous benefits. Movies have the potential to enrich and influence the lives of gifted students in constructive ways. . . . When an appropriate movie is combined with a discussion and supportive follow-up activities, gifted students may view their situation through a more positive lens, enabling them to appreciate multiple aspects of difficult situations they may encounter."

These are just a few of the many movies that depict the joys and struggles of gifted kids and teens.

Matilda: Sensitive, moral, and bright, Matilda's only friend is her teacher—until, suddenly, everything changes

October Sky: A group of teens from coal country get mesmerized by space and take their lives in new, unexpected directions

Ferris Bueller's Day Off: A classic depiction of a highly skilled underachiever who challenges authority at every turn in his "borrowed" Ferrari

Billy Elliott: Ballet instead of boxing? The struggles of a young man whose dad expects something more macho than dancing from his talented son

Finding Forrester: A talented young writer—and basketball player—finds an unexpected mentor in an older author

The Hunger Games trilogy: A strong and skilled teenage girl takes on a fight to the death disguised as a televised game and becomes a source of inspiration and leadership to her nation

August Rush: An orphaned musical prodigy uses his gift as a clue to finding his birth parents

The Fault in Our Stars: Two teens with sharp, unconventional minds bond in the face of cancer

Phoebe in Wonderland: A bright young girl who struggles to follow the rules uses her intense and vivid imagination as an escape

Any Harry Potter movie: Need we say more?

Thomas P. Hébert and Daniel R. Hammond, "Guided Viewing of Film with Gifted Students: Resources for Educators and Counselors," *Gifted Child Today*, vol. 29 no. 3 (2006).

a facilitator (you) and a participant (your student). In other words, if you're going to suggest books to your students, and you want to have meaningful discussions about them afterward, you need to read the books yourself. Judith Wynn Halsted, author of *Some of My Best Friends Are Books: Guiding Gifted Readers,* explains:[5]

Rather than merely recommending a book to a child, [bibliotherapy] includes three components: a reader, a book, and a leader who will read the same book and prepare for productive discussion of the issues the book raises. To be effective, the leader must be aware of the process of bibliotherapy: IDENTIFICATION, in which the reader identifies with a character in the book; CATHARSIS, the reader's experiencing of the emotions attributed to the character; and INSIGHT, the application of the character's experience to the reader's own life. The leader then frames questions that will confirm and expand on these elements.

Bibliotherapy is an effective way to introduce gifted students to fictional peers and mentors—people who are like them (at least in certain ways) whose lives, struggles, and decisions are revealing and affirming. (See pages 128–129 for a list of ten great books that feature kids with gifts.) It certainly does this more positively than the usual depictions of gifted kids in TV shows and movies. For some gifted kids, reading about "someone like me" is their first exposure to the fact that they're not alone and they're not "weird."

What kinds of questions can you formulate and ask your students about a particular book you've assigned? That depends on the book, your student, and

what you hope to achieve through bibliotherapy. For example, if your student needs help with relationships, you might choose a book with that theme. As you read it, jot down questions you think of along the way. Try to come up with questions that lead to thoughtful discussion as opposed to simple yes or no answers. Helpful question starters are: "What did you think when . . . ?" "How did you feel about . . . ?" "If you were [a character in the book], what would you have done differently?" You might also ask your student to comment on, evaluate, or journal about a character, event, or turning point in the book.

Or, have the student choose a quote from the book that speaks loudly to him or her and compose an essay, journal entry, or other writing using that quote as a jumping-off point. In *Bookmarked: Teen Essays on Life and Literature from Tolkien to Twilight*, teacher Ann Camacho collected dozens of student essays written on this theme. She prompted kids to use the quotes they chose "as the foundation or seed to developing your personal philosophy about how you live your life." She suggests doing the same with your students, saying, "In the process of reflection on what we have read, and then committing our own thoughts to the written world, we connect with the greater world around us."[6]

STRATEGY Schedule Weekly Conferences

Weekly conferences may provide just the right amount of attention, in just the right format, for certain students in need of temporary or periodic counseling. Naturally, if the student has serious emotional or psychological problems, he needs to see a professional counselor in addition to talking with you. But as a classroom or special services teacher, you are right to be concerned if a student is having trouble in your class. And before you refer a student to someone else, the weekly conference is a good first recourse. Regular office hours can be set up after school for any student to visit you on an as-needed, first-come, first-served basis. Or you can invite particular students to come in for scheduled appointments.

The purpose of student conferences changes, of course, with the student. For some kids, the issue may be breaking away emotionally from parents who don't understand their need to be independent. (Independence, for them, may be symbolized by being different—or, in some cases, by being totally average. A kid who's been pushed too hard for too long may assert his independence by being "ordinary.") For others, it may be trying to rekindle interest in school, or slowing down and focusing on only a few tasks at once. For still others, it may be the pressure of grades, lack of friends, or lack of role models. Students may be weighed down by heavy-duty expectations, or multiple college or career options. The outcomes of your conferences will vary, from improving their academic performance to tempering their productivity; from changing (or individualizing) assignments to recommending extracurricular activities.

Although the specific goals will change from student to student, individual conferences can accomplish several things.

- They give kids a chance to vent, beyond group discussions (in which they may not be participating fully anyway),

about whatever personal problems are interfering with their work or life.

- They give you a chance to confront the student whose grades or participation levels are slipping; the student who is becoming increasingly negative; the student who seems anxious or depressed. Confrontation, in this sense, means communicating this message: "I see that something is going on with you. Will you tell me about it? We're going to have to work something out here. . . ." The act of intervention alone tells the depressed student that his feelings have been noticed; the irresponsible student that her "act" isn't fooling anyone; and the passive student that his lack of participation is cause for concern.

- They show that you care about the student as a person. You're listening; you're taking her feelings seriously.

- They enable you and the student to problem-solve different situations together.

- They provide direction and support as students go about implementing solutions.

Condensed guidelines for weekly conferences are difficult to suggest when the issues at stake, and the age and type of learner, are so variable. But perhaps the simple approach described here will lend direction to your already evolving practices. Keep in mind the common problems of gifted students. Keep in mind their particular needs for self-knowledge, acceptance by others, and understanding of others. Your observations, questions, feedback, and especially your affirmation of them as people will help them gain these forms of knowledge. Specifically, you may wish to:

1. Use the first session (or two or three) as a time to "get the full story"—to hear and understand the student's perception of herself, her challenges, and all that is related.

2. Clarify what you (the teacher) feel may be misperceptions on the student's part. Feelings depend in part on cognitive reasoning. Sometimes they are based on perceptions and assumptions which may or may not be correct. Ask the student to clarify fuzzy statements by rephrasing them. Ask for examples and verification.

3. Suggest ways in which a student might test his own perceptions. For example, you might ask: "Have you asked your mother directly whether she cares about you attending an Eastern college?" "If you're convinced that the English teacher thinks you can't write, perhaps you ought to ask for a conference and get a fuller evaluation." "You say other kids don't like you. Is there any way you could test that conclusion and find out if it's really true?"

4. Ask the student what she wants to do about the problem—what she would like to see happen.

5. Get a sense of when the student is ready to think about solutions. Even after gathering new information and new insights into a problem, the student may not be ready to let go of it. Chronic problems can give people a sense of identity, and changing them (or changing one's response to them) can cause anxiety. But when students seem ready to admit that there just

might be a solution to their problem, brainstorm like crazy. Back up the ideas with measurable goals, concrete plans, and dates for keeping in touch. During the follow-up conferences, find out what happened: Did the solution work? Why or why not? Does the strategy need readjustment? Or does the problem need to be reanalyzed and redefined?

6. Set behavioral guidelines for some students while they work on problems that can't change overnight. Students may not be ready to work on solutions for quite some time, but they still need to conform to certain expectations now. For example, it may take years to turn a really discouraged kid around. Perhaps the underlying problem is perfectionism, transfigured into fear of failure. You might meet with him regularly to reinforce his efforts, and to reinforce your minimum expectations (staying in school, not missing class, maintaining a C average, doing required work, and so on).

7. Ask the student what she is learning about herself by having this conflict, by experiencing the emotions it causes, by examining the perceptions she forms, and by testing the solutions she generates. Conflict in life is not always avoidable. What matters is how she deals with it and uses it to grow internally. Some of our greatest opportunities for growth come from conflict, if we only have the courage to meet it with both eyes open.

If deeply rooted issues such as chemical dependency, family conflict, child abuse, or suicidal feelings emerge, refer the student to more formal evaluation and make sure it happens. The school psychologist or principal should be consulted before you mention anything about this to a student or to parents. Continue to be a listener and an advocate, but demand honesty. You may not be the person who will work with the student on a deeper emotional level, but you can at least confront him on behavior in your class, and any delusions that are disrupting your teaching and his learning. You might say, "I may not know the answer to your problem, Jake, but you and I both know that's not true." You can also reinforce the positive steps the student takes. Stay committed to your course of action, which is to observe, set limits, provide encouragement, respond to needs when possible, and tell the truth.

📌 STRATEGY Use Growth Contracts

Growth contracts are written agreements between individual students and teachers, specifying a plan for personal change or growth within a set period of time. Goals generally focus on affective issues of concern to the student. In this respect, they differ from learning contracts, which are essentially academic. (Changing one's attitude about school, or improving performance in a particular area, would be an appropriate growth contract goal, however.) Both the high achiever, wishing to meet new friends, and the underachiever, wanting to find something that holds his or her interest (a goal which inevitably involves risk-taking), can benefit from the process of setting intentions and strategies down on paper.

Growth contract timelines may be as short as one week or as long as a year.

Contracts can be initiated by either the student or the teacher. Whether you'll require them of all students, use them only with kids meeting with you for weekly conferences, or for a single student in a special situation will depend upon your own set of circumstances.

One key to making growth contracts successful is helping the student articulate something that is really important to him or her. The goal of the contract should reflect a felt need. A second key consists of finding strategies that are reasonably small and concrete, easy to monitor and evaluate. A third key is a time commitment from you; the teacher must stay involved. Even the most motivated student needs the reinforcement of having someone to talk to about his or her progress and problems.

A reproducible "Growth Contract" is found on pages 114–115. You might use this as is or adapt it as you see fit.

Along the way, you'll want to talk with the student about the progress being made on the contract. Here are some suggested questions:

- How easy or how difficult have you found it to work on this contract?

- Is the goal still worthwhile to you? Have other goals replaced it?

- If you had to do this over, would you take different steps? Why or why not?

- Do you need to think of other ways to overcome these obstacles? What can you do? Who can help you?

- What has come as the biggest surprise to you while working on this contract?

- How do you feel about the reactions you've been getting from other people, now that you're making these changes?

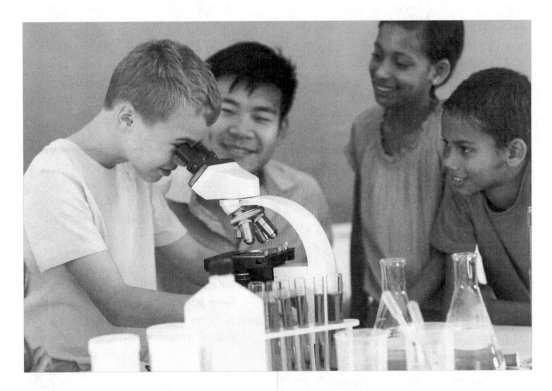

- How are you feeling about yourself these days?

- Do you remember how you felt when you first started to work on this contract?

- Have there been any changes?

    In summary, keep in mind that whether students fulfill their contracts down to the letter is less important than the information and skills they gain in the process. Achieving complete success is wonderful, but any measure of progress is worth celebrating. Meanwhile, setting goals, designing strategies to meet those goals, working on those strategies, improvising, and seeing what works are skills students will use throughout their lives in an infinite number of settings.

STRATEGY Form Peer Alliances

For the gifted student who is emotionally troubled, socially "ungifted," or withdrawn, large groups may seem safe because they're large. Small groups seem threatening when sharing and participation are required, and one-to-one partnerships the most threatening of all. But small groups and peer teaching (or "alliances") may also give the loner the individual attention he needs. They may offer the best, most private arena for him to try out his newly acquired social skills and to learn about other people.

    Partnerships can be short-term (limited to the length of one learning project or exercise) or long-term (as with a year-long study partner). They can be formed between students at the same academic or age level, or between students of different ages and abilities. Tutoring younger or less advanced students is a good variation of one-to-one learning.

Using assigned partners or small teams (of three or four members) can build social awareness and skills either directly or indirectly. If addressing communication skills, values, attitudes, or feelings directly, start partners off with low-risk activities and work toward exercises requiring more intimacy and self-disclosure.

In our experience, there are several factors that seem to affect the success of peer alliances. They include:

- **Compatibility of members.** Age, sex, backgrounds, and personalities are all important. Students of various ages can be grouped together, but not indiscriminately.

- **Awareness and acceptance of ground rules for working together.** Students can help develop these rules. They usually appreciate having established guidelines.

- **Length of time allowed for the relationship to develop.** Kids can't become close immediately just because they're gifted. In fact, they may never be as close to some in their group as others.

- **Expected outcomes of the alliance.** Not all partners will necessarily benefit or get along. Determine in your own mind what minimum outcomes you're looking for.

When given the option, kids usually rush to be with their friends when choosing small groups or partners. As you know, this is not always a good thing. Use your discretion when placing students together; ideally, their strengths and limitations will balance each other out. Students should have some rapport (or the potential for it) but not be so close as to preclude any challenge or opportunity for new experiences.

Think ahead of time about guidelines your students will need to work together productively. How long will the students be working together? What is the purpose of the alliance, the task? What terms will they have to work out themselves (such as division of labor, agreement on topics or methods), and what will they need to work out with you? What should they do if and when they get stuck?

Keep in mind that short-term partnerships are very useful for serving immediate purposes, but they won't make long-term changes in a withdrawn or antisocial student. You may not always be able to find the right person to team up with a particularly lonely, socially inept kid, but when you do, give them enough time to get to know each other and become more comfortable working with each other. On the other hand, don't be afraid to terminate a partnership that isn't doing either student any good.

Ask yourself what you expect to happen for the students as a result of the alliance. Better study habits? More confidence? A friendship? Learning to work in a team? Support for each other? What are the signs of success, and the symptoms of dysfunction?

STRATEGY Recommend That Students be Referred to Counseling

Although this option is the last one described here, by no means should you consider it the option of last resort. If you suggest that a student be referred for professional counseling or therapy, that does not mean you believe that he's beyond other forms of help, or even that you and he have exhausted the alternatives. Therapy is more than a form of treatment for the emotionally conflicted; it is potentially a unique form of education in the interpersonal and intrapersonal realms. Any introspectively inclined person can benefit. Professional individual counseling or psychotherapy is undoubtedly one of the best ways gifted students can learn more about themselves and their conflicts with the world, whether these conflicts are severe or not.

But individual (or group) psychotherapy is expensive and not always covered by medical insurance. School psychologists may or may not be qualified or available. In large urban public schools, they typically have heavy workloads and limited time. For these reasons alone, you probably should explore a number of options for students in addition to psychological counseling.

Keep in mind that for some students, the suggestion of therapy itself can greatly affect their self-concept. They may see it as a punishment or feel there truly is something wrong with them ("I must be really weird"), and therefore be doubly ashamed and angry. Others will approach it fearfully but also with relief.

Your own attitude about therapy is very important here. If you communicate by your words, actions, attitude, or body language that therapy represents failure or disgrace (either yours or the student's), it will be more difficult for the student to accept it. It helps if a teacher can say, "I was once helped greatly by a counselor," or "I'm really happy that you're going to be getting some help with this. Good for you for having the courage to work on it."

If your school does not already provide counseling for the gifted, strongly encourage them to do so. **Remember:** It's the job of a school psychologist or counselor to make a referral, *not* your job as a teacher. The proper arena for support groups for the gifted is really in the counselor's office. Psychologists or counselors are better equipped to sort out the variety of problems in students' lives, whether they're related to the home, career options, finances, drugs, peer group or identity, gender, or school and intellectual concerns. These problems are inevitably intertwined, particularly when one or more is chronic.

As was mentioned earlier in the section on weekly conferences, your job will be to maintain contact with the counselor while continuing to meet with the student and solve school-related problems together. Resist the temptation to feel overly responsible for your students. It's easy to become too wrapped up in their lives and affected by their struggles. And although teaching is a caring profession, you'll need to define the limits of your involvement and not feel guilty for doing so. Don't hesitate to recommend that a student be referred to a professional counselor when you feel there is something going on that needs to be looked at, and which requires more time and more specialized training than you've got.

Growth Contract

1. *Target area for growth*: Something I want to change about myself or my life.

   I'd like to be _____

   _____

   _____

   _____

2. Steps I'll take to reach my goal:

   a. _____

   _____

   b. _____

   _____

   c. _____

   _____

3. Resources that will help me along the way (including people I can turn to for support):

   a. _____

   _____

   b. _____

   _____

   c. _____

   _____

4. Possible roadblocks or things that will stand in my way that I'll need to get around:

   a. _____

   _____

→

Growth Contract, continued

b. _____

_____

c. _____

_____

5. *Evaluation*: How will I know when things are better?

I'll know when _____

_____

_____

_____

How close to my goal did I come? Explain: _____

_____

_____

_____

Did I achieve as much as I hoped or expected? Explain: _____

_____

_____

_____

Did I achieve less than I hoped or expected? Explain: _____

_____

_____

_____

CHAPTER 5

Understanding Gifted Kids from the Inside Out

 You're always with yourself, so you might as well enjoy the company.
—Diane von Furstenberg

At fifteen, Christine was asked to share her views on what it means to be a gifted adolescent. "The thought did cross my mind," she said, "to write profoundly on the topic, but I quickly dismissed it. I'm trying to cut down on the number of deep and meaningful thoughts I have before breakfast." Instead, Christine talked about herself and her giftedness by posing a series of questions, including:

- "Why is giftedness linked to achievement—that is, what I can or cannot do—instead of what and how I feel?"

- "Why do teachers act as counselors if they can't listen or stand not having a quick solution?"

- "Who says that growing up gifted necessarily means wanting to get high grades, going to college, and getting a good job?"

- "Have you noticed that adults expect kids to wear the label 'gifted' when they won't?"

Like many who came before her (and many who will follow), Christine was grappling with issues of self-image and self-acceptance. But isn't that true of all adolescents? Don't all teenagers question their place in the ocean of existence?

Of course they do. (So do many younger kids, especially younger gifted kids, who tend to be more sensitive, perceptive, and introspective than their peers.) But when giftedness is added into the "Who am I?" and "Where do I belong?" equation, the need for answers may be more intense, powerful, and acute.

Being smart doesn't inoculate a person from the fear of being bypassed by friends or overshadowed by self-doubts. Indeed, the gifted child may be more aware than others of the need for these issues to be resolved if one is to have a happy and fulfilling life.

Self-Image vs. Self-Esteem

If you can't tell the difference between a $50 cabernet and a $5 bottle of rotgut red, your self-image as a wine connoisseur may be low. Likewise, if your trigonometry skills are limited to knowing that a cosine isn't the person who underwrites a loan, your self-image as a mathematician might be lacking. Still, if you're not a wine drinker, you probably don't care that your palate is poor, and if sines and cosines don't play a major role in your professional life, it may not matter to you that you can't determine the area of a right triangle.

Herein lies the difference between self-image and self-esteem:

- **Self-image** = your perception of your ability to do a certain task, like cook a meal, write a term paper, or make a friend.

- **Self-esteem** = the importance you place on your ability (or inability) to cook a meal, write a term paper, or make a friend.

Even if your self-image as a mathematician is lower than absolute zero, this might not impact your self-esteem in the least. However, if your self-image for doing math is low and it's important to you to do well in math, your self-esteem could be negatively affected.

It's important to know and understand this distinction, and to explain it to your students. Here's why:

- Counselors or teachers may talk about a student's high or low self-esteem as if it were a singular, all-encompassing trait when, in fact, it's content-specific. To say that "Maria has low self-esteem" is a generalization, and, like all generalizations, isn't accurate. So, Maria's self-esteem as a scholar might be high, while her self-esteem as a socially relevant person could be low.

- Gifted kids often tend toward perfectionism,* so helping them see both the connections and distinctions between self-image and self-esteem may allow them to see the importance of being selective in their quest for excellence.

- Knowing the difference between self-image and self-esteem often helps students understand their motivation (or lack thereof) to improve a certain skill. For example, a student may wonder, "Why should I work hard to improve my social relationships if I don't believe that friendships are worth

---

*For more on this topic, see pages 63–66 and pages 204–207.

the hassle?" While this might be a sad admission on the part of a potentially lonely person, at least it helps us understand the reasoning behind his actions or inactions.

Explaining, through example, this fine-line distinction between self-image and self-esteem to parents of gifted kids is also a good idea. Not only may it help them understand their smart kids a little better, it may also make for more pleasant and productive dinnertime conversations about achievement, motivation, and priorities.

Gifted Kids Speak Out

We asked gifted kids, "What are some things adults do and say that are supposed to help you—but *don't* help?" Here's what they said:

"Oh, it's okay, Eric." (No, it's not.)

"Good try, Eric!" (Yeah . . . right.)

"You'll do better next time, Eric." (As if.)

"Get the football, Eric!" (I'm trying.)

—Eric, 10

"There's always a next time!" (In truth, I really don't care about next time yet. I wanted to do well now!)

"You're smart. Don't worry." (Okay, I'm smart, but that doesn't automatically guarantee that I know the answer or will get an A. I still need to work and worry.)

—Mei, 19

"Don't take everything so personally."

"You're too (smart, sensitive, opinionated, etc.) for your own good."

"Don't be so hard on yourself."

"Don't work harder. Work smarter."

"Lighten up once in a while."

"You'll get over this in time."

Gifted Kids Are Different

"To be yourself in a world that is constantly trying to make you something else is the greatest accomplishment."

—Ralph Waldo Emerson

More than half a century ago, psychologist Abraham Maslow proposed a hierarchy of human needs. He defined our most basic needs as physiological: food, water, sleep, shelter, exercise, and other essentials of life. Our highest needs have to do with self-actualization: developing our talents, being true to our goals, and becoming everything we're capable of being.

Maslow understood that self-actualization (and, just below it, self-esteem) are possible only when we've had enough to eat, we feel safe, and we have formed close, accepting relationships with others. Once these needs are covered, the higher needs such as self-esteem and self-actualization take on increasing importance.

For gifted children, the desire to belong and to be accepted is as strong as in other children, but they may experience more anxiety about it. Some of the specific intellectual issues gifted children and adolescents face include:

1. **Understanding and accepting what it means to be gifted.** ("Everybody tells me I'm gifted, but nobody tells me what that means. Help!")

2. **Evaluating one's life relative to different measures of success.** ("If I don't become a doctor or a lawyer, will I be perceived as a failure?")

3. **Recognizing the difference between "better at" and "better than."** ("Does my being able to do things other kids can't do make me a more valuable member of society?")

4. **Coping with the frustration of having too many options.** (How do you prepare for a future in which many available jobs are likely to be very different from the present? And how do you know if your dreams are going to match what your future holds?)

5. **Overcoming the barriers of others' expectations.** ("No matter how well I do, there is always someone telling me that I could have done better.")

6. **Understanding the concept of asynchronous development.** ("I'm twelve years old with the mind of a sixteen-year-old, the body of a ten-year-old, and the social skills of a 1,000-year-old Druid. Where do I fit in?")

7. **Becoming an advocate for one's own self-interests.** ("I find school so boring, but nobody seems to care. There's got to be a better way to learn.")

8. **Understanding the role of socialization.** ("All of my good friends are older or younger than I am. Why is this? Is it okay to have friends of varying ages?")

Obviously, questions about one's intellect interweave with questions that deal with social and emotional growth. This is to be expected, as few of life's uncomfortable or unclear situations inhabit only one domain of our existence. Each of us is both a thinker and a feeler. To disassociate one element from the other is an artificial separation, at best.

What this means for you, the teacher who's trying to understand the gifted students in your classes, is that you should be ready to talk about and explore issues with your students that begin as school issues but end up as life issues. The academic world of gifted students is often the one in which they have experienced the most success; therefore, they feel most comfortable talking about it. But as you reveal other aspects of your students' lives—social, emotional, vocational, intellectual (as opposed to academic)—you'll likely notice more vulnerabilities than you ever saw in that comfortable classroom context where A's often come easily and homework is a breeze.

Following are eighteen activities related to the eight specific intellectual issues listed on page 119. These will start you on the path of getting to know your gifted students from the inside out—and helping them know, understand, and respect themselves. The first two activities should be done early in the school year; they set a solid

tone for "deciphering" what giftedness is. The others can be scheduled in any order throughout the year as part of your curriculum for gifted students. Remember, exploring this social and emotional territory is just as important (if not more important) as covering core subject matter. But don't think that you have to do all the activities—this is not a test!—as you might find some more age-appropriate than others for the particular students with whom you work.

Understanding and Accepting What It Means to Be Gifted

What does it mean to be gifted? This is the springboard from which all other discussions of giftedness are launched.

✏ ACTIVITY Ups and Downs

One of our favorite ways to get children to consider their personal reactions to being gifted is to ask them to complete a bubble chart.

Give each student a copy of "Everything Has Its Ups and Downs!" on page 145. Have them work alone or in pairs to consider some of the positive and negative aspects of growing up gifted. Once they complete their charts, invite them to walk around the room and compare their responses to those of their classmates. Follow this with a class-wide discussion of the ups and downs of being gifted—and be ready to hear some interesting banter. Don't be surprised if the children express a positive aspect of something negative. In the sample shown at right, two fifth-grade boys, Teddy and Cody, note that being teased allows them to "come up with a good comeback." This "Ups and Downs" activity seems to work best with younger gifted students—those in grade five or below.

Name: Teddy and Cody

ACTIVITY Gifted Is . . .
Gifted Means . . .

Here's a simple but effective way for students to share how they feel about the "gifted" label. Give each student a copy of "Gifted Is . . . Gifted Means . . ." on pages 146–148. If they need a few prompts to get started, you might offer one or more of the following:

- "Gifted is . . . hard to explain to other people."

- "Gifted means . . . having to do homework that you already know how to do."

- "Gifted is . . . a lot of fun, if you know what to do with it."

- "Gifted means . . . having friends who act more grown-up than they are."

Make sure that your students understand how to complete the second part of the handout: by imagining what *other people* in their lives would say.

The ensuing discussions can be a reflective overview of how and why different people have such varied views on what it means to be gifted.

Students may mention some of the less-than-pleasant names that gifted kids (and adults) are sometimes called: brainiac, nerd, teacher-pleaser, wonk, snob, know-it-all. They may point out that on television and in movies, gifted people are often portrayed as weird—consider Sheldon Cooper on *The Big Bang Theory* or the main character from *Akeelah and the Bee*, who tries to hide her intelligence in order to fit in. Even Hermione in the early Harry Potter films was ridiculed for her strict attention to everything academic.

Ask your students to think about this: What is it about the word "gifted" that causes people to have such strong reactions? No one seems too concerned about the terms "athletic" or "artistic" or "talented," all of which mean that someone has capabilities in other domains of living. So what is it about this singular word—"gifted"—that is such a turn-off to many?

You likely won't come to a firm conclusion or resolution, since this question has been around for almost as long as our field of study has existed. Still, it's good to have this discussion so that your students can air their views.

Gifted Kids Share Their Views

Here's how some of Jim's sixth-grade students responded to the "Gifted Is . . . Gifted Means . . ." activity.

To us, gifted is . . . / gifted means . . .

- Being special, even if others don't think so

- Being smart enough to think of a comeback for a bully who picks on you because you're smart

- Thinking all the time
- Being role models to younger siblings and nerds to your older siblings
- Smarting off to teachers when you don't mean to
- Being smarter than others but still being human
- A reason for people to make fun of you
- You are an ordinary kid with speedy learning skills
- Being intense
- You are different (not in a bad way, necessarily)
- Having classes that everyone says are hard but you think are easy
- Me

To our parents, gifted means . . .

- Being outrageously smart
- Having to live up to their high expectations
- Being just like them
- Having a special gift from God

To our best friends, gifted means . . .

- Being cool
- Wishing they could do the things we do in our class

To our worst enemies, gifted means . . .

- Being goody-goody freaks
- Being stuck-up

To a teacher who "gets it," gifted means . . .

- Getting respect
- Having a talented brain that is hungry for knowledge
- Knowing that smart kids are often ignored by schools

→

To a teacher who doesn't "get it," gifted means . . .

- "You just got a lucky score on a second-grade test"
- Kids who get unfair privileges
- Someone completely different from other kids
- Not someone worth respecting

To our grandparents, gifted means . . .

- "A good thing on your record"
- Good grades, which means more $$$
- Smart kids who want books instead of money (wrong!)

To a TV producer, gifted means . . .

- An exaggerated stereotype put together to win ratings
- Someone easy to make fun of in a situation comedy

Considering Different Measures of Success

In today's era of high-stakes testing and performance-based standards, students are pressured to produce. Whether it's high test scores that will allow a school to call itself "effective" or "exemplary," or three-dimensional projects that are hung in the school halls for visitors to admire, kids are bombarded with a pervasive yet false bias: that one's worth is primarily determined by one's scholastic achievements.

In a climate such as this, it's easy for gifted students to lose sight of the fact that not everything that can be measured matters, and not everything that matters can be measured. As teachers, let's encourage students to concentrate on what they *learned* rather than what they *earned*.

"What was educationally significant and hard to measure has been replaced by what is educationally insignificant and easy to measure. So now we measure how well we taught something that isn't worth learning."

—Arthur Costa

ACTIVITY Coffee for a Cause

It was a rainy, warm night in May. The lava lamps were in place, the lattes were steaming hot and smelling great, and more than 200 parents, students, and community members were gathered at a local coffeehouse for an evening of student readings and musical performances.

Seventh grader Stevie began the night by reading his selection, "Poetry Is ..."

Poetry Is . . .

What is poetry?

It is such a simple word, yet so hard to define.

Far from just rhyming

Poetry is a portal between destinations.

Poetry takes you away from normal life and into a rebirth,

Into imagination.

Poetry creates a division

Between those who are poets

And those who are not.

Poetry is a work of art that has a mind of its own.

Poetry describes what does not exist, yet always has.

Poetry opens your eyes to see what is invisible.

Poetry lets you hear the silence.

At the poem's end, people started clapping. Stevie stopped them, reminding his audience that "at a real coffeehouse, people do this" and snapping his fingers like a beatnik from an earlier era. Everyone laughed, then the snapping began.

More than sixty students shared their work that night. Little of it had been graded, and much of it had been completed outside of class time. Students merely chose something to share that made them proud—a story they'd written, a flute-and-piano duet, a scene

Ownership of Learning

David Conley, CEO of the Educational Policy Improvement Center (EPIC) at the University of Oregon, seeks solutions to educational problems, with a strong focus on making sure that students are college- and career-ready by high school graduation. He starts by asking students this essential question: "Think about something you became good at through effort. What did you have to do? What challenges did you have to overcome?"

Conley hopes to instill student ownership into the learning equation. Here are his core elements of owning one's learning:

- Be self-aware—discover your interests, passions skills, and ambitions

- Set goals—know what you need to achieve based on self-awareness

- Be motivated—have the mindset to achieve your goals

- Persist—don't give up, especially when something does not come easily to you

- Monitor performance—know how well you are *really* doing by gauging your true skill level

- Ask for help—know when you are stuck, then get help—and don't view this as a weakness

- Show self-efficacy—learn how to control the things you can control, and then control them

from *Hamlet*. A portion of the money raised that night from the sale of coffee and pastries (plus an end-of-the-evening passing of the hat) netted almost $400 for a charity of the students' choosing: a summer camp for children with severe burns that was sponsored by a local children's hospital. Coffee for a Cause is now in its second decade of operation at Twinsburg, Ohio's public library, and its performers have raised more than $35,000. Some of the music has changed—Bruno Mars and Taylor Swift now hold a place in the program, as do the old standbys of Beethoven and Nirvana—but the underlying purpose of Coffee for a Cause remains the same: no tests, no homework, no competition, just a chance for children to reveal their talents and benefit others.

Is there a coffeehouse in your school community? You, too, can offer Coffee for a Cause.

ACTIVITY Quotables

Sometimes the fewest words convey the most meaning. Such is the case with many quotations (from people famous and not) that leave meaningful and poignant impressions. For example, how would your students respond to the following?

- "When you come to a fork in the road, take it." —Yogi Berra

- "No person is your friend who demands your silence or denies your right to grow." —Alice Walker

- "The respect of others' rights is peace." —Benito Juarez

- "Birds sing after a storm, why shouldn't we?" —Rose Kennedy

- "If you hear a voice within you say, 'You cannot paint,' then by all means paint, and that voice will be silenced." —Vincent van Gogh

- "We learn more by looking for the answer and not finding it than we do from learning the answer itself." —Lloyd Alexander

- "If you don't like change, you're going to like irrelevance even less." —General Eric Shinseki

- "The key is to fail quickly. Flush out ideas and let go of the ones that fail." —Josh Linkner, author of *Disciplined Dreaming*

This selection barely scratches the surface, of course. Countless books and websites offer a wide variety of quotations for students to consider. And once you've found suitable examples, the possibilities for projects are endless. A few ideas to try:

- Have students select a quote and write an essay on its importance in their lives.

- Ask students to locate a photo or draw a picture that brings to life the quote they have selected. Share these in small groups.

- Have students work with the art teacher to learn simple calligraphy. Afterward, have them copy their quotes on a shield made from construction paper. The shield represents the students' "defense" against other people's angry, demeaning, teasing, or otherwise inappropriate words. Students can use the back of the shield to compose an essay on the importance of the quote in their lives and in their interactions with others. (If calligraphy instruction isn't available or convenient, students can print out their quotations in fancy computer fonts.)

■ Locate some quotes from fictional characters in literature and complete a classroom collage of their wisdom. Some ideas:

- Katniss Everdeen in *The Hunger Games* by Suzanne Collins: "You don't forget the face of the person who was your last hope."

- Albus Dumbledore in *Harry Potter and the Sorcerer's Stone* by J.K. Rowling: "It does not do to dwell on dreams and forget to live."

- Gandalf in J.R.R. Tolkien's *The Fellowship of The Ring:* "All we have to decide is what to do with the time that is given us."

- Quentin in *Paper Towns* by John Green: "If you don't imagine, nothing ever happens at all."

- Tris in *Divergent* by Veronica Roth: "Sometimes, the best way to help someone is just to be near them."

Recognizing the Difference Between "Better at" and "Better than"

Few people would argue against providing special assistance to students diagnosed with a learning disability

Raising the Ceiling

Chester Finn and Jessica Hockett examined 165 public high schools that have selective admission policies, where the needs of gifted and/or high achieving students are paramount to the schools' missions. Why do we need such schools? Finn and Hockett explain[1]:

"First, is the United States providing *all* of its young people the education that they need in order to make the most of their capacities, both for their own sake and for that of the larger society?

"Second, have we neglected to raise the ceiling while we've struggled to lift the floor? As the country strives to toughen its academic standards, close its achievement gaps, repair its bad schools and 'leave no child behind,' is it also challenging its high-achieving and highly motivated students—and those who may not yet be high achievers but can learn substantially more than the minimum? Are we as determined to build more great schools as to repair those that have collapsed?

"Third, is America making wise investments in its own future prosperity and security by ensuring that its high-potential children are well prepared to break new ground and assume leadership roles on multiple fronts?

"Finally, at a time when we're creating new school choices and individual learning opportunities of many kinds . . . are we paying sufficient attention to *this* kind of choice: the academically selective high school, and the learning opportunities it offers to youngsters with the capacity and inclination to benefit from them?"

or a developmental handicap. Fewer still would say that there is something "undemocratic" about providing differentiated educational services that allow these children to realize their potential.

Unfortunately, this attitude does not always apply when special education options for gifted students are under discussion. While some people do acknowledge and espouse the need to provide extra intellectual stimulation for these high-end learners, many others see such provisions as wasteful expenditures on "kids who will make it anyway." Sometimes the term "elitist" arises, as critics contend that any separation of smart children from others will create one group of "haves" and several other groups of "have nots." Combating these biases—indeed, prejudices—against gifted children has been a constant battle for gifted child advocates for generations.

Addressing this issue directly with children, gifted or not, can result in valuable learning for all.

✎ ACTIVITY Top Ten Favorite Reads

Bob Seney—a gifted education colleague, friend, and book connoisseur—selected these books as his all-time favorite reads for children and their teachers. They feature children with gifts—children who are better at certain things than those around them but who still face struggles. Consider setting up a book club with your students, giving them the option to vote on which book they read and holding regular meetings to discuss, especially focusing on topics relevant to them as gifted kids. Also be sure to check online and with publishers to see if study guides or reading group guides are available for the books you choose.

#10: *A Solitary Blue* by Cynthia Voigt. Love, loss, family, friendship: big issues for Jeff Greene, who comes to understand his parents and himself after some emotionally trying experiences.

#9: *Welcome to the Ark* by Stephanie S. Tolan. Four brilliant misfits are thrown together in an experimental group home they dub "The Ark." They soon discover each other's extraordinary powers—and the gifts they offer each other.

#8: *Interstellar Pig* by William Sleator. A sci-fi novel in which sixteen-year-old Barney is resigned to another boring summer—until some curious neighbors move in, bringing with them a game called "Interstellar Pig." But is it only a game?

#7: *The Invention of Hugo Cabret* by Brian Selznick. A graphic novel starring Hugo, an orphan, clockkeeper, and thief who lives in a Paris train station. Surviving through his wits and anonymity, Hugo finds that everything is in jeopardy when he meets a bookish girl and the bitter owner of a toy shop. Through them, he learns wonderful secrets of his deceased father.

#6: *The Van Gogh Café* by Cynthia Rylant. Anything can happen here! Food cooks itself and poems foretell the future. Clara's dad owns this magical café where the unexpected is to be expected.

#5: *Bridge to Terabithia* by Katherine Paterson. Two lonely kids create a magical forest kingdom. Leslie is a smart, outgoing tomboy and Jesse is a fearful and angry artist. But when their lives meet, both are transformed. (Note: This book was the twenty-eighth most challenged book from 2001 to 2008, according to the American Library Association.)

#4: *Dogsong* by Gary Paulsen. A fourteen-year-old Eskimo boy sets out with his dogs to find himself after the ways of the modern world upset him. On the way, he meets a girl who, like himself, is disaffected by life's challenges. Their journey together leads to some remarkable discoveries.

#3: *Gathering Blue* by Lois Lowry. A companion to *The Giver*, this book finds Kira, a physically disabled and orphaned teen who lives in a future society that kills off its elderly and disabled. Thanks to her amazing talent in embroidery, the elders of the community keep her alive for their own purposes. In the process, Kira learns much about her society that causes her concern.

#2: *Fade* by Robert Cormier. In 1938, Paul Moreaux discovers he can "fade," but this invisibility is not the great gift it first appears to be.

#1: *What Child Is This?* by Caroline B. Cooney. On Christmas Eve, eight-year-old Katie wants only one gift: a real family, not the foster family where she currently lives. Can sixteen-year-old Liz and seventeen-year-old Matt grant a wish that seems impossible?

ACTIVITY Exploring Elitism

In certain school activities, particularly athletics and music, it's both accepted and expected that strong performances will be rewarded. At rallies before big football games, students cheer wildly for the star quarterback. Roses are thrust on stage after a particularly stirring Beethoven opus is performed by a talented pianist, or a hard-to-reach high note is sustained by a student vocalist. Strong abilities that make us stand up and take notice prove that people—including children—are neither ashamed nor intimidated by the presence of others' gifts . . . as long as they're not *intellectual* gifts.

For some reason that we have yet to understand fully, gifted athletes are served well in our schools with nary a hint of "elitism" attached to the special provisions provided for them. But a class for gifted students selected to participate in a special program matched to their intellectual abilities is viewed as suspect by many people—including many educators—who consider this separation of gifted students as being harmful to the democratic nature of our schools. (As Jim has written elsewhere, however, it can at times be empowering to be "elitist" if it means acknowledging in the distinct needs of gifted students.)

Since students in gifted programs or classes are sometimes subject to derision by those who find such options elitist, it is a good idea to approach this issue up-front. Following are two activities to try with your students. The first is best done with older students, and the second is more appropriate for younger students.

For older students: Divide your class into two groups of equal size. Have one group research the viewpoints of those who promote separate gifted programs (like George Betts and Linda Kreger Silverman), while the other group examines the writings and opinions of some of gifted education's main critics (like Alfie Kohn and Mara Sapon-Shevin). Then have students address several specific questions. For example:

- In what ways is it beneficial to separate gifted students in schools for at least part of the day? In what ways is it worse to do so?

- When gifted students are placed in regular education classes, who does this help? Who does it hinder? Which group's needs are more important to consider?

- What is the real meaning of the word "elitist"? In what ways can it be considered positive to be an elitist? In what ways is it negative?

- Are gifted programs elitist by the nature of their existence, or are gifted programs merely a positive expression of the idea that every person should be allowed to reach for their highest potential? Defend your position with examples.

- What is the difference between "equal" and "the same"? How does this distinction have an impact on gifted child education—its rationale and its practice?

If your discussions lead where we think they might, you may want to record your debate for a future school board or faculty meeting where the schools' gifted programs are being highlighted for review.

For younger students: Create a bubble chart. (See page 121 for an example.) Write "Gifted Programs" in the middle bubble. Have students cite the positives and negatives of gifted programs in the surrounding bubbles. Follow with discussion.

You might ask your students, "What if we replace the words 'Gifted Programs' with the words 'Sports Programs' or 'Music Programs'? Does that make a difference?" Invite their thoughts and opinions.

Coping with the Frustration of Having Too Many Options

In a particularly poignant moment of insight, Charlie Brown came to a personal revelation about his life: "There is no heavier burden," he sighed, "than a great potential." Many gifted students, from very young ages, are told something like this: "You are so lucky! You can become anything you want to be when you grow up because you're so smart!" This sounds like a compliment, but to many gifted students who suffer from multipotential— the ability to enter many careers due to diverse interests and multiple strengths— the pressure begins building from early on to choose a profession that befits someone "who is blessed with high intelligence."

Gifted Kids Speak Out

When asked about the importance of opportunities designed for gifted kids, here's what a few students had to say:

"A gifted program stimulates a gifted student's mind to learn about other gifted children and how they feel about being gifted."
—**Isabel, 12**

"I'm one of those people who has trouble finding good friends, and being gifted makes it tougher. But now that I'm in a Challenge program, it's gotten easier. I've found two or three friends there that I can really trust, and probably five or six kids that I get along with okay."
—**Hiro, 10**

"I don't like not being able to work ahead in school. I don't feel mentally challenged. It's like being thrown in jail never to escape. That is, until I got to go to GT [gifted and talented] classes."
—**Sofia, "9¾"**

"It's key to group gifted kids together in classes based on their abilities rather than a one-size-fits-all mentality."
—**Jack, 13**

The list of "acceptable" occupations generally looks something like this:

- doctor (a real doctor, not one of those Ph.D.-types)
- scientist (a Ph.D. will do here, but only if it's from a place like MIT or California Polytechnic or Cornell)
- lawyer (anything but a public defender)
- high-tech wizard (who starts a company and becomes a billionaire overnight)
- professor (only if the previous options fall through—the pay is too low)

But what if you, as a gifted student, have ambitions to be an actor, not an architect? A teacher, not a techie? An advocate for the homeless rather than a Wall Street hedge fund manager? Where are the adults around you who should be saying, "I'll support you all the way"? These rare individuals are the solace sought by many gifted adolescents trying hard to determine all that they want to be when they grow up. And as much as it might seem like a blessing to have so many more choices than others your age, it can actually grow to become an embarrassment of riches, where decisions are complicated by both internal and external factors that push against one another.

Multipotential and the decisions to be made about one's far-off future are the basis of the following two activities. We encourage you to share these letters with your students, then just open up the floor for general discussion.

▌ ACTIVITY What Are You Going to Do with the Rest of Your Life?

Give students a copy of "A Valedictorian Speaks Out at His High School Graduation" on page 149. Explain that it was written by an eighteen-year-old named John. After everyone has read the letter, open the floor to a general discussion. You might also ask your students to write letters of their own—as if they, too, were eighteen, just graduating, and looking ahead to their future.

Here are a few points you might want to raise and invite your students to comment on:

- Many college freshmen change their majors before graduation. The only reason to declare a major in high school is to apply for scholarships directed at certain areas, such as the arts or sciences.

- Some people are ready to announce at eighteen what they want to do and be when they're forty. Others aren't. Either way, the option to switch gears should always be left open.

- John, the valedictorian, seems wise beyond his years. He realizes that not getting too serious about one's

On Becoming a Teacher
by R.G. McCune, 52

I was the only one in my family to graduate from college. My father was a mechanic and my mother stayed at home. When I was in high school, I belonged to the FTA—Future Teachers of America—during my senior year. I grew up in a small, rural county in West Virginia and there were no substitutes for absent teachers, so when someone was absent in the elementary schools, I was sent to substitute. I spent over sixty days of my senior year out in the schools and still managed to maintain all my own schoolwork.

When graduation came, someone asked me what I was going to do (this was the high school counselor), and I said I was going to college to train to be a teacher. She said, "How do you know that is what you want to do? Wouldn't you rather get a job that makes a lot of money? Besides, most men do not want to go into teaching."

Fortunately, I didn't follow her advice and began college at fifteen and finished up at age nineteen. Now, after all these many years, I have never regretted how I have spent my life.

economic future while still a teenager is a good way to approach life. Financial responsibility will follow soon enough.

✎ ACTIVITY Celebrity Majors Match-Up

This fun activity reinforces the message that it's good to keep one's options open—because you never know what the future will bring.

Give each student a copy of "Celebrity Majors Match-Up" on page 150. Chances are, they won't be able to match any of the celebrities with their college majors. (If they can, their matches will most likely be lucky guesses.) For this reason, don't wait too long before explaining that the point of this exercise isn't to score high, but to see how life can take new and unexpected directions. Then share the answers, allowing for brief discussion.

Celebrity Majors Match-Up Key

- Ashley Judd, French and classics, University of Kentucky

- Ashton Kutcher, biochemical engineering, University of Iowa

- Barack Obama, political science, Occidental College and Columbia University

- Bill Gates, pre-law, Harvard University (did not graduate)

- Sean "Diddy" Combs, business, Howard University

- Lady Gaga, music, New York University (did not graduate)

- Conan O'Brien, history and American literature, Harvard University

- Denzel Washington, journalism and drama, Fordham University

- Mick Jagger, economics, London School of Economics

- Julia Roberts, veterinary studies, Georgia State University

- Gloria Estefan, psychology, University of Miami

- J.K. Rowling, French and classics, Exeter College

Overcoming the Barriers of Others' Expectations

When you're gifted and others (parents, teachers, friends, etc.) know it, they have high expectations of your performance and behavior at school, at home, and in other areas of your life. Meanwhile, you have high expectations of yourself. The benefits of being bright are paired with the fear of being imperfect—of not measuring up to anyone's high standards, including your own.

With so many chances daily to "fail" or succeed, gifted children often come up short in their own minds. Their thinking goes something like this:

- "That B-plus might have been an A-minus if I'd studied for ten more minutes!"

- "If I don't make the Honor Roll this quarter, it'll be my first failure in two years!"

- "I've got to do well on these college essays. My parents and my school are counting on me!"

Surrounded by potential pitfalls, gifted children worry constantly about disappointing others. A peak performance is seen as a fluke, a precursor to an academic plateau. This fear, often unstated, may affect academic decisions. For example, a top student may choose not to take an advanced course, fearing that he or she

might not get an A. The grade becomes more important than mental stimulation and intellectual rewards. Learning takes second place to earning that all-important A. As teachers, we need to help our students evaluate themselves and their achievements more realistically. Here are several ways to accomplish that.

ACTIVITY Fill in the Blanks

Open-ended statements that allow children to respond from a base of personal truth are a great way to gauge feelings and attitudes. Give each student a copy of "Fill in the Blanks" on page 151. Tell them that they may respond with a word or phrase, but longer answers now will require less explanation later.

If students feel comfortable doing so, ask them to swap lists with classmates they trust. Allow time for sharing and discussion. Then invite them to comment on particularly surprising or revealing responses. Conclude by asking students to create their own open-ended sentence stems and have other classmates complete them.

With younger students, have them team up with a classmate to illustrate one of the statements on "Fill in the Blanks" for which they wrote similar responses.

ACTIVITY Bottom of the Top

It happens to each of us eventually: As smart as we think we are, we get into a situation that makes us feel dumb. As adults, we have the capacity to excuse ourselves to another venue, a more comfortable one that restores our sense of accomplishment and worth. Equilibrium returns, and we're happy. Children often don't have as much freedom to move from one setting to the next. They're required to tolerate an uncomfortable situation or reevaluate themselves by a new set of standards. Cases in point:

- The first time a child enters a gifted program. Always used to being number one in her particular classroom, she's now just one among many number ones, so the academic pecking order changes.

- The first time a smart high school student enrolls in an arduous course with cutthroat competition among its students. "Is it worth competing with them," the student asks himself, "or should I settle for something less?"

- The first time a gifted child participates in a summer enrichment program for gifted students or an academic competition at school. "Everyone seems so much smarter here," she wonders. "I'm not sure if I fit in."

The feeling and belief that you don't fit into an academic setting where everyone else is also smart (and, from your estimation, a lot smarter than you) is called the Bottom-of-the-Top Syndrome (BTS). In BTS, you realize that you had to have some brain power to get accepted into the mix initially, but after evaluating the others around you, you determine—often with no basis in fact—that you're the least intelligent of an intelligent bunch.

Share this BTS description with your students and ask them if they have ever been affected by it. Then ask how they responded to this experience. Here are three questions to start with:

- Did you strive harder?

- Did you give up entirely?

- Did you talk yourself out of your negative feelings and just plow ahead in an effort to learn?

Such questions (and their answers) can go a long way toward achieving the ultimate goal of this activity: helping your students realize that almost everyone feels like the bottom of the top at some time, even if it's seldom discussed openly. Just knowing that you have company in your search for an academic comfort level is emotionally beneficial.

Understanding the Concept of Asynchronous Development

We've all seen it happen: A gifted five-year-old has a picture in her mind of what she wants her hand-drawn house to look like. The trouble is, her mind has developed far in advance of her fingers' drawing capacities. The result? Tears at the table, crumpled-up pages of "bad houses," and an underlying feeling of stupidity in a bright young child who doesn't understand that some parts of the body (and mind) develop more quickly than others.

Asynchronous development is a concept that parents, teachers, and counselors of gifted children need to understand, and they need to share this understanding with the gifted children in their care—the same gifted children who experience asynchronous development from the inside out because they live it every day.

In 1991, a group of educators, counselors, and researchers involved with gifted children met in Columbus, Ohio, to explore new ways to define giftedness apart from IQ scores or high achievement. Led by Dr. Linda Kreger Silverman, one of the leading experts on the emotional development of gifted children, the Columbus Group began today's focus on looking at giftedness as more of an inner quality than one manifested in school work or high grades. They coined the term "asynchronous development" and came up with this definition:[2]

Giftedness is asynchronous development in which advanced cognitive abilities and heightened intensity combine to create experiences and awareness that are qualitatively different from the norm. This asynchrony increases with higher intellectual capacity. The uniqueness of the gift renders [children] particularly vulnerable and requires modifications in parenting, teaching, and counseling in order for them to develop optimally.

Although not universally accepted as a way to define giftedness, the asynchronous development idea rings true with many parents and educators. Children whose minds are developing at one rate while their bodies and emotions are developing at another need to accept that this uneven progression through childhood, though frustrating, is perfectly normal for them, even if atypical for most.

ACTIVITY The Ideal Me

Sometimes, in order to see what's most important in your life, it helps to also consider some things that aren't so important.

Give your students copies of "The Unables" on page 152 and ask them to follow the instructions at the top of the form. Then start a discussion using some or all of these questions:

- What's the most frustrating unable on your list?

- Why do you think being able to do this thing is so important to you?

- Have you actually tried to do it? What happened when you couldn't do it? How did you feel?

- What's the least frustrating unable on your list?

- Why don't you care if you can do it or not? Why is it unimportant to you?

- Have you actually tried to do it? What happened when you couldn't do it? How did you feel?

- How many of your unables are within your control?

- Which unables will take more time and practice to master?

- Which unables do you simply have to wait to do until you're older? Is it hard to be patient? Why or why not?

Somewhere during the discussion, make the point (or wait for students to discover) that as much as they might like to do it all, some things are beyond their personal control.

> "The absolute best part of being gifted is being accepted into adult conversations on politics, ethics, and world events. I used to be always told to go play with the other kids, but once people found out I was gifted, my 'adult' interests were accepted."
> —Ellen, 16

ACTIVITY Pitching in at Preschool

This is less of an activity and more of an experience. It will help your students recall and appreciate what it's like to be *really* young—a time when life is full of "unables" and other things that are hard to do. It will also broaden their understanding of asynchronous development. (We suggest you share the asynchronous development definition with your students in advance of this preschool experience.)

Contact a teaching colleague who works in a preschool. Plan a time when you and your students can visit and spend forty-five minutes to an hour with the children. The students will work in pairs—one of your students with one of your colleague's students. Prior to your visit, have each of your students choose one of the following and make appropriate plans:

- Select a favorite picture book to read to the young child

- Choose a dot-to-dot or coloring page to complete with the child

- Select a simple board game, like Chutes and Ladders, to play with the child

- Locate a website featuring suitable games to play or activities to do together with the young student (find out first if the preschool has Internet access and computers or tablets)

- Write the first half of several familiar adages or proverbs that the children will complete (examples: "When the cat's away . . ." "There's no fool . . .")

- Plan a hands-on science experiment or demonstration

After your visit, ask your students about the fun they had and the frustrations they felt. Several will probably mention things like, "The little kids didn't understand my directions" or "They couldn't hold the pencil long enough to connect the dots" or "They have such short attention spans!" As they note these frustrations, chart the area of development each one relates to: physical, intellectual, or emotional. It should then be fairly easy to start a discussion of what asynchrony looks like in little kids, which is a natural bridge to discussions related to similar developmental lags that exist even in older students.

Follow up by having your students make thank-you cards to send to the preschoolers who helped them learn more about themselves.

Becoming an Advocate for Your Own Self-Interests

Even though the roles of student and teacher are clearly defined in most schools, there are times and places for role reversals. Some students know their needs and interests at least as well as their teachers do, and this is especially true with gifted students.

Teachers would be wise to understand that their gifted students can often provide insights into their own educational needs. You don't have to wait until you hear the words that make conscientious educators cringe ("I'm bored!") before modifying the curriculum for your most able learners. Also, don't let students put you on the defensive by claiming boredom. We sometimes share this quote with our students:

*"Someone is boring me.
I think it's me."*

—Dylan Thomas

As teachers, we can help our students become more than passive recipients of our teaching. With some enlightened self-exploration into their own educational agendas, your students will become partners with you in an enterprise that was never meant to be a one-way street: education.

Gifted Kids Speak Out

We asked gifted teens to describe their perfect school day. Here's what some of them said:

"In a perfect school day, the teachers would ask you what you want to learn and then provide the resources to do just that. Then, you would discuss your work directly with the teacher."
—Alexei, 16

"I can go slow if I want, fast if I'm so inclined, or skip right to the end and work backwards sometimes, too. A perfect day is where I am free to think flexibly and act at my own pace. Can you even do this in school?"
—Jennifer, 17

"A perfect school day would go by quickly and involve no homework, leaving me time for a long bath until I fall asleep reading."
—Chandra, 13

"A team of experts helps me design an experiment or project that I get to work on as long as I want—without being graded!"
—Jon, 15

ACTIVITY Focus on the Positives

Sometimes students remember what they dislike about school more readily than they recall the positive events that occurred in the classroom or schoolyard. To encourage your students to look back on activities or lessons that were especially meaningful to them, set aside time each week for journal-writing. Have them respond to these questions:

- What is the most important lesson I learned this week that had to do with school?

- What is the most important lesson I learned this week that had to do with myself?

- Who was the most influential person in my life this week? Why?

Continue this journal-writing activity for a month or longer, depending on how your students respond. Have them start each week's writing by rereading their comments about the previous weeks.

You may also want to do this activity yourself. It will keep you focused on the week's brightest spots.

ACTIVITY Taking Charge of Your Own Education

If students need help convincing some of their teachers that a change in their curriculum or assignments would be a change for the better, they may need some guidance in requesting specific modifications.

The "Ten Tips for Talking to Teachers" on pages 153–154 have guided thousands of students since they were first written more than 25 years ago. By following this simple advice (and working with responsive teachers), students can make substantial improvements in their lives at school. The "Ten Tips" describe realistic and respectful strategies students can use to approach almost any teacher about almost any education-related issue. Best of all, students play a major role by acting as their own advocates.

And what about when even those strategies don't work? That's when students can turn to "What to Say When Teachers Say No," page 155, for help and ideas.[3]

Give each of your students a copy of the "Ten Tips" and "What to Say" handouts. Let them know that you're open to talking with them about their specific educational wants and needs.

Understanding the Role of Socialization

More than seventy years ago, psychologist Leta Stetter Hollingworth wrote that "isolation is the refuge of genius, not its goal." What she meant then remains true today; gifted students don't seek to separate themselves socially from classmates, but sometimes it does happen. Usually it's for one or more of the following reasons:

- Gifted children, from a young age, often prefer complicated, rule-based games that others their age don't understand or care about.

- Gifted children are often concerned with world problems and other "big issues" that may not interest other kids their age.

- Gifted children's advanced vocabularies inadvertently isolate them from age peers who don't comprehend their words.

- Gifted children seek out others whose minds operate at the same fast pace as their own. Finding few, they may gravitate toward older children or adults, making them appear aloof or snobby to their classmates.

- Gifted children who feel distanced from their age peers may resort to solitary play or a world of electronically connected playmates, making them even less available for social interaction.

In an effort to fit in, some gifted children will "dumb themselves down" to appear more appealing to classmates. They may alter (lower) their vocabularies, get a poor grade on purpose, refuse to participate in "uncool" activities like the gifted program, or deliberately "lose" completed homework. As a teacher, you'll want to be alert to these behaviors and aware of the underlying reasons why your gifted students may be choosing to "opt out" of certain interactions, especially those with classmates who are developing more typically.

Self-Advocacy for Gifted Teens

Deb Douglas, a former gifted coordinator and tireless advocate for gifted children, authors a website titled "GT Carpe Diem" (www.gtcarpediem.com). There she offers this definition of self-advocacy:

"Self-advocacy is the process of recognizing and meeting the needs specific to your learning ability without compromising the dignity of yourself or others."

She goes on to highlight four steps of self-advocacy, as follows:

- **Step 1: Understand your rights and responsibilities.** You have the *right* to a rigorous education, which stretches your skills and thinking every day. Your *responsibilities* include taking an active role in creating your educational plan and developing the attributes of good character.

- **Step 2: Assess and reflect on your learner profile: abilities and interests, strengths and weaknesses, learning styles and habits.** Consider your traits in five different areas: cognitive functioning information; learning strengths information; personality characteristics; learning preferences; and interests.

- **Step 3: Match your attributes to options and opportunities.** What would you like to change? What are you looking for? More challenging work? Interaction with like-ability peers? Time to explore personal interests? Changes at home or school that support your unique needs?

- **Step 4: Connect with advocates who can support your goals.** It's important to know who you can turn to and how to be diplomatic yet effective when asking for help.

▌ACTIVITY What's a Regular Kid?

> "Nobody realizes that some people expend tremendous energy merely to be normal."
>
> **—Albert Camus**

> "For a long time, I tried to manage an honesty and openness about my personal life because I'm human and I'm normal—well, semi-normal."
>
> **—Johnny Depp**

> "Normal is not something to aspire to, it's something to get away from."
>
> **—Jodie Foster**

It seems that every book, article, or news story about a young person who's done something amazing or shocking—starred in a movie, made a hit record, performed a heroic act, or committed a crime—includes at least one claim of being a "regular kid" after all.

Somehow it's comforting to know that Daniel Radcliffe, the star of the Harry Potter films, still had to do chores like a "regular kid." And that rapper Bow Wow (real name: Shad Moss), whose debut album went multiplatinum when he was just 14, missed being a "regular kid." And that Vino Vasudevan, the first 12-year-old to score a perfect 1,600 on the SATs, wanted to remain a "regular kid."

Yet what's so great about being "normal"—a regular kid? Why do so many people insist that they're regular (or wish they were) when they're clearly not? And what does it mean to be regular, anyway? Explore these questions with your students in this activity. You'll learn more about them—and they'll learn more about themselves.

Divide the board into two columns by drawing a vertical line down the center. At the top of the left-hand column, write:

A "gifted kid" is someone who . . .
Ask your students to quickly complete the sentence. Write down their responses as quickly as they offer them.

Next, at the top of the right-hand column, write:

A "regular kid" is someone who . . .
Ask students to complete this sentence. Write down their responses.

Afterward, have your students look at the two lists and think about what they imply. Start a discussion with questions like these:

- What does it mean to be a gifted kid?
- What does it mean to be a regular kid?
- How are gifted kids different from regular kids? How are they the same?
- Have you ever wanted to be a regular kid? Why or why not?
- Have you deliberately acted like a regular kid? If so, what did you do? Why did you do it? What happened as a result?
- Do you think you might have more friends if you were a regular kid?
- Some gifted kids say they "just want to be normal." Does this imply that being gifted is an abnormal condition?
- If you substitute the word "typical" for "normal," does this make being different from others your age any easier to accept? Why or why not?

Talk with your students about how we all sometimes make compromises to fit in and be accepted by others. For gifted kids, these compromises may include pretending they're not smart and hiding their real abilities. Ask them to think about one person with whom they can be themselves, without worrying about being "gifted" or "regular" or anything else. Suggest that this person is probably a real friend.

ACTIVITY Going Along with the Crowd

Going along with the crowd may result in changing a view, attitude, opinion, or behavior that was once held dear. This can create some inner turmoil.

Have students read the "Do you ever do anything just to go along with the crowd?" comments that follow. Then, invite students to tell about a time when they gave in to group norms—if ever. What did they do? How did they feel? Would they do it again? Next, ask them to describe a time when they didn't give in. If they're slow in responding to either request, you might start things off by sharing examples from your own life.

Lead into more general questions about when it's okay to go along—and when it's best to stand your ground. Students may raise such determining factors as safety, morals, personal preferences,

Gifted Kids Speak Out

We asked gifted kids, "Do you ever do anything just to go along with the crowd?" Here's what some of them said:

"I never pretend to be dumb. If that was the case, I'd pretend to be smart."
—Terrell, 14

"Yes, I have done things just to go along with the crowd before, because I was tired of being 'so special . . .' and so alone. I just wanted to belong to the big crowd for a while. (It never worked out very well, though.)"
—Gabi, 13

"No, I've learned it's better to do things for myself. If other people want to jump off a bridge, I hope they have fun."
—Carlos, 15

"If you really knew anything about middle school social politics, you wouldn't want to go along with the crowd."
—Natasha, 13

"Sometimes, 'dumbing down' is a misnomer for a life skill strategy. It is time to recognize how 'smart' it is to adjust your communication style to your audience in order to socialize."
—Esther, 17

and fear of punishment. All are worth exploring further as you discuss topics both trivial and vital in one's development as a social being.

✎ **ACTIVITY** Looking Ahead, Looking Back

Plenty of gifted kids feel different and alienated. To help them feel more comfortable with standing out from their age peers, give them a firsthand look at what it's like to go from gifted kid to gifted adult. Locate a former student from the gifted program, or an adult in the community who has been identified as gifted and accomplished, and invite the person to speak to the class. Ask him or her to address issues pertaining to peers, challenges with isolation, connecting with a profession or avocation, and fitting in socially. You'll want your guest to talk about the rest of his or her life as well, but make sure the person understands that you're looking for an adult role model who can talk about instances of feeling isolated from the norm, and can share stories of growing up feeling different from other kids. Have students prepare for this speaker by writing down questions in advance. After the speaker's prepared discussion is over, facilitate group discussion between your guest speaker and kids, and encourage students to ask their questions.

Suggested Questions

1. Can you talk about your current profession, or avocation, or interests?

2. How did you figure out what you wanted to do in life?

3. Were you in any special program(s) at school? Did you receive any special instruction?

4. How were you different from other kids? How were you similar to them?

5. Who were your friends? How did you go about making good friends? Did you have a lot of close friends, or just a few?

6. How did you get along with your siblings and parents? If and when there were issues, did any relate to giftedness (such as conflicts with people who had super-high expectations of you)?

7. Sometimes it feels like being gifted doesn't pay off until you're grown up, while as a kid, you may feel penalized for it. Is that true in your case?

8. What advice do you have for gifted kids? Is there anything you'd do differently if you had your school years to do over again?

ACTIVITY **A World of Equals**

In Kurt Vonnegut's short story, "Harrison Bergeron," the title character is a tall (very tall), intelligent (*very* intelligent) fourteen-year-old who lives in the year 2081. The United States Handicapper General has made it law that no one shall be different from anyone else—not smarter, not more athletic, not better looking. Those who naturally are any of these things are given artificial handicaps so they're more "equal" to their less able peers. For example, a prima ballerina is forced to wear weights on her ankles so she can't jump any higher than the average dancer. Everyone is the same . . . except Harrison, who refuses to play this game.

Vonnegut's story shows what happens when a spunky adolescent chooses to stand out as a singular entity rather than being one more lemming in the crowd. It doesn't have a happy ending (that's putting it mildly: Harrison—spoiler alert!—is gunned down by the Handicapper General on national television), but it will definitely prompt much discussion about what it means to be an individual, and the price that is sometimes paid for taking the social road less traveled. If you think it's appropriate, you might have your students read "Harrison Bergeron." You'll find it in Welcome to the Monkey House, a collection of Vonnegut's shorter works, or online at tnellen.com/cybereng/harrison.html.

A Few Final Thoughts

We began this chapter with the words of a fifteen-year-old. In the pages that followed, you "met" other young people who had something to say about growing up gifted and the stamina it takes to keep both one's heart and one's mind intact.

The issues today's gifted kids face are not that much different from issues that intelligent people have struggled with since time began: self-understanding and acceptance, social meaningfulness, and the desire to learn and succeed in life. During the thirteenth century, a poet named Rumi wrote about two kinds of intelligence: one acquired in school and one already inside the individual—"a freshness in the center of the chest." As we seek to understand the gifted kids in our care, let's not forget to look for and celebrate the freshness within them.

Everything Has Its Ups and Downs!

Name: _____

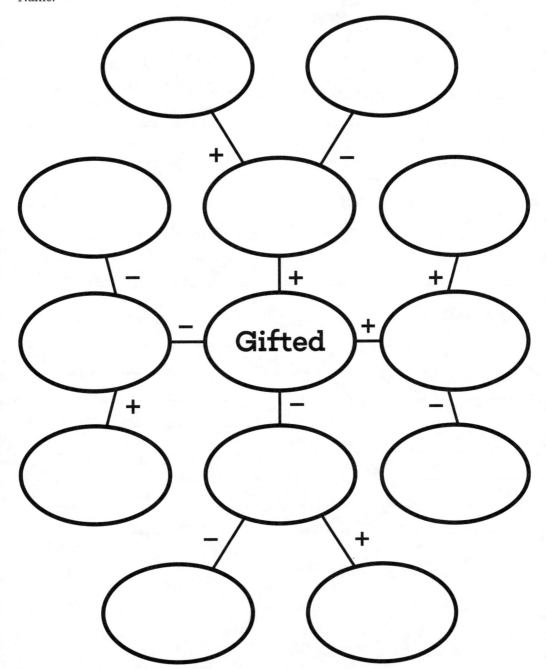

Gifted

Gifted Is ... Gifted Means ...

To You

Complete each sentence with at least three personal responses. Write what *you* think gifted is and means.

Gifted is ...

1. _____

_____

2. _____

_____

3. _____

_____

4. _____

_____

Gifted means ...

1. _____

_____

2. _____

_____

3. _____

_____

4. _____

_____

→

Gifted Is . . . Gifted Means . . . , continued

To Others

Think about how *other people* react to the term "gifted." How would each of the following complete the sentence "Gifted means . . ."?

Your parent(s): "Gifted means _____

_____

_____

_____

_____."

Your best friend: "Gifted means _____

_____

_____

_____

_____."

Your worst enemy: "Gifted means _____

_____

_____

_____

_____."

A teacher who "gets it": "Gifted means _____

_____

_____

_____

_____."

→

Gifted Is . . . Gifted Means . . . , continued

A teacher who doesn't "get it": "Gifted means _____
_____
_____
_____
_____."

Your grandparent(s): "Gifted means _____
_____
_____
_____
_____."

Your brother(s) or sister(s): "Gifted means _____
_____
_____
_____
_____."

A TV producer of a show about gifted kids: "Gifted means _____
_____
_____
_____
_____."

A Valedictorian Speaks Out at His High School Graduation

by John T. Ross

Like countless people have asked countless other graduates, a man asked me, "What are you going to do with the rest of your life?"

But as I stood there dumbfounded, eyebrows bent, mind perplexed, I realized I had no idea. And I realized, too, that it was good not to know and good not to have any idea.

It was good not to know where my money will be invested in ten years or where I will be working in five. Good not to know for whom I wanted to work or where and why. It was good not to know how big my house will be or what car I'll drive. Good not to know about retirement or IRAs or 401K plans.

As I stood there with that curious man, who was asking a question I couldn't answer, I realized that not knowing was good because if you aren't careful, you can grow up too fast, and die too early, thinking only of security, planning, jobs, and things. It's too easy to lose what matters.

To lose: the beautiful innocence of youth, the wild fun of running in the rain, going to amusement parks to eat cotton candy and ride rides, staying up late on purpose, going to ball games, fishing all day in dirty rivers and swimming, the purity of dancing, and singing loud off-key notes behind the comfort of a closed door.

To lose: Turning with friends to the wisdom of classic rock-and-roll to learn about life and women. Hanging out. Doing nothing. Making believe. Walking barefoot in the woods. Climbing trees with ball caps, sweatpants, and dirty T-shirts. Skipping rocks and spitting. Sitting, building sandcastles, asking questions about weird, crazy people, places, and things.

When you plan too much, you lose important things like watching cartoons and not caring that Wile E. Coyote comes back after every ill-timed attempt with boulders. Laughing at least thirty-seven times every day. Loving everything and everybody because the world seems like one of those books that you save for a rainy day and a soft, high-backed chair by the window.

It was good not to know what I wanted to do, because when you're young and fresh and innocent, you can't go wrong. Someone once wrote, "When you're young, you're golden." So, wherever I go and whatever I do with the rest of my life, I'll always stay young and I'll always stay golden.

Thank you.

End note: John Ross loves staying up all night so he can listen to music, write, meet people, and find out what has been going on during the nights he slept through. John loves his family and his friends, and pretty much everyone else.

Celebrity Majors Match-Up

Who majored in what? Where? Try to match the following celebrities with their majors and colleges. Good luck!

J.K. Rowling (*Harry Potter* author)

Lady Gaga (musician and actress)

Bill Gates (inventor, technology and business magnate, and philanthropist)

Sean "Diddy" Combs (musician, record producer, actor, and entrepreneur)

Ashley Judd (actress and political activist)

Barack Obama (president of the United States, lawyer, and community organizer)

Conan O'Brien (comedian, television host, writer, and producer)

Denzel Washington (actor, director, and producer)

Mick Jagger (musician and actor)

Julia Roberts (actress and producer)

Ashton Kutcher (actor, producer, and investor)

Gloria Estefan (musician, actress, and entrepreneur)

Business, Howard University (did not graduate)

Veterinary studies, Georgia State University (did not graduate)

Psychology, University of Miami

History and American literature, Harvard University

Journalism and drama, Fordham University

Biochemical engineering, University of Iowa (did not graduate)

French and classics, University of Kentucky

Economics, London School of Economics

Pre-law, Harvard University (did not graduate)

Political science, Occidental College and Columbia University

French and classics, Exeter College

Music, New York University (did not graduate)

Fill in the Blanks

Name: _____

When I get an A . . .

_____

_____

When I don't get an A . . .

_____

_____

When I bring my report card home . . .

_____

_____

If I forget to do my homework . . .

_____

_____

My parents expect me to . . .

_____

_____

Most of my teachers expect me to . . .

_____

_____

Most of my friends expect me to . . .

_____

_____

No one expects me to . . .

_____

_____

The Unables

Read the following list of "unables." Cross out anything you *are* able to do.

Add other things to the list that you'd like to be able to do, or think you'll be able to do someday but can't right now.

Then rank all the items you did not cross out, from most frustrating ("I'd love to do it but I can't yet") to least frustrating ("It's really not important to me if I can do this or not").

Right now, at this point in my life, I'm unable to:

_____ Swim

_____ Understand some adult conversations

_____ Draw well

_____ Do something I want to do because I'm "too young"

_____ Be taken seriously by older kids

_____ Get straight A's in everything

_____ Speak a foreign language

_____ Play basketball (or another sport) with the bigger kids

_____ Attend college because of my age

_____ _____

_____ _____

_____ _____

_____ _____

_____ _____

_____ _____

Ten Tips for Talking to Teachers

Are you having a problem with a class or an assignment? Can you see room for improvement in how a subject is taught? Do you have a better idea for a special project or term paper? Don't just tell your friends. Talk to the teacher!

Many students don't know how to go about doing this. The following suggestions are meant to make it easier for everyone—students *and* teachers.

1. Make an appointment to meet and talk. This shows the teacher that you're serious and you have some understanding of his or her busy schedule. Tell the teacher about how much time you'll need, be flexible, and don't be late.

2. If you know other students who feel the way you do, consider approaching the teacher together. There's strength in numbers. If a teacher hears the same thing from four or five people, he or she is more likely to do something about it.

3. Think through what you want to say before you go into your meeting with the teacher. Write down your questions or concerns. Make a list of the items you want to cover. You may even want to copy your list for the teacher so both of you can consult it during your meeting. (Or consider giving it to the teacher ahead of time.)

4. Choose your words carefully. *Example:* Instead of saying, "I hate doing reports; they're boring and a waste of time," try, "Is there some other way I could satisfy this requirement? Could I do a video instead?" Strike the word "boring" from your vocabulary. It's a negative and meaningless buzzword for teachers.

5. Don't expect the teacher to do all of the work or propose all of the answers. Be prepared to make suggestions, offer solutions, even recommend resources. The teacher will appreciate that you took the initiative.

6. Be diplomatic, tactful, and respectful. Teachers have feelings, too. And they're more likely to be responsive if you remember that the purpose of your meeting is conversation, not confrontation.

7. Focus on what you need, not on what you think the teacher is doing wrong. The more the teacher learns about you, the more he or she will be able to help. The more defensive the teacher feels, the less he or she will want to help.

→

Ten Tips for Talking to Teachers, continued

8. **Don't forget to listen.** Strange but true, many students need practice in this essential skill. The purpose of your meeting isn't just to hear yourself talk.

9. **Bring your sense of humor.** Not necessarily the joke-telling sense of humor, but the one that lets you laugh at yourself and your own misunderstandings and mistakes.

10. **If your meeting isn't successful, get help from another adult.** "Successful" doesn't necessarily mean that you emerged victorious. Even if the teacher denies your request, your meeting can still be judged successful. If you had a real conversation—if you communicated openly, listened carefully, and respected each other's points of view—then congratulate yourself on a great meeting. If the air crackled with tension, the meeting fell apart, and you felt disrespected (or acted disrespectful), then it's time to bring in another adult. *Suggestions:* a guidance counselor, the gifted program coordinator, or another teacher you know and trust who seems likely to support you and advocate for you. Once you've found help, approach your teacher and try again.

What to Say When Teachers Say No

If your teacher says . . .	You might respond . . .
"I can't make an exception for you."	"That's okay with me, since I think there are a number of students who might benefit from being allowed to [fill in here with whatever it is you're suggesting]."
"It's always been done this way."	"I know. And I'm sure there are probably some very good reasons for that. But how about letting me try this one time, and if it doesn't work, I'll agree to go back to the way it's been done in the past?"
"It would cause chaos in my classroom."	"I'd be willing to help see that chaos doesn't prevail. I could form a small committee of students who really care and who would help set some guidelines that would keep order in the classroom. We'd agree that if things got out of control, we'd lose this opportunity."
"You're a straight-A student. Why not be satisfied with that? After all, what more could you ask for?"	"I know I get straight A's, but the thing is, I feel I could be learning so much more. If it were possible to get a higher grade than an A, just think of the possibilities! You know the old cliché—'The sky's the limit.' I'd like to aim higher, and I really need your help and support."

CHAPTER 6

Underachiever or Selective Consumer?

What is an underachiever made of? . . .
an unexpressed idea . . . an unpainted picture,
an unsung song, a safely hidden poem,
unused talent. These make an underachiever.

—E. Paul Torrance

Few situations are more frustrating for teachers than working with children who don't perform as well academically as we know they could and we think they should. Their potential is obvious. Why won't they just do their work? Why don't they get better grades? Why don't they participate more?

Often, we get so frustrated that we label these children underachievers. Once this label has been applied, remedial strategies may be employed, most involving contracts, verbal agreements, and losses of privileges for students who stubbornly refuse to live up to our expectations. We bargain. We cajole. We punish. We nag and scold:

- "You're a smart kid—if only you'd apply yourself."

- "I don't care if the homework is boring. An assignment is an assignment! Everyone else has to do it. Why shouldn't you?"

- "If you'd argue less about your work and just plain do it, you wouldn't be having these problems."

■ "When you get a job in the real world, you'll have to do stuff you don't want to do. Just think of boring school assignments as practice for your adult years."

Change, we insist, is up to the student. It's his choice, his responsibility, his burden. (Most students labeled underachievers are boys, hence the "his." Often they're just not willing to play the school "game.") So much for the theory that education is a positive partnership involving school, home, and students!

Matt's Story

When Jim met Matt, Jim was a first-year teacher and Matt was a fifth-grade student. To Matt, school was irrelevant, and he told Jim so every day by writing that very word—in red crayon—across the top of any worksheet he found either distasteful or unrelated to the needs he perceived he had. More often than not, Matt then formed a paper airplane out of his worksheet and sent it on a nonstop flight to Jim's desk. Thanks to this behavior, among others, Matt spent much time in the hall, at the principal's office, or off-task.

Then, one day, a miracle occurred: Matt got sprayed by a skunk in his backyard—a common event in northern New England, where this story took place. Actually, Matt's spraying was a harbinger of good things to come. Skunks emerge from hibernation in early spring to seek mates. Also, maple sap starts to flow as the days get warmer but the nights remain cold. Matt was a maple-sugar farmer, and his unfortunate and smelly meeting took place when, in the process of tapping a tree, he interrupted a couple of amorous skunks.

Matt and Jim talked (downwind, at Matt's suggestion) and decided that maple-sugar farming would become part of Matt's curriculum. Thus, his math assignments went from rote drills to making change and converting quarts to pints. His reading and writing assignments involved completing invoices and preparing posters and flyers to advertise his product (he made $65.50 after expenses). His social studies assignment was a photo essay of his skills at maple-sugar farming. Matt even spoke at a Rotary Club luncheon, where he listened to old war stories and contributed a (possibly tasteless) joke or two of his own to the colorful discussion.

Was Matt an underachiever who suddenly came to appreciate school under the guidance of his skilled first-year teacher? It's tempting to think so, but the answer is probably no. More likely, Matt was "selective" about his education, not "turned off" to education in general. His learning never stopped, even during difficult times. He needed a reason to learn, a purpose, and he was not finding that purpose in the regular curriculum. Rather, like Dorothy in *The Wizard of Oz*, Matt found the magic of learning in his own backyard—not, in his case, a Kansas cornfield, but a New Hampshire sugar-maple grove.

This chapter distinguishes between the identification and treatment of two types of low performance by gifted students: underachievement and nonproduction, which we prefer to call "selective consumerism." We review the literature and research on what has historically been called underachievement. Then we suggest strategies for reversing patterns of underachieving and selective consumer behaviors through curricular and counseling interventions.

Underachievement: The Research Perspective

In a national study[1] of gifted child educators and advocates, the number one issue cited that needed resolution was reversing underachievement. That study took place in 1990—and we have no doubt that a similar study done today would yield the same results.

Ever since the term "underachievement" entered our vernacular, researchers and practitioners have sought reasons for its existence. Thomas P. Hébert and F. Richard Olenchak[2] studied adolescent males who underachieved and found that many of them tried to maintain a masculine identity by sacrificing their own potential and adapting to more peer-accepted norms of "average." Barbara Kerr[3] took a similar position from a slightly different angle when she defined "kindergarten red-shirting," which is the practice of delaying a boy's entrance into kindergarten so that in later years he will be larger in body mass, enhancing athletic performance. The problem is, if you are red-shirting a gifted five-year-old boy, when he finally does enter school, the material he's supposed to learn is that

much more boring, increasing the likelihood of underachievement. Psychiatrist Jerald Grobman[4] examined underachieving adolescents and young adults and found that his subjects developed anxiety in trying to reconcile their giftedness with age-appropriate aspects of their lives: social/sexual development and struggles with dependence/independence.

But we're getting a little ahead of ourselves by describing the problem of underachievement before we've properly defined it. Let's take a step backward and do so.

Defining Underachievement

Both early researchers and more recent authors have defined underachievement in terms of a discrepancy between a child's school performance and some ability index, such as an IQ score.[5] Such "discrepancy" definitions, though clean-cut and precise, are actually quite limiting. When underachievement is seen from the vantage point of test scores versus daily performance, it becomes associated exclusively with academic, school-based endeavors. Yet, as Maple-Sugar Matt and the research subjects previously cited clearly show, underachievement is often more a symptom of a deeper set of concerns that can involve intellectual, social, and emotional areas of development, not simply academics.

Defining underachievement more holistically is important because the term itself is a buzzword among educators. The mere mention of "underachievement" generates many images (all of them negative) about the child in question. We picture the underachiever as belligerent, difficult to work with, smart but not motivated, or a "poor-me" type who could get good grades with some effort but just doesn't want to try. These mental images can transform quickly into mental blocks, as we may begin to resent the apparent unwillingness of the student to perform on cue and may accuse the student of creating problems that could be resolved with a little extra effort. Such oversimplification of a complex issue seldom leads to positive results.

The bottom line is this: Where underachievement is concerned, the name of the game is blame. Everyone involved (including the student) may try to make the issue seem like someone else's fault, and therefore someone else's problem.

A New Approach

If the discrepancy formula is too narrow a definition for underachievement, how else might it be described? In fact, there are several useful ways to consider underachievement without getting overly precise about defining it. For just as the term "gifted" has multiple meanings, so does the term "underachievement."

Indeed, many people believe there is "safety in numbers," so if we state that performing in school two years below your measured aptitude constitutes underachievement, then we will look no further or deeper than that. The approach to defining and reversing underachievement that we will take, however, is more complex and less focused on precise numbers or academic/aptitude discrepancies. We'd like to think that most educators will be open to considering the following new approach to defining underachievement,

but we also realize that we can't convince everyone. However, since we've been trying to fix underachievement for generations using techniques that simply don't work, we hope you will consider the following conceptual framework for underachievement as something worth looking at.

Underachievement Is a Behavior and It Can Change Over Time

Too often, underachievement is seen as a problem of attitude ("He's just being stubborn; he can do the work") or personality ("If she weren't so lazy, she could pass that course"). However, neither attitude nor personality can be modified as directly as behaviors can. To speak of underachieving behaviors is to pinpoint those parts of children's lives they are most able to alter: actions.

Underachievement Is Content- and Situation-Specific

Gifted children who do not succeed in school are often successful in outside activities—sports, social events, after-school jobs, talents, or hobbies. Also, even children who do poorly in *most* school subjects often display a talent or interest in at least *one* school subject.

When we label a child an under-achiever without specifying the *specific areas* of underachieving behaviors, we disregard anything *positive* that the child displays in other areas and endeavors. Since it is more useful to label the student's behaviors than to label the student, we should identify a child as "underachieving in math and language arts" rather than as an "underachieving student."

Underachievement Is in the Eye of the Beholder

For some students (and educators), as long as a passing grade is attained, under-achievement does not exist. "After all," this group would say, "a D isn't failure!" To others, a grade of B+ constitutes under-achievement if the student in question was expected to get an A.

When it comes to academic grades, we all have different thresholds of pain. A grade of B might elate one student and devastate a classmate of equal ability. Recognizing that the definition of under-achievement varies with each person is the first step in understanding this complex phenomenon.

Understanding Underachievement

This excerpt is drawn from *The Essential Guide to Talking with Gifted Teens* by Jean Sunde Peterson. Use the following discussion activity to explore students' thoughts and feelings on underachievement. Peterson also advises:

> *Avoid preaching or cheerleading when dealing with gifted underachievers. Quietly affirm intelligence and worth. Acknowledge that they may be in control of their achievement—unless there is a learning disability, depression, or another factor not controllable by will. Avoid implying that they could do better if they tried. They have heard that before, and it might not be true. If achievement is within their control, one approach is to encourage them to be pragmatic—and use the school to get what they need for later life: academic credentials.*

1. As an introduction, mention that many students with high capability are not academic achievers. Some experts have estimated that half of those with

high ability do not perform well in school. Although many educators are pessimistic about the future of gifted underachievers, success and satisfaction are indeed possible.

Next, ask students to define underachievement (usually defined as a student who scores high on achievement or ability tests, but doesn't perform as expected academically).

2. Ask, "How do achievers usually feel about underachievers?" Allow for responses before asking, "And how do underachievers usually feel about achievers?" Then ask, "Do you think achievers and underachievers have anything in common?" (Possible shared characteristics: Feeling stress from expectations, sensitivity, family situations, social difficulties, and concern about the future.)

3. Ask the group what they think contributes to underachievement. Ask if any underachievers are willing to talk about when their school performance began to decline. What was going on in school or elsewhere for them at the time? Did they get good grades up to that point?

4. Depending on the level of trust and honesty in the group and whether you think it is appropriate, ask members to identify whether they think they are perceived by teachers as achievers or underachievers. Then invite them to consider some of the following questions. You may want to have achievers and underachievers respond to the questions separately, with the achievers answering first. Underachievers might be surprised by the achievers' responses.

- Everyone in this group is quite intelligent. Where do you let it show?

- Who in your life believes you are an intelligent person?

- On a scale of 1 to 10, with 10 being "high level," how much do you focus on academics?

- What is the most comfortable part of school for you? The most uncomfortable?

- How would you rate your "social savvy" and "street smarts"?

- What would you gain if you started (under)achieving in school? What would you lose?

- How would members of your family react if you started (under)achieving in school?

- When you achieve or underachieve, who gives you attention?

- What do (under)achievers get out of (under)achieving?

→

- How many gifted (under)achievers are in your family? In your circle of friends?

- How much of your school achievement (grades) is in your control?

- What is your attitude about life in general? What is your level of self-confidence, well-being, physical health, or energy?

- How much influence might you have over the achievement of others?

- How do you respond to competition, especially in school?

- What affects your school achievement the most?

5. Ask the underachievers how they could use the system to their advantage without sacrificing themselves to it. Although all underachievers are not rebels, this kind of question may raise new possibilities in their minds. (However, they might not yet be comfortable talking about actual changes they could make.)

6. Depending on interest, make a brief detour and examine the terms "success" and "failure," which are part of the school and broader cultures. Ask the group to define the terms. Then ask them some of the following:

- How much do success and failure depend on other people knowing about them?

- Can successful people feel like failures?

- How might success in academics and activities affect adult life—if at all?

- How might poor performance in these areas affect adult life—if at all?

- When have you experienced success? Failure?

- Who and/or what has influenced how you think about these?

- Whom do you want to tell when you feel successful?

- How much do you worry about failure?

- A popular view is that it is important to learn how to fail. Do you agree?

- Do males and females define success and failure differently? Do adults and teens?

- What will help you feel successful when you are thirty? Fifty? Retired? (*Examples:* Being respected; using talents; feeling content; having a successful relationship; having lots of money; being healthy.)

- What could contribute to feeling failure at those ages?

- How does society, in general, view success?

From *The Essential Guide to Talking with Gifted Teens* by Jean Sunde Peterson, Ph.D. (Minneapolis: Free Spirit Publishing, 2008), pp. 55–58. Used with permission.

Underachievement Is Tied Intimately to Self-Image Development

A child who learns to see herself in terms of failure eventually begins to place self-imposed limits on what is possible. Thus, any academic successes are written off as lucky accidents, while low grades or achievement serve to reinforce her negative perceptions about herself.

This self-deprecating attitude often results in such comments (spoken or unspoken) as, "Why should I even try? I'm just going to fail anyway," or "Even if I do succeed, people will say it's because I cheated," or "Nothing I do is ever good enough, so why bother?" or "This is so boring to me I just can't make the effort. I might as well shut my brain off."

The end product is a low self-image, in which the student sees herself as weak in academics. Under this assumption, a child's initiative to change or to accept a challenge is limited.

Underachievement Implies That Adults Disapprove of a Child's Behavior

Underachievement is a problem for children because it is recognized as such by adults. Students who are labeled underachievers suffer the pangs of knowing that they are disappointing parents, teachers, and other people who are significant in

Putting Failure into Perspective

- Albert Einstein didn't speak until he was four years old, and some of his teachers thought he had learning disabilities or was lazy. At one point he was expelled from school.
- Steve Jobs was ousted from Apple—the company he founded—before returning and creating the iPad, iPhone, and iPad.
- When Lady Gaga first got signed to a major record label, they dropped her just three months later
- *Harry Potter and the Sorcerer's Stone* received more than a dozen rejections.
- John Grisham's first novel, *A Time to Kill*, was rejected by twenty-eight publishers.
- William Golding's *Lord of the Flies* was rejected twenty-one times.
- A successful actor is turned down twenty-nine out of thirty times when auditioning for TV commercials.
- Colonel Sanders's fried chicken recipe was rejected by more than 1,000 restaurants.
- The greatest quarterbacks complete only 60 percent of their passes.
- The best basketball players make only about 50 percent of their shots.
- Most major-league baseball players get on base about 25 percent of the time.

their lives. Thus burdened, these children learn to assess their abilities relative to what they have not accomplished instead of what they are capable of doing.

Similar to the frustration felt when attempting to deepen a hole in wet sand, the underachiever sees each victory squelched by the collapse of other unmet goals. So, when a trusted adult in this child's life praises the so-called underachiever for a successful grade or project, the child may dismiss this compliment as meaningless. "After all," the child might think, "it probably won't happen again."

Sadly, the overall disapproval felt when things don't go well overrides the occasional success, which the child notes as an exception—nothing more.

> "My greatest fear is that I am really not gifted, and the only reason for my placement in advanced classes is due to my parents pushing me. I often feel like an intellectual imposter."
>
> **—Evelyn, 14**

> "After rejection number forty, I started lying to my friends about what I did on the weekends. They were amazed how many times a person could repaint her apartment. The truth was, I was embarrassed for my friends and family to know I was still working on the same story, the one nobody apparently wanted to read."
>
> **—Kathryn Stockett, author of The Help, which was rejected sixty times before becoming a published best seller and the basis of an Oscar-winning film**

Underachievement Is a Learned Set of Behaviors

Underachievement can be learned by gifted students for whom "school" and "education" exist in separate spheres.

In five studies of education in the United States, published over decades, criticism was leveled at state and national policies that do not support gifted children, as well as at curricula designed strictly by grade-level norms with little regard for individual rates of learning. Let's begin with a classic study conducted nearly half a century ago.

In 1970, a congressional mandate required the Commissioner of Education to determine the extent of programs for gifted and talented students. Published in 1972, the Commissioner's report—known as the *Marland Report*—noted, "The boredom that results from discrepancies between the child's knowledge and the school's offerings leads to underachievement and behavior disorders affecting self and others."[6]

In 1983, the National Commission on Excellence in Education published *A Nation at Risk*, the first of many national critiques of the practice of education in America. Speaking specifically to the education of gifted students, the commission concluded that:[7]

- "Over half the population of gifted students do not match their tested ability with comparable achievement in school."

- "Only 31 percent of high school graduates complete intermediate algebra; 13 percent complete French I; and calculus classes, though available in 60 percent of U.S. high schools, are completed by only 6 percent of the students."

- "Textbooks are too easy for able students, and rigorous texts remain unavailable because of the 'thin market' for sales that is perceived by publishers."

In 1993, *National Excellence: A Case for Developing America's Talent* presented similar bad news about the state of U.S. education as it serves gifted children, including:[8]

- Economically disadvantaged and minority students are offered the fewest opportunities for academic advancement and are the most at risk for underachievement.

- Students are not asked to work hard or master a body of challenging skills. Adequacy prevails over excellence.

- Exceptional talent is viewed suspiciously in America. It is seen as a valuable resource, but it is noted by many as a troublesome expression of eccentricity.

Although *National Excellence* was as much a political document as an educational manifesto (for example, the word "gifted" was replaced by "talented"), it did refocus attention not only on underachieving behaviors, but also on the underachieving curriculum. Still, little change was noted even after this well-received report was published.

Then, in 2004, yet another report on the state of educating gifted children in America was released, titled *A Nation Deceived: How Schools Hold Back America's Brightest Students*. The title itself was controversial, but the report's authors defend its use:[9]

"We know *deceived* is a very strong word . . . the title is provocative—and accurate. This title is our honest

message to America and that message is this: deceiving ourselves and deceiving our brightest students is no longer defensible."

Focusing especially on acceleration practices and the infrequency of their use in America's schools, the authors address the overwhelming degree of underachievement for many gifted students, not just those who fail to achieve at all. Their solution begins with just one word: "Yes."

"Yes to giving bright kids complex math problems. Yes to letting them learn another language. Yes to letting them accelerate to take classes that are ahead of their age group. Yes to letting them fly.

"Instead, we say no. And by saying no, we undermine the motivation of bright students and hurt ourselves. We cling to the idea that all children are better off with children who match them in age. We don't even question it. And the cost to our country, to our communities, and to our children is enormous."[10]

The underlying message of this report was this: underachievement by gifted

students in America is not sporadic. It's epidemic.

A more recent report analyzed the policies used by various states to fund gifted child education and support gifted children in their schools. The 2011 report *State of the Nation in Gifted Education* used data collected from forty-four states and one territory, beginning with a message that sounds familiar: "A half-century after winning the Space Race, our nation's competitiveness is at risk." Citing the increasing achievement gap between students of color and poverty and their non-minority peers, as well as the patch-work of ways that individual states do (or don't) provide for gifted children, the report concludes with another ominous warning:[11]

"Our collective failure to prioritize the development of our most talented students is a crisis for the nation, one that looms larger with each passing school year, as students languish unchallenged."

Each of these reports, spanning two generations, points to the same conclusion: our nation is losing much of its intellectual capital by ignoring the needs of its most capable students. Perhaps even sadder is the personal loss felt by students and their families each time a gifted kid gives up on him or herself because school becomes tedious, trivial, or intellectually painful to endure.

Underachievement Is Taught

The year before *A Nation at Risk* was published, an eleven-year-old boy wrote a poem that's still appropriate today:[12]

Teachers told me I was rude,
Bumptious, overbearing, shrewd.
Some of the things they said were crude
I couldn't understand.
And so I built myself a wall,
Strong, solid, ten feet tall.
With bricks you couldn't see at all.
So I couldn't understand.

Gifted Kids Speak Out

We asked gifted kids, "What is the biggest challenge in school for gifted students?" Here are some of their answers:

"School itself. It isn't flexible enough to allow us to grow as individuals. Everything is very structured and if you ask for any differences you are seen as bucking the system, looking for trouble."
—Hector, 13

"Schools need to stop repeating the same thing year after year. I wish they would just move on. I wish the schools would just teach me at my level, not theirs. I wish I could have learned Latin starting in first grade, but I have to wait until high school."
—Mikaela, 11

How ironic: Gifted children, who often receive curriculum and instruction that is unchallenging and lacking in rigor and creative appeal, have come to be seen as the source of their own difficulties. In fact, the real problem lies in a lackluster set of academic offerings which leave students pleading for more. Perhaps in the final analysis, underachievement is *learned* because it is *taught* so well, year after year.

We know this hurts, and we realize, too, that if you are reading this book, you're probably not one of those offending educators who teaches a "one-size-fits-all" curriculum. Still, with so many highly able students turned off to learning, it's obvious that some teachers neither believe in nor practice curriculum differentiation that benefits gifted students.

Now, we're not saying that differentiation is easy! Nor do we believe it is the panacea that will serve to engage *all* disengaged gifted students. However, if teachers are willing to consider education from the student's side of the desk (even if it involves a skunk and some maple sugar), they can forge the foundations for positive change.

You can also help (even more than you already do) by supporting workshops about the needs of gifted students, or by conducting your own. Sponsor a panel of gifted students who are willing to talk to staff about their school experiences—the good, the bad, and the downright ugly. Provide resources for teachers to borrow that can help them know and do more for these students. Invite staff to visit your class so they can witness firsthand the ways in which gifted kids learn differently.

Underachievers vs. Selective Consumers

> "Don't mistake activity for achievement."
>
> —**John Wooden**

As we mentioned earlier, the problem of underachievement begins with its definition. There is no consensus on what underachievement actually is, where it starts, and how or when the metamorphosis to achievement occurs.

Another stumbling block is this: Any child who is not working up to potential, however that potential is defined, can be dubbed an underachiever. Too seldom do the people who attach that label actually consider the source of the problem. They see the result—the lack of achievement—and rush to label the student as something she or he may not be.

In many cases, the child in question is not an underachiever but is, instead, a selective consumer, adept at taking the best from what school and teachers have to offer and leaving the rest behind.

Two case studies can help us understand the distinctions between an underachiever and a selective consumer.

Case Study: Stephanie

Stephanie is a fifth grader whose report card comments read like a list of missed opportunities: "Stephanie is bright, but seems insecure about her ability to do well"; "Stephanie's perfectionism prevents her from pursuing new topics or projects."

In class, Stephanie seldom causes trouble; in fact, you hardly know she's there. She pursues her work with caution, and when her teacher hands her an assignment, Stephanie's out-loud comment is, "This is too hard for a stupid-head like me." Often, she is her own worst enemy. When she receives a high grade on a project, she attributes it to "being lucky," and when she doesn't do well, she internalizes the failure and calls herself "dumb."

Socially, Stephanie fits in with one or two friends she's had since first grade, but most students don't know her well. It's not that she's totally withdrawn, but she is *very* quiet.

Stephanie would like to do better in school but claims she can't. She insists she's not as smart as everyone says, and she can prove it by showing you all her low grades and poor papers.

To the casual observer, Stephanie is a nice, quiet girl who just lacks confidence. To the careful observer, Stephanie is a sad girl who seems to have little hope of ever being anything more than she is right now: self-critical, self-deprecating, and unable to chart her own course, socially or academically.

Case Study: Mark

Mark is a student most teachers hear about before they ever meet him. His reputation precedes him because Mark is the source of constant teacher-lounge banter: "You've got to approach him just so, or else he'll walk all over you"; "He's a smart kid, and he knows it—*that's* his biggest problem"; "He can do great work one day and no work the next."

In class, Mark's performance and behavior are sporadic. On some days, he's the most animated discussant in a review of current world events. On other days, he just sits there, completing seatwork when he feels like it and turning in homework when the mood strikes him.

Mark dislikes "busy work" and teachers who assign it. Although he can and does succeed on projects that pique his interest, he often concentrates solely on this work to the exclusion of other tasks. This, of course, makes it difficult for teachers to assign grades. They know that Mark understands the concepts of his lessons, but if he refuses to turn in all of his required work, how can they possibly reward him with high grades? It wouldn't be fair.

Socially, Mark has few problems, and some students may even see him as a leader—a rebel with a cause, an agent with a mission: to take the best from school and leave the rest behind.

Almost everyone is frustrated with Mark's sporadic performance, except for one person: Mark. He does know he's smart and he realizes, too, that if he "played the game by the rules" he could be a straight-A student. Somehow, though, getting high grades isn't necessarily one of Mark's personal goals. He's into learning, but it doesn't naturally follow that school is the place where lots of learning occurs.

To the casual observer, Mark is rebelling for the sake of rebelling. If he isn't willing to change his attitude, then "he can just sit there and get Fs." To the careful observer, Mark is a selective consumer of education. He knows what he knows, and he doesn't want to have to keep proving it through homework and "dumb" assignments that do little more than fill time. Mark could improve his school performance dramatically and almost overnight. He knows what the hoops are, but he's just not willing to jump through them.

Conclusions

If you compared the report-card *grades* of Stephanie and Mark, the similarities would outweigh the distinctions.

If you compared their report card *comments*, you'd find that teachers have very different impressions of these two "underachievers."

A Child's Fate
by Abel Lopez

This poem was composed by educator Abel Lopez at a workshop where he learned about the difference between being an underachiever and a selective consumer (his word: "nonproductive"). In the poem, he remembers his early education.

What happened on that dreadful day
Is something I just realized here today.

A nonproductive child just sat and stared
At a teacher who just did not care.

Although considered gifted, smart, and all that stuff,
This teacher thought it was all a bluff.

The nonproductive child sat in awe
Because the teacher only saw
A poor student without the right clothes
A poor student who didn't know.

The nonproductive child knew what was going on
The self-fulfilling prophecy was quickly turned on.

She just didn't know, she just didn't care
The nonproductive child was not treated fair

("Abel, I have spoken to the counselor and WE have agreed that you will be better off if we move you out of the accelerated classes and put you in the remedial courses . . .")

That nonproductive child sits here today
And realizes what happened on that one dreadful day.
If that teacher knew then what exists today
There may never have been that dreadful day.

In fact, Mark is not an underachiever, despite grades that indicate otherwise. He is a selective consumer: a student very much in touch with both himself and the world of learning but unwilling to do much of his assigned work because he sees little purpose in doing so.

Stephanie does display underachieving behaviors. She is a lost soul in the academic miasma called school. She desperately wants to do better—and feel better—but is at a loss about how to begin.

Differences at a Glance

The chart below is a fairly simple way to present the similarities and distinctions between students like Stephanie and Mark. As is true with any such side-by-side comparison, each trait or behavior listed is etched in soap, not stone. Although a particular student may seem to fit one pattern more than another, some of the items listed under that pattern will probably not apply. This chart is provided more as guidance than gospel and should, therefore, be regarded as more relative than absolute. Nonetheless, the overall idea that some so-called underachievers are actually selective consumers is legitimate and worth exploring further.

What are some characteristics that underachievers and selective consumers

Underachievers . . .	Selective Consumers . . .
Do not understand causes or cures	Can explain both the problem and possible solutions
Are dependent and reactive	Are independent and proactive
Tend to withdraw	Tend to rebel
Respect or fear authority figures	See teachers as adversaries; can be contentious
Need both structure and imposed limits	Require little structure; need "breathing room"
Exhibit uniformly weak performance	Exhibit performance that varies relative to the teacher and/or content
Generally require family intervention	Can usually be dealt with using school resources
May change over the long term	May change "overnight"
Are often perfectionistic; nothing they do is ever good enough	Are frequently satisfied with their accomplishments
Have a poor academic self-image	See themselves as academically able

may have in common? There are at least four:

1. Their socialization with classmates may be impaired, albeit for different reasons or in different ways. (Stephanie is too quiet; Mark is too "mouthy.")

2. They prefer a "family" versus a "factory" classroom atmosphere, as they see learning as an interactive, social activity.

3. They need to change both their behaviors and their attitudes.

4. They may need individual guidance or counseling to achieve academic success.

Many Studies, Few Conclusions

When Jane B. Raph, Miriam Goldberg, and Abraham Tannenbaum reviewed thirty years of research studies on underachievement (1931–1961), they analyzed more than ninety empirical studies—and could not find any one unified explanation of underachievement.[13] In 1974 and 1977, C. Asbury and Avner Ziv concluded that no specific psychosocial factors seem consistently associated with underachievement.[14]

More current research on underachievement indicates that both its definition and treatment remain complex. Sally M. Reis and D. Betsy McCoach mention the need to "individualize programs for achieving gifted students."[15] They also emphasize the need to focus on factors within the family, school, and home if underachievement is to be reversed—a finding consistent with work done by other researchers.[16]

Creativity researcher Kyung Hee Kim postulated that many gifted underachievers may, in fact, be highly creative but unrecognized as such. Placing them into a learning environment that is nurturing—allowing freedom of expression and true understanding of their learning needs and capabilities—often results in a reversal of underachieving behaviors.[17]

When all is said and done about the causes and treatment of underachievement, though, it seems that we know as little now about reversing it as we did when Raph, Goldberg, and Tannenbaum threw up their arms in frustration in 1961.

How can decades of research result in so little progress in understanding a phenomenon that everyone agrees exists? We believe this is due to two issues previously described here: the unfocused definitions of underachievement, and the lack of recognition of the distinctions between the underachiever and the selective consumer.

In their extensive review of underachievement as a multifaceted set of behaviors, Gary Davis and Sylvia Rimm allude to this distinction between the underachiever and the selective consumer, though they do not use those exact terms.[18] Rather, they create composites of specific (but fictional) children such as "Manipulative Mary," "Rebellious Rebecca," "Taunted Terrence," and "Dramatic Dick." What distinguishes the varieties of underachievement within these children is their unique levels of dependence and dominance.

Seen from another vantage point, these children could represent the characteristics of underachievers versus those of selective consumers. Davis and Rimm

go on to explain the circumstances and environments that prompt the emergence of the "Depressed Donnas" and "Dramatic Dicks" of the world, including school climate, inflexible and competitive classrooms, negative expectations, and an unrewarding curriculum.

In her review of decades of research studies on underachievement, Barbara Clark arrives at sixteen characteristics of children with underachieving behaviors:[19]

1. They have low self-concept and give negative evaluations about themselves. These feelings of inferiority are demonstrated by distrust, lack of concern, and/or hostility toward others.

2. They are socially more immature than achievers, lacking self-discipline and refusing to do tasks they deem unpleasant. They are highly distractible.

3. They harbor feelings of rejection, believing that no one likes them and that parents are dissatisfied with them.

4. They have feelings of helplessness and may externalize their conflicts and problems.

5. They do not see the connection between effort and achievement outcomes.

6. They are rebellious, have feelings of being victimized, and have poor personal adjustment.

7. They have few strong hobbies or interests.

8. They are unpopular with peers and have few friends.

9. They are hostile toward adult authority figures and distrust adults, generally.

10. They are resistant to influence from teachers or parents.

11. They have lower aspirations for their future, lacking future plans or career goals.

12. They may withdraw in classroom situations and be less persistent or assertive in these situations.

13. They lack study skills and have weak motivation for academic tasks.

14. They dislike school and teachers and choose companions who share similar feelings.

15. They often leave schoolwork incomplete and nap during study time.

16. They perform at higher levels on tasks requiring synthesizing rather than detailed computational or convergent responses or those tasks requiring precise, analytic processing.

Some of these characteristics show a resemblance to the items previously listed on page 170—with one important exception. Clark's list does not differentiate between behaviors (for example, items 6, 9, 12, and 15) and attitudes (for example, items 1, 3, 5, and 11).

What Next?

At this point in our knowledge (or lack thereof) about underachievement, it seems important to take a few steps back before trying to take any more steps forward. That is, before we begin to offer solutions to reverse the patterns of underachievement, educators need to reexamine—again—what they mean by that term.

It is our suggestion, based on both our clinical experiences as teachers and counselors and our review of pertinent research, that underachievement be subdivided as described in the chart on page 170. Once it is acknowledged that some so-called underachievers have nearly total control of their academic lives but merely choose not to perform, while others cannot change their behaviors because of a lack of self-regulation or inner resources, then the general strategies that are used to address the specific behaviors will become more on-target and focused.

When approaching any problem, there are two general lines of attack: the "shotgun" approach, where strategies are applied willy-nilly in hopes that something will hit its target, and the "spotlight" approach, where a sharp, precise beam is focused on a specific situation or problem. In issues as complex as these, time and effort spent on locating the target will ultimately result in more effective, efficient treatment strategies.

As a final comparison between underachievers and selective consumers, let us offer two analogies. The child who chooses not to perform up to others' expectations—the selective consumer—reminds us of the adage, "You can lead a horse to water, but you can't make him drink." With just a little editorial license, this new proverb describes such a case: "You can lead a child through school, but you can't make him think." On the other hand, the child with underachieving behaviors, who has little control over or understanding of his or her depressed performance is reminiscent of Narcissus, the Greek mythological character, who, upon seeing his reflection in a pond, pined away for the lovely creature he saw. In his case, Narcissus was longing for something that he already had, so his was not a problem of attainment but of realization. And just as Narcissus was eventually transformed into a beautiful flower, so might the child with underachieving behaviors come into full bloom, given the proper mix of support and nurturance.

Strategies to Reverse Behaviors and Attitudes

"There is one factor that has been shown repeatedly to make a difference in the life of an underachieving child: a caring, sensitive teacher who recognizes the child's true potential and is determined to help the child. Children respond to those who believe in them."
—Shelagh A. Gallagher

Since both selective consumerism and underachievement are noted especially in academic situations, it makes sense to look toward the roles played by schools in the treatment of these problems. This is not meant to either deny or downplay the important influences of the family, but rather to focus attention on the situations and structure most amenable to change by educators: school.

Although many strategies work better with selective consumers than they do with underachievers (and vice versa), there are some common denominators

that apply to both groups. Joanne R. Whitmore, in *Giftedness, Conflict, and Underachievement*—considered by many to be the most comprehensive treatment of underachievement ever published—classified these strategies into three clusters:[20]

1. **Supportive strategies.** These "affirm the worth of the child in the classroom and convey the promise of greater potential and success yet to be discovered and enjoyed."

2. **Intrinsic strategies.** These are "designed to develop intrinsic achievement motivation through the child's discovery of rewards available . . . as a result of efforts to learn, achieve, and contribute to the group."

3. **Remedial strategies.** These are "employed to improve the student's academic performance in an area of learning in which (s)he has evidenced difficulty learning, has experienced a sense of failure, and has become unmotivated to engage in learning tasks."

These three families of strategies all focus on one central theme: putting the child back in charge of his or her own education. Only when students feel academically capable and internally motivated to learn will school success occur. And since success is more likely to breed additional success, the child who learns early on that he or she has a good degree of power in determining learning outcomes will be more ready to absorb knowledge independent of adult supervision once the structured parameters of school are in the past.

Case Study: Mark

Let's see how the three types of strategies Whitmore described might work with Mark, the selective consumer.

Some people might surmise that Mark doesn't need much in the line of supportive strategies ("Surely his cockiness is a sign of a strong self-image"). But, just as looks can be deceiving, so can bravado. Mark's rebellious attitude toward authority may be a well-disguised front to cover for the inadequacies he fears he might have.

Mark probably does need support—who doesn't?—to show him that it's okay to show a vulnerability; a need for others to like and accept him for himself, not for someone he is trying to be. Therefore, a supportive teacher would acknowledge and thank Mark whenever he showed a glimmer of cooperation or whenever his independence was demonstrated in a positive or helpful way.

Intrinsically, Mark already knows that he is the "real teacher" in the sense of controlling when and if he learns, and he needs to be rewarded for these insights. At the same time, Mark and his teacher need to come up with some type of agreement that leads to the following accord: As long as Mark learns what he needs to learn (by the teacher's standards) via his own methods, the teacher won't interfere. However, if Mark's methods fall short, or he is at a loss as to how to proceed, then his teacher will intervene on Mark's behalf—by mutual consent.

Mark may have few areas in need of remediation, but if they do exist, they should be approached in an up-front manner by his teacher: "I know you don't like to write note cards before doing a report, but I need to see one set from you just so I know you have that skill. Then I'm off your back." This gives Mark a chance to demonstrate a skill he says he has, and it satisfies his teacher's need to know how close Mark's perception is to reality.

The Making of an Underachiever

Here's how an intelligent high school senior explains his academic frustration:

"School is ugh. Today, in sociology, we got into the topic of whether nature or nurture was more responsible for development. What better way to teach us than to give us a worksheet. It gave an opinion on the nature argument and one on the nurture, and then asked us to answer questions about the opinions. It had the same question phrased three different ways. I looked at it and got so pissed. This teaches me nothing. I learn to copy stuff from the front of a worksheet to the back. As I said, school is ugh!

"High school is basically around teaching us to take tests. Read a book for English (which I can never bring myself to do), take a test, write a paper about what the teacher wants us to say. In doing this, school is trying to create the passive, submissive mold of a student that will do whatever teachers want for the sake of a grade. That's not me."

Case Study: Stephanie

Could Whitmore's strategies also work with an underachiever like Stephanie? Let's find out.

One minute, one hour, one day at a time, Stephanie needs to hear that she is a valuable person, regardless of the grades she attains. Supportive comments such as, "It's so great to have you in class, Stephanie. When you smile, it lights up the whole room!" need to be interspersed with accolades for Stephanie's attempts (not necessarily successes) at academics: "I saw you practicing spelling with Julie. Thank you for helping her out." In subtle and obvious ways (for example, words and smiles), both one-on-one and in group settings, Stephanie needs to be reminded that she is able, valuable, and responsible.

Stephanie's true need is to feel that she is an active participant in rather than a passive recipient of her education. When she does a good job on a project or paper, the teacher should ask Stephanie how and why she thinks she succeeded. If Stephanie claims it was due to luck or fate, a few words of rebuttal will help: "I bet you studied—even a little," or, "The way you put this report together shows me that you have fine organizational skills." The more specific the comments, the better, since it is harder to deny direct

What Learning *Could* Be

Jane Goodall, world-noted naturalist, received a toy gorilla from her father as an infant. Some eighty years later, "Jubilee" still sits on her bedroom dresser. At the age of four, Jane hid in her family's henhouse for several hours to investigate where eggs came from, unaware that the police had been called in to find her. When she reunited with her mother, her mom didn't scold her; instead, noting Jane's excitement, her mother listened to Jane tell her story about the eggs. Upon high school graduation, unable to afford college, Jane became a typist at Oxford University. When a family friend invited her to their farm in Kenya, Jane quit her job, moved back home, and waitressed until she could afford the boat fare to Africa. At age twenty-three, she visited Africa for the first time, met with anthropologist Louis Leakey, and became his assistant. In her 2013 book, *Seeds of Hope*, Goodall recalls a personal learning experience:

"I came across a 'Nature Notebook,' in which the twelve-year-old Jane, with great attention to detail, had sketched and painted a number of local plants and flowers. Beside each drawing or watercolor I had handwritten a detailed description of the plant, based on my careful observations and probably a bit of book research.

"This was not a schoolbook. This wasn't done for an assignment. I just loved to draw and paint and write about the plant world."

Jane Goodall, *Seeds of Hope* (New York: Grand Central Publishing, 2013).

statements than it is to dismiss or disregard a general "Good job, Stephanie!"

If there is any remediation to be done, Stephanie needs to know that it's okay to be better at some things than others. The catchphrase to apply to Stephanie should be "Less than perfection is more than acceptable." Should she need help with handwriting, research skills, or any other area related to school success, Stephanie needs to be told that even she—a gifted child—isn't expected to know everything.

Stephanie cares about and respects school a great deal. It's the prime source of her attitudes toward herself and learning. Knowing this, the concerned teacher will take great care in acknowledging Stephanie's efforts and will support her both directly (through words) and indirectly (through gestures) so that Stephanie's attempts to succeed are noted as the brave efforts they are.

Strategies at a Glance

Specific distinctions between supportive, intrinsic, and remedial strategies for addressing the behavior of underachievers and selective consumers are found on pages 178–179.

Notice that the teacher is a supportive partner in the learning process in both cases. When working with students who underachieve, the teacher is more directive and in control. When working with selective consumers, the teacher adopts a more relaxed, "how-can-I-best-help-you-learn?" attitude. Either way, the teacher is fully in charge of the events transpiring in the classroom and the conditions under which learning is most likely to occur for specific, individual students.

The approaches used to attain success give new meaning to the phrase "The end justifies the means." In this case, it does. Students who may appear at first glance to be similar because of the commonality of their poor academic performance may be, in fact, very different from each other. Thus, the strategies used, the demeanor displayed, and the degree of autonomy provided by the teacher may (and should) differ considerably from student to student.

The idea of individualizing curriculum and instruction for different students is hardly revolutionary. Even the most staunch traditionalists would agree that since children learn at different rates, some degree of consideration may be given to the possibility that what works for one pupil won't work with another.

	For Selective Consumers	**For Underachievers**
Supportive Strategies	Eliminating (or at least significantly reducing) work already mastered	Holding daily class meetings to discuss student concerns and progress
	Allowing independent study on topics of personal interest	Directive atmosphere shows the student that the teacher is in charge and is competent
	Nonauthoritarian atmosphere	Daily/weekly/monthly written contracts of work to be completed
	Permitting students to prove competence via multiple methods	Free time scheduled each day to show importance of relaxation and free choice
	Teaching through problem-solving techniques over rote drill	Using instructional methods that are concrete and predictable
Intrinsic Strategies	Students help determine class rules	Students are aware of specific rewards for attempting and/or doing their work
	Assigning specific responsibilities for classroom maintenance or management	Allowing students to evaluate work prior to the teacher assigning a grade
	Teacher practices reflective listening—comments to students serve to clarify statements, not evaluate them	Frequent and positive contact with family regarding child's progress
	Students set daily/weekly/monthly goals with approval of teacher	Verbal praise for any self-initiating behaviors

	For Selective Consumers	**For Underachievers**
Remedial Strategies	Self-selected, weekly goals for improvement determined between student and teacher	Programmed instruction materials, where students grade their own papers immediately on completion
	Private instruction in areas of weakness	Peer tutoring of younger students in areas of strength
	Use of humor and personal example to approach areas of academic weakness	Small-group instruction in common areas of weakness (e.g., spelling, sequencing, phonics)
	Familiarizing students with learning-styles research and its personal implications for classroom performance	Encouraging students to work on projects which don't involve a grade

"In second grade, I was asked to cut out the rising and setting times of the sun from the newspaper. After the first few times I refused to do it—once I understood the concept, I saw no point to it. That year the teacher announced to the class that I was passing by the skin of my teeth. I remember sitting there thinking that teeth don't have skin."

—Meg, a teacher

"The drive I have to learn is overwhelming, but I can't learn in the classic school environment. I feel I would best learn in the presence of someone who actually could expand on everything in depth. I think I would learn best talking to someone one-on-one. Just talking to someone about what I'm searching to learn would help me—not only academically, but in another way: I'm searching for a purpose, and when I find it, it will guide me."

—Justin, 19

A Modest Proposal

The work of Jane B. Raph, Miriam Goldberg, and Abraham Tannenbaum was cited earlier in this chapter. One can almost read the disappointment in the words Tannenbaum used to summarize

their three decades of research on underachievement: "Added together, the studies yield a tangle of conclusions that are more puzzling than revealing."[21] There is no way that a phenomenon such as underachievement—or its reversal—could remain that elusive for so long except for one reason: the term itself was (and is) ill-defined.

In their review of research on underachieving gifted students, Cynthia Dowdall and Nicholas Colangelo conclude that "the inescapable result [is that the variability] in definitions is of a magnitude that makes the concept of underachieving gifted (students) almost meaningless."[22]

With a single exception—Joanne R. Whitmore's analysis of underachievers based on years of classroom intervention and research—it is our belief that it might be best to throw out what we think we know and start over with a *tabula rasa* on which we draw conclusions based on new research, new beginnings, and a new set of guidelines regarding underachievement. Specifically, we propose the following:

1. That clear distinctions be made between underachievers and selective consumers, as explained in this chapter.

2. That studies look at student behaviors over a span of time, not merely over one school term or one testing situation.

3. That underachievement be defined specifically and painstakingly by individual researchers, so that those who use this research will not generalize a study's findings to other groups of similarly labeled (yet very different) students.

Passion vs. Achievement

by Jason, 14

To some teachers, *passions* are as important as *achievements*. Thank heavens! Some of us just don't seem to be able to make high grades like we should be able to—for whatever reasons—but we still have passions.

Usually, this "failure" is met with two responses:

1. "He's not really gifted or he would be making better grades," or

2. "He's just not trying hard enough."

Me? I just hope that gifted people can be happy. If you have an IQ of 160 and if learning every bit of knowledge and going to college at age 12 and making straight A's is your passion, then go for it! But if you are like me and find that being with people, playing video games, reading about stuff that is interesting, having fun, and laughing a lot is your passion, then I think we should be allowed to do that without feeling guilty that we are letting society down. Bunches of gifted people don't seem to have much fun unless, as I said before, their view of fun has to do solely with books and laboratory mice. Fine for them, just not for me.

4. That you, as a caring educator, come to understand and appreciate the central role you play in the academic and emotional lives of gifted children who are not performing at levels that all agree they are capable of reaching.

By recognizing the vast and important distinctions between underachievers and selective consumers, and by altering our approaches to working with these children, we will have a better chance of achieving success with smart kids who love to learn, even if their grades and behaviors might lead us to believe otherwise.

A Few Final Thoughts

We wish we could provide you with a nice, tight definition of underachievement to end this chapter. Unfortunately, that's not possible. Underachievement and selective consumerism are constructs that take on personal interpretations—always. Like other big ideas—justice, beauty, respect—their definitions cannot be fully appreciated on paper. Like beauty, they are in the eye of the beholder; like justice, they seem to vary somewhat depending on the circumstances; and like respect, you know it when it's there, though explaining exactly what makes it so remains elusive.

Still, having difficulty defining beauty doesn't diminish our enjoyment of seeing it in a painting, a person, or a relationship. And not being able to accurately pinpoint what we mean by justice doesn't keep us from critiquing the latest Supreme Court decision.

So must it be with the underachiever and selective consumer. For even if we can't define them to our own satisfaction, that doesn't diminish our responsibility to Matt, whose passion to make maple sugar is surpassed only by his ability to do so, or to any other student who "does not go to school well" and is, therefore, labeled as something that no one wants to be.

CHAPTER 7

The Eight Great Gripes of Gifted Kids

 I like seeing what other gifted kids have to say about stuff, because it gives you a different point of view, and it makes you happy to find out you're not the only one who feels like that.
—Dylan, 11

The Eight Great Gripes of Gifted Kids evolved from surveys Judy has conducted with gifted kids over the past thirty-plus years.[1] And Jim, in more than twenty years as a teacher of gifted kids from grades four to twelve, has witnessed similar sentiments from kids throughout those decades. Indeed, it's amazing to both Judy and Jim how similar many (but not all) of these Great Gripes are today as they were when they were first introduced.

The Eight Great Gripes of Gifted Kids

(from *The Survival Guide for Gifted Kids, 3rd Edition*)

1. We miss out on activities other kids get to do while we're in GT [gifted and talented] class.

2. We have to do extra work in school.

3. Other kids ask us for too much help.

4. The stuff we do in school is too easy and it's boring.

5. When we finish our schoolwork early, we often aren't allowed to work ahead.

6. Our friends and classmates don't always understand us, and they don't see all of our different sides.

7. Parents, teachers, and even our friends expect too much of us. We're supposed to get A's and do our best all the time.

8. Tests, tests, and more tests!

As we mentioned, some of these gripes have changed over time. For example, gifted kids report that they are teased less and face less of a negative stigma than our surveys showed in earlier years. This improvement may be due to the fact that services on behalf of gifted kids have become more numerous, and being identified as gifted has grown more common. In addition, kids may feel more comfortable with the gifted label as a result of greater opportunities to talk with teachers and parents about growing up gifted.

Other gripes—such as #7—*haven't* changed. Gifted children and teens continue to feel strong pressure to be perfect on many levels. All the more reason for teachers (and other people in kids' lives) to address perfectionism and why it's important to have a healthy perspective of what success is (and isn't). In fact, kids truly benefit from the opportunity to explore *all* of the Great Gripes. Activities, conversations, and journaling all help kids experience a kinship with each other, since many share most—if not all—of the Great Gripes. If nothing else, kids feel better when they know that they're not the only ones feeling a certain way or experiencing certain situations.

Group Discussions of the Eight Great Gripes

Gifted kids need to talk about the challenges, issues, and problems in their lives—and they need to talk with people who will listen, empathize, and understand. There's no better place to do this than in a small group of their peers, led by a teacher or counselor with knowledge of and experience in gifted education. In this setting, gifted kids can be themselves, without worrying about appearing "too smart."

Gifted Kids Speak Out

Success means . . .

"Not having to worry about my manifest destiny."
—Jessie, 13

"Reaching a manifest destiny."
—Jason, 13

(From a board in a GT Resource Room)

Preparation

If you haven't already asked your students to complete the "Student Questionnaire" on pages 37–43, we suggest that you do so before beginning any of the discussions that follow. It helps to know ahead of time how your students feel about the Great Gripes, and this questionnaire will provide you with that information.

You may also want to review the "Creating a Supportive Environment" section in Chapter 4: Being a Gifted Education Teacher and use the first four strategies described there:

- "Clarify Your Role as Teacher and Your Students' Roles as Learners" (pages 98–99)

- "Clarify Expectations—Yours and Theirs" (pages 99–100)

- "Set Ground Rules" (page 100)

- "Decide What to Reward and How" (pages 100–103)

These will help set the stage for a positive group experience for everyone.

Because these discussions touch on personal topics, and talking about personal things takes a certain amount of risk and trust, you may want to go beyond the basic ground rules. Give every student in the group a copy of the "Group Guidelines" on page 210.* Read them aloud or ask group members to read them. Ask if anyone has questions about any of the guidelines. Tell the students that everyone is expected to follow these guidelines—including you.

*These guidelines are adapted from Jean Sunde Peterson, Ph.D., *The Essential Guide to Talking with Gifted Teens* (Minneapolis: Free Spirit Publishing, 2008), pp. 18–19. Used with permission.

You might introduce the Great Gripes discussions by saying something like this: "Remember the 'Student Questionnaire' I asked you to fill out [*last week, last month, at the start of the year*]? The questionnaire had a section that asked about the conflict in your lives and how often you have certain feelings or frustrations, like being underchallenged in school, feeling misunderstood, or believing that people expect you to be perfect all the time. In fact, gifted kids everywhere have those same feelings or problems. Over the next several [*days, weeks*], we're going to talk about each one and figure out ways to handle it."

We recommend that if you discuss one Great Gripe, you discuss them all. We envision this as a series of eight discussions in whatever order you prefer. One method we've used is to ask for a show of hands indicating how many kids have felt or dealt with each Gripe, begin with a discussion of the Gripe that most kids feel affect them, and work our way through the other Gripes after that. If students need reminders of what the Great Gripes are, you can write them on the board or create a handout listing them.

● DISCUSSION OF GREAT GRIPE #1

We miss out on activities other kids get to do while we're in GT class.

Purpose

To review the purposes of GT classes and opportunities and help kids remember why these are valuable and important. Also, to give kids a chance to talk about the types of things they feel they miss out on, which in turn will give you information about what might be done differently.

Note: This gripe is most common among gifted students in elementary school, who participate in pull-out programs. If you're working with older students, however, your group can still benefit from a discussion about how they may feel their participation in the gifted program isolates them or deprives them of fun experiences that they see as part of "normal" teenagers' lives.

Preparation

Gather your school or district mandate or goals related to meeting the needs of gifted kids. Prepare a handout for students with that information, along with any additional information you think they'd benefit from, such as definitions of giftedness from your program and other sources or readings. Feel free to also share your personal definition of giftedness.

In addition, find out if there are any patterns to the sorts of things gifted kids miss out on, and whether such patterns truly create unfair divides. For example, if gifted kids routinely miss out on art, movies, or other activities that most kids enjoy, this situation creates a clear dilemma.

Procedure

Ask students to arrange their chairs in a circle (or to sit on the floor). Have each person name one reason he or she thinks gifted and talented programs and classes exist (in general, as well as at your school in particular). Keep going until no one can think of another reason to add. Do this quickly; just have students name one element after the other, off the tops of their heads. Then distribute the handout you prepared listing goals for gifted programs and various definitions of giftedness.

Discussion Questions

1. Why do you think gifted programs exist?

2. What are your favorite things about being in GT class?

3. What are your least favorite aspects? What do you wish you didn't miss when you're away from your regular class?

4. Now that you've read some definitions of giftedness, which ones do you like the most?

5. How do you define being gifted?

6. Why are there so many different views of what gifted means?

7. Do you have any questions about this program or what's expected of you?

8. What expectations do you have of me, your teacher?

9. What, if anything, could be done differently so you don't have to make a choice between two opportunities, being here versus staying in your regular class?

Discussion Guidelines

The group may not reach a consensus on the purposes and importance of the gifted class, much less the meaning of giftedness in one discussion. (Adults certainly haven't, so we can hardly expect students to!) Aim to demystify the word *gifted*, and to clarify why students are in the class or program. Emphasize that we're still learning a lot about exceptional ability and talent. The "gifted" label isn't meant to typecast people as much as it is to recommend certain kinds of instruction in certain fields.

Gifted Kids Speak Out

When we asked gifted students, "What are the best and worst parts of being a gifted child?" here's what they said:

"Best: Our GT program is really fun and challenging, and our teacher is very encouraging. It's one of my favorite things about school, and I feel lucky to have been chosen for the class."
—**Manuel, 10**

"Best: I feel proud to be in the gifted program. I think self-esteem, and learning how to keep it, are really important for being pleased about who you are just the way you are. That's not to say that you can't or shouldn't try to be even better. But you need to believe in your own basic worth in order to take advantage of the positives of giftedness."
—**Scott, 11**

"Worst: A negative of being gifted is that there's nothing higher than a 4.0 grade point average. I don't get excited about my perfect report card (all A's and 1's), yet all my friends would be ecstatic to even get all B's. I wish there was something higher for me to strive for."
—**Annie, 13**

"Worst: One of the worst parts about being gifted is boredom in school. We have a lot of slow learners in our class, and my teacher has to explain (and explain, and explain) things. This is very frustrating to those of us who get it the first time."
—**Janelle, 10**

You'll want to summarize that gifted people are not "better" people, but that other people may be angry about the superiority which the label can imply. Gifted students may be superior academically or in specific areas of talent, but there are many other valuable qualities in human beings, and intellectual or creative abilities are only some of them. How any student develops his or her abilities is what's important, and people at all levels of ability make significant contributions to our world.

For fun, and if time allows, you may want to share "More Possible Meanings for the Acronym IQ" on page 46 with the group.

Finally, tell students that the "gift" they have is theirs, to nurture and share as they can. They don't owe society for having been born with a high potential. They don't owe the world anything more than any other citizen does. (Some kids may say something along the lines of, "But my parents say, 'to whom much is given, much is expected.'" If this type of idea comes up, open this topic for discussion, too.)

💬 DISCUSSION OF GREAT GRIPE #2
We have to do extra work in school.

Purpose
To determine in what ways gifted kids have to do extra work in school, or perceive that they do; to come up with some coping strategies or ways to balance schoolwork to be more equitable if there are inequities.

Preparation
Talk with regular education teachers to find out what their typical expectations are of the gifted kids in their classes. For example, determine whether students are expected to complete all of the regular class assignments on top of the work they're assigned in their gifted education classes. Or, are students able to test out of things they already know and can do? Are they allowed to skip certain assignments so they don't have to do double the work?

Procedure
Arrange students in a circle, introduce the topic, and invite students to comment on this Great Gripe. Is it relevant to their lives? If so, in what ways? If not, why not? You may want to have a student volunteer to be a recorder for this discussion and list remarks on a board or on a large sheet of paper.

Once all comments have been made, take each unique response and determine, as best you can, if each complaint about having to do more or extra work is objectively accurate. For example, if students voluntarily do extra-credit work, that's obviously their choice. But if they're *required* to do extra-credit work because they're in the gifted class, it's not surprising that they may view this as a punishment for being smart. If students

complain about special or fun things that seem to be planned when the gifted class is scheduled, ask them to elaborate. Sometimes gifted kids simply don't want to miss out on *anything*. In other cases, they are genuinely (and understandably) frustrated at missing out on movies, parties, and other fun stuff because of going to the gifted class.

Discussion Questions

1. What kinds of extra work are the most frustrating for you? What would help you feel less annoyed by this?

2. Are any accommodations made for you so that you don't have to do extra work on top of the work you do in this class? If so, what are they?

3. When you're frustrated about the amount of work you have to do, have you talked with your regular teacher to let him or her know how you feel? If you have, what was the result?

4. If you have talked with your teacher and did not get a positive result, what ideas do you have that might help the situation?

Discussion Guidelines

Remember that sometimes kids just need to talk and be heard. Other times they may have legitimate complaints. You can help by empathizing with their frustrations, and by acknowledging that sometimes things just aren't fair. You can also advocate on students' behalf if what you discover clearly shows they're not being permitted to test out of what they already know and can do. You can also offer them guidance on how to advocate for themselves (you might check Deb Douglas's website, www.gtcarpediem.com, for tips). In addition, you can talk with teachers

about instances in which the gifted class could possibly be scheduled for a different time if that would allow gifted students to participate in a special or particularly fun activity. And you can try to get teachers to avoid assigning gifted students MOTS* work. When these instances occur, it could be that educators in the school would benefit from in-service training about the social, emotional, and educational needs of the gifted. Without this background knowledge, they may not really know how to differentiate for gifted kids.

Refer students to "Ten Tips for Talking to Teachers" (on pages 153–154) and "What to Say When Teachers Say No" (on page 155). If you can, role-play various scenarios so students can practice this assertiveness with each other, and with you.

● DISCUSSION OF GREAT GRIPE #3
Other kids ask us for too much help.

Purpose

To give students an opportunity to talk about situations when other kids ask them for help; to brainstorm ways they can respond if they don't want to help, or if they want to help but don't have time.

Preparation

Ask students to keep a log for a week or two that documents times when kids ask them for help. They should simply note what types of help were requested, and when (during particular classes, after school, and so on). Have them bring their logs to class when you're ready to discuss this Great Gripe. Ahead of time, create a graph on which they can record dates, times, and situations when help is asked

---

*MOTS = More Of The Same

for. Once students fill in their graphs, the whole class can view and compare these records.

Procedure

Give students the graph you've prepared and ask them to transfer the data from their logs to the graphs. Discuss whether or not students notice any patterns. For example, is help requested more often in certain subject areas? While students are doing project work? Shortly before tests? On the board or a sheet of paper, make notes on any such patterns, as well as any unique situations that students observe or report.

Discussion Questions

1. Why do you think other kids ask you for help? How do you feel about it?

2. Are there instances when you feel like it's totally okay for kids to ask you for help, and other times when it's not? Please be as specific as possible.

3. Have you ever asked another student to help you with schoolwork? What was his or her response, and what was the outcome? Have you ever asked someone for help and he or she said no? How did that feel, and what did you do?

4. When you don't want to help others, for whatever reason, what are respectful ways of saying no? (*Examples:* "I have so much homework myself right now I don't have time to help you. Maybe you could ask our teacher to help you." or "I really prefer to work by myself. Maybe someone else in class can help.")

Discussion Guidelines

If possible, encourage students not to name specific kids who ask for help. You don't want to have particular students targeted because they need help (or think they need help). Also emphasize the importance of responding respectfully to requests for help. It's okay to say no, as long as it's done in a polite or caring way. Gifted kids often learn more easily and quickly than other kids. They may need help empathizing with students who struggle to learn.

🗨 DISCUSSION OF GREAT GRIPE #4
The stuff we do in school is too easy, and it's boring.

Purpose

To understand what feelings underlie boredom; to clarify what students find boring; to help students acknowledge their own responsibility for being bored.

Preparation

Gather several large photographs showing close-ups of human faces—people of various ages, and from various ethnic and cultural backgrounds. Photography books, websites, magazines, and so forth are all good resources. Ideally, you'll have enough that you can assign each student a different photograph.

Procedure

This exercise is composed of two parts. First you'll introduce the topic of boredom, find out how prevalent it is among your students, discuss what they think causes boredom, and hear their feelings about boredom. Then you'll ask them to write about a face in a photograph. This writing exercise will take at least 15 minutes. Afterward, you'll follow up with a summary discussion. Depending on your schedule, you may need to spread the discussion of Great Gripe #4 over two days.

Part One

Have students take their usual seats or find a comfortable spot. Tell them you'll be discussing the subject of boredom.

Discussion Questions

1. Does anyone in here ever feel bored? If so, what is that feeling like?

2. Are there other feelings that seem to go along with boredom? What are they? Can you describe or name them? (*Examples:* anger, disappointment, frustration, resentment)

3. When do you feel most bored? Can you predict which things—which events, subjects, people, obligations, or tasks—will bore you most? Has this type of thing always bored you, or have your "boredom triggers" changed over time?

4. What can you do about being bored?

Discussion Guidelines

Try to get students to look at all the feelings that go along with the phrase "I'm bored." Kids often say they're bored when they really mean something else, such as "I'm afraid to make the effort," "I'm lonely," "I really don't know how to focus or get involved," "I'm angry they're making me do this again," or "I'm mad about something unrelated." By probing and rephrasing, you should be able to reveal some of these feelings. If students are angry about schoolwork, they're also probably frustrated and depressed that other people don't recognize that the work is boring, or don't trust them to work on something more meaningful.

Knowing specifically what one finds boring is useful self-knowledge. Not everyone will be interested in everything.

Try to get students to list precisely what bores them. Is it chemistry (or just molecular chemistry)? School dances? Cars? Television (or just reality TV)? Math? Basketball? Conversations about feelings? Politics? Being told what to do? Being thirteen years old? If "the whole system" bores them, this may point to a larger problem involving anger and self-esteem.

Write down the various actions students say they can take when they're bored, but hold your comments until you've finished Part Two.

Part Two

Have each student choose a photograph of a face, study it, and write about it. Tell them they'll have 15 minutes to do this. Explain that their "essay" doesn't need to have a beginning, middle, or end. Also stress that their writing won't be judged on literary or grammatical merit. Encourage students to focus, stay engaged, and keep looking for interesting qualities to observe and describe.

This exercise is about seeing, and realizing there is always something *more* to be seen if one looks long enough and carefully enough. For this reason, the writing task needs to last long enough to stretch students' usual period of concentration. Depending on your group, 15 minutes may or may not be long enough. When students start looking around as though they're bored, press them to keep looking and keep writing, even when they think they've said it all.

Discussion Questions

1. What kinds of things did you write about?

2. As you spent time looking at the person's face, did you discover anything

about it that surprised you? Anything that you didn't see at first?

3. How many people found it hard to keep writing? Did you reach a point when there seemed to be nothing new to say?

4. For those of you who kept writing, how did you keep yourself interested and involved? What did you do to keep going?

Discussion Guidelines

Discuss what kinds of observations, descriptions, and stories students wrote. Were their essays imaginative in nature? Factual? Personal? Emphasize how many different approaches students took to the same task. If they *all* say they were bored,

try the exercise again, this time providing specific tips on how to stay engaged. For example, "Highlight what you see visually." "Use your imagination. What is the person thinking or feeling? What kind of life has the person had?"

If students were able to push themselves beyond initial observation and discover or explore something new, reward them for their efforts. Ask them to relate their discoveries and describe the feelings they experienced.

The take-away of this discussion is, of course, that we are all somewhat responsible for our own boredom. Sometimes our boredom is in direct proportion to the amount of effort or energy we invest in a subject. Typically, we choose not to invest much of ourselves in a subject that is difficult, threatening, or simply unappealing—thus automatically lessening the return we might get from it.

A constantly bored kid may be a fantastically brilliant and accelerated student. He may *also* be unwilling or unable to risk self-disclosure, failure, or personal energy. What's more, many kids are used to being passively entertained. Yet all the best strategies for combating boredom require action.

Stress the concrete steps that students can take when they're bored. Refer to the suggestions they made themselves during the discussion. Also encourage them to find out more about "uninteresting topics" and to take risks by trying new approaches to old problems. Generally, solutions boil down to "Change what you can change, avoid what you really need to avoid, and make it interesting whenever you can." Reinforce the notion that they have more power over their boredom than they think.

Creative Tips for Battling Boredom in School, at Home, or Wherever You Are!
by Felice Kaufmann, Ph.D., and Sahil Gogtay

Felice Kaufmann is a research assistant professor at the New York University Child Study Center and an independent consultant in gifted child education. Sahil Gogtay is (at the time of this writing) sixteen years old and a junior at Georgetown Day School in Washington, D.C. They came up with these unusual ways to combat boredom—because they both know what it is like to be bored! Share these with your students and see if they have any creative ideas of their own.

- Alternate your school supplies. Use different-colored notebook paper every day. Write with a different pen. Similarly, when doing your homework on a computer, vary fonts, backgrounds, and templates to make your assignment look like a page from a magazine, newspaper, billboard, or menu.

- Use "idea traps" (such as self-sticking notes) to record ideas that occur to you while you are listening. (Later, collect your ideas in a note-taking app or notebook so you have them all in one place.) Challenge yourself to keep up with what's going on in class while paying attention to your own thoughts. Think of questions and topics you want to explore later. Who invented the pencil? Was Mahatma Gandhi married? What causes cell respiration? Be as random as you want. *Extra credit:* Think about how you'd connect all of these ideas in a two-dimensional flowchart or concept map.

- While listening to the teacher or doing your work, use another part of your brain to turn your classroom into a movie set. Think about how the room would look from different camera angles. Imagine scenery and costumes. For example, picture your class taking place on the moon. If you're a visual artist or photographer, think about how to express your ideas in images. If you're musically inclined, think about the soundtrack you'd create.

- Ask yourself fun questions about whatever topic is being discussed. How might a superhero use this information? How might your favorite movie star use this information? How could you use it in different seasons or at different times of day? How might you use it ten years from now? What might someone living 100 years ago think of this information? What might someone from the future think?

- Make lists of *everything*. Gifts you want to buy for someone else (or yourself). Science fair project ideas. Places you want to visit. Slogans for your presidential campaign. Keep all your lists in one file, notebook, or app. Each week review your lists and decide which ideas you want to pursue

➡

now, which you want to set aside for later, and which you want to toss. Try creating a daily log or long-range plan for the things you definitely want to accomplish.

- Mentally create inventions using random things you see around you—a clock, a shoe, a cell phone, a desk. How might you combine two or three of these to make something new? A clock you wear on your feet? A desk with a built-in cell phone dock?

- Ask your teacher to let you sit in a different chair or a different part of the room when you get bored. Sometimes making small changes in your environment can help you stay alert and focused.

- Play the game of opposites. If you're learning about multiplication, reflect upon how it is similar to, and different from, its opposite, division. How is a comedy like and unlike a drama? How are girls like and unlike boys?

- Suspend the rules of logic. Wonder about how a noun feels about being a noun, or whether a tree would rather be a bird, or whether the number three would rather be the number five. What might an orange have to say to an apple? What might you ask your house if it could talk?

- Take a "three-minute vacation." Think of somewhere you've always wanted to go—a place you have seen, read about, or imagined—and let yourself BE there for three minutes. Notice how people go about their daily lives—what do they eat? Where do they live? Who are their friends? What do they do? Come back after three minutes and see how energized you feel!

- Look at an object in the room and imagine what it would be like if it were gigantic or maybe very, very small. What else might it be used for? What if there were ten of them in a row? What if it were cut in half? What could you add to it to make it more interesting?

- While paying attention to what's going on in class, test yourself on other "subjects." Without looking, do you remember who is sitting in which desk? How about what each student is wearing today? Check to see how you did when class is over.

- Imagine that you're the teacher. How might you present the same material differently? What questions would you ask students? What projects could you assign? Are there ways you might communicate the same information as a game? How could you use technology (video, apps, etc.) to present the material?

🔵 **DISCUSSION OF GREAT GRIPE #5**
When we finish our schoolwork early, we often aren't allowed to work ahead.

Purpose
To air feelings about not being able to work ahead and at your own pace in school, and come up with possible remedies.

Preparation
Compile a list of ways teachers can differentiate for gifted students. Given their advanced cognitive abilities, these students learn at rates and in ways that can be significantly different from those of their age peers. Your list might include, for example:

- **Pace:** For gifted students, this can mean spending less time on background knowledge; doing fewer exercises or viewing fewer examples of how to do particular tasks; and receiving less direct teacher instruction. Students should be given the opportunity to work more independently and be challenged in ways that focus on their learning needs.

- **Complexity:** Teachers can support and develop gifted learners' complex and higher level thinking skills by giving them authentic tasks that require problem solving. Gifted students will also benefit from learning divergent thinking (the idea that there's more than one way to do things), and from having interactions with others that involve negotiation, collaboration, and strong verbal skills.

Take a look at "Ten Strategies to Differentiate Pace" (below) and "Tips for Creating Complex Learning Tasks" on page 199. These lists may introduce you to

Ten Strategies to Differentiate Pace

An accelerated pace is an essential part of differentiation for gifted students. Pace refers to the rate of instruction and management in the classroom. Following are ten proven strategies for differentiating the pace with gifted students:

1. Create the course syllabus with clear objectives, including what students will know, understand, and be able to do after each lesson, so that they know what to expect and focus on in the lesson.

2. Have students do reading and preparation as homework, using either print or online material. Class time should be used primarily to review and zero in on new learning points. (This is often called a "flipped" classroom.)

3. Make students responsible for noting homework in daily planners, or post the homework for each day on a website. Don't spend class time disseminating homework.

4. Implement a "study buddy" program. Partner each student with at least one other student in the class. The study buddies are responsible for keeping each other posted on work, assignments, and notes missed when they are absent.

➡️

The study buddies also answer each other's questions about the material whenever possible. This frees up teacher time to instruct. Of course, if neither student can answer the question, they pose it to the teacher. Every pair will also need a backup in case both partners are absent on the same day.

5. Use the "anticipatory set" idea [a question, statement, or other "hook" that connects students' background knowledge to a lesson and gets them interested in what's to come] wisely. Begin lessons with a short activity that focuses the learner on the material to be covered or the new skill/strategy to be developed. This activity should last no more than two to five minutes, should be highly charged and engaging, and should pique interest.

6. Along with or instead of the anticipatory set, use brain warm-up activities at the beginning of the class to set the stage for the lesson. Warm-ups can be brainteasers, questions about controversial issues, logic problems, or creative situations seeking a solution that are done for two to five minutes as students arrive. Students can post their answers to a website, email them to the teacher, or write them in their personal journal. At the next class meeting, quickly review the answers for no more than two minutes.

7. Have all the resources for the unit readily available to students prior to starting the unit. This will encourage gifted students to consider their own prior knowledge or investigate the topic before the unit begins. Or, prior to the unit, offer students a list of websites that can introduce the topic or extend the material.

8. Be prepared for every class session before the students arrive. Have all the lesson materials arranged and ready, or designate students to prepare the materials. Keep in mind that students will mirror the attitudes and behaviors you display at the beginning of class. The more focused on the learning you are, the more focused the students will be.

9. Design, teach, and practice classroom protocol for an efficiently run classroom. Avoid letting interruptions take you off task, and prepare the students for interruptions that are inevitable (such as fire drills, office announcements, and latecomers/early departures). Teach students how to quickly refocus on the task after the interruption.

10. During lessons, offer one or two examples or models and then move forward. Gifted students don't need as much practice as the general population. Move on to new learning as quickly as possible. Spend most of your time investigating and wrestling with controversial issues, complex problems, and in-depth conversation. This is where gifted learners blossom!

Adapted from *Differentiation for Gifted Learners: Going Beyond the Basics* by Diane Heacox, Ed.D., and Richard M. Cash, Ed.D. (Minneapolis: Free Spirit Publishing, 2014), p. 18. Used with permission.

new ideas, as well as spark innovations of your own.

Procedure

Ask students to write about several instances when they've felt they weren't allowed to work ahead in class. Request that they be as specific as possible. If some students are inclined and if time permits, they may also create illustrations or other artwork depicting their experiences.

Next, ask for a volunteer or two to record responses to the questions that follow. Ask some or all of these questions and have an open, honest discussion. Feel free to adjust or add to these questions depending on your school's approach to gifted education. Ask the recorder(s) to draw as many columns as there are questions on a board or large piece of paper. Then have them place the responses to each question in the appropriate columns. If the same answer is given more than once, use hash marks to indicate and tally up these duplicates. So, for example, if two students express feelings of frustration

about not being able to work ahead, a recorder will write "frustrated" in the column for Question #1, and make two hash marks next to the response.

1. How do you feel when you can't work ahead?

2. Do you have any classes in which you *can* work ahead? If so, what are those subjects?

3. In our class, do you feel you can work at your own pace? Why or why not?

4. Have you ever asked your teachers about working ahead? How did they respond?

5. What happens when you work ahead on your own, without the teacher's permission?

6. Can you think of ways teachers could help you learn at your own pace?

7. What types of projects or activities would you most like to work on if you didn't have to complete the same number of assignments as the rest of the class?

Gifted Kids Speak Out

"I do not want busy work in school. I would rather work ahead, but the farther I get ahead, the farther I must come back at test time. In some units, I don't necessarily know all of the material, but I can move through it much faster than the rest of the class."
—**Nate, 14**

"It's an awful feeling when you have nothing to do. You might as well turn your brain off."
—**Allison, 11**

Discussion Questions

1. Looking at your responses to the questions, what patterns do you see? Are there any surprises? If so, what are they?

2. Can you think of ways you could get teachers to more often accommodate your rate and preferred ways of learning?

3. What will it take for you to feel comfortable asking teachers about this issue? For example, would a minicourse on assertiveness and self-advocacy be helpful to you?

Note: If possible, share with students any school or district initiatives and efforts to differentiate for varying learning abilities, including those of gifted students. In what ways can you advocate on behalf of these students to better meet their educational, social, and emotional needs?

💬 DISCUSSION OF GREAT GRIPE #6
Our friends and classmates don't always understand us, and they don't see all of our different sides.

Purpose
To tell stories about friendship; to contrast loneliness with aloneness and popularity with friendship; to share common questions about friendship (especially as it may relate to giftedness), and possible answers; to introduce ideas for making and keeping friends that students can try.

Preparation
Make copies of "Questions and Answers About Friends and Friendship" on pages 212–213 and "Twelve Tips for Making and Keeping Friends" on pages 214–215.

Procedure
Tell students that for the first part of this discussion, you're going to divide the group into two or three teams, depending on the size of your group. Explain that each team will spend ten to fifteen minutes sharing stories about friendship. Then you'll reconvene to discuss the differences between friendship and popularity, and between aloneness and loneliness.

Before breaking the large group into small groups, give the students these instructions:

Each person in your group is to think of a situation, real or imaginary, involving a friend.

This can be either a positive or negative situation. You can describe the ideal friend or the worst possible friend. The situation can express what you long for in a friendship, what you fear about friendship, what you don't understand, or what you regret.

When you have your situation in mind, tell it to the group.

While someone is talking, the other group members are to listen without interrupting until the speaker is finished.

When the speaker is finished, the group may comment on or ask questions about the story.

While the students are working in their small groups, circulate among them and listen to their stories. Ask questions like these:

1. Why did you choose to tell that particular story?

2. How many other people have had an experience like that, or imagined that kind of incident?

Tips for Creating Complex Learning Tasks

1. Ensure all students are fully aware of the learning goals and objectives. For students to work within a complex task, they need to thoroughly understand the expectations and outcomes of the learning task.

2. Make all resources and materials readily available to students, or ensure that they can gather the resources and materials themselves.

3. Prepare activities that are authentic (real-world) and involve ambiguous and somewhat abstract problems.

4. Develop tasks that allow for trial and error so students will eventually automatize the skills. Automatization occurs when students repeatedly practice using strategies successfully.

5. Use "reverse problem finding" to help students develop problem-finding and divergent thinking skills. Reverse problem finding is a brainstorming process that first explores what causes a problem rather than beginning with how to solve it.

6. Ensure that tasks will use both affective (emotional) and content knowledge strategies and skills. This is called the "Whole Task Method" of learning. Within a holistic scenario, students must consider not only how to create a solution, but also how the solution may affect people, the environment, animals, and so on.

7. Design tasks that encourage students to develop unique products or reinterpret old ideas or sophisticated methods of designs that involve creative thought.

8. Urge students to seek advice from experts in the field or to gather multiple perspectives on the problem before them.

9. Set up problems that require students to cross disciplines as they solve the problem. For example, when researching the effect of inexpensive sewer systems on developing nations, students will use the principles of civil and environmental engineering, economics, chemistry, biology, and anthropology.

Adapted from *Differentiation for Gifted Learners: Going Beyond the Basics* by Diane Heacox, Ed.D., and Richard M. Cash, Ed.D. (Minneapolis: Free Spirit Publishing, 2014), p. 20. Used with permission.

Gifted Kids Speak Out

"I don't always know how to handle my giftedness around my friends. Who should I tell, who shouldn't I? When am I bragging, and when am I just telling them the truth?"
—**Max, 13**

"A good friend is always there for you, not just in the good times."
—**Maddy, 9**

"Sometimes, people will try to falsely be my friend just to get answers."
—**Shane, 10**

"I try not to let the fact that people think I am gifted affect my social life. I want to be like my friends, just another person, because being different sets you apart. Anyone who is different gets laughed at."
—**Jayla, 14**

3. Why do you suppose the friend behaved that way (so disrespectfully, so generously)?

4. How do you (the speaker) feel now, when you think back on that situation?

5. What kind of friend does that make you want to be?

Once you've reconvened the large group, ask a couple of students if they would share their stories. Ask them if they have any additional comments; ask them if they learned about some common feelings and experiences.

Next, write these two pairs of words on the board as large headings above blank columns:

Loneliness/Aloneness

Popularity/Friendship

Tell students that you want to discuss the differences between loneliness and aloneness, and between popularity and friendship. During the discussion, list the attributes of each beneath its appropriate heading.

After students have voted on the most important qualities for a friend to have (discussion question 9 on page 201), hand out copies of "Questions and Answers About Friendship." Tell the students that these are questions that many gifted kids have. You might want to go through the handout one question at a time. What do your students think of the questions? Do they sound familiar? What do they think of the answers?

Finally, say that you have a list of ideas you'd like to share with them. Hand out copies of "Twelve Tips for Making and Keeping Friends."[2] Invite students to try one or more of these ideas before the group meets again. Maybe they can report back to the group next time on what worked and didn't work for them.

Depending on your schedule, you may need to spread the discussion of Great Gripe #6 over two days.

Discussion Questions

1. How do you feel when you're alone? When you're lonely? What's the same? What's different?

2. Does anyone like being alone? Or lonely?

3. Is it possible to be alone without being lonely?

4. How can you tell when other people are lonely?

5. Name some examples of famous people in history or fiction, TV programs, movies, or whatever whom you suspect are or were lonely. Explain why you chose them.

6. What personal qualities make a good friend? What qualities make a good friendship?

7. What personal qualities make someone popular? Are the qualities the same as those you look for in a good friend? Which characteristics overlap and which are unique?

8. Are there aspects about you, besides being gifted, that you really want people to know and understand? Why is this important to you?

9. What are the most important qualities for a friend to have? Let's vote ...

Discussion Guidelines

Telling tales of friendships past and future is a positive way to ease into some pretty intense feelings. If students need coaxing to open up, be ready with an anecdote of your own to start the group rolling. Or bring a few passages from literature (fiction or biography) to serve as examples. One of our personal favorites is the "Loneliness" chapter from E.B. White's classic story, *Charlotte's Web,* but you'll have to decide what's appropriate for your group.

Summarize what the groups discover in terms of common human needs. In friendships and groups, we seek such things as acceptance, identity, loyalty, support, companionship, advice, solace, and power. Relate how the situations they described underscore any of these human needs.

Some of the sting can be taken out of aloneness if students realize its benefits. Solitude can be a wonderfully creative state; it provides time and space for reflection and integration. Artists,

inventors, musicians, writers, and presidents learn to tolerate solitude, and many people crave it. Aloneness should not be feared as an unnatural state, for solitude is not a problem; loneliness is.

Remind students that one doesn't necessarily need a lot of friends. One or two close friends may be enough. Great popularity usually falls to outgoing people who possess qualities others admire and wish to emulate, yet who remain within the range of "normal" or familiar. Popular leaders represent the more dominant values of the group. Popular

Helping Kids with Big Questions

When we did our most recent survey of gifted kids, one of the old gripes that didn't make the new list was this:

We worry about world problems and feel helpless to do anything about them.

Even though it's not among the top eight gripes anymore, this topic is still an important one that affects many gifted kids and teens, and you may still want to hold a discussion in which you invite students to discuss their feelings about world problems and generate possible ways to respond to these problems. Introduce the conversation by saying:

Today we're going to talk about how affected we feel by certain world problems. It's been said that technology such as online communication and satellite television brings the world closer together; that the world is becoming a "global village." Although this may be good in some ways, it also makes us more aware of how difficult and stressful life can be. Violence from around the world comes into our living rooms via the Internet, TV, newspapers, and radio.

Discussion questions could include the following:

1. Are there any world problems you feel especially concerned about?

2. How have you learned about this problem? From your parents? From school? From the media? What do these sources have to say about it?

3. Is this a confusing issue for you? Do you understand why it's a problem?

4. Would you like to learn more about this subject? Where or how could you get information?

5. Do people at home or in this room have strong feelings about this topic? What are they?

6. Are there other social problems, perhaps closer to home (in your neighborhood or city), that concern you?

After discussing these and other questions, say:

Now that we've talked about the kinds of problems that worry us, and some specific questions we have about these problems, let's take one of these concerns and brainstorm what you, individually or in a group, could do about it.

Write the problem on the board and list the ideas students brainstorm.

In leading this discussion, be prepared for two types of challenges. One is the student who is so overly sensitive to world problems—particularly suffering and violence—that she can't separate herself from them and feels overly responsible for them. It's very difficult to accept millions of people starving in a faraway country, or the threat of nuclear war emanating from certain nations. But a student shouldn't feel the suffering of others to the extent that it immobilizes her, or feel such extreme anxiety for a future when the future is not yet determined. Work to relieve this student of her guilty feelings and help her put in place some healthy separation between the situation and herself. Invite her to learn more about the issues (both the positive and negative aspects) and to take constructive social action. But remind her also that she has time to grow up and deal with these problems as an adult, and that she is not expected to take them on single-handedly. Empirical evidence shows the world will probably continue to turn, even in the face of truly terrible events.

The second kind of problem concerns the opposite type of student, one who is apathetic and lacks sensitivity toward people suffering in remote places in circumstances he can't relate to. This student is probably uncomfortable discussing world problems. He doesn't want them to concern him, and therefore believes that they don't. Or he believes the government or some superpower is controlling things, which means—for better or worse—that matters are out of his hands. For this student, you may want to emphasize how important individual efforts can be. Ask students whether they can think of a time when the work of people or groups changed history (or life in their city, town, neighborhood, school, or family). Emphasize how similar all human beings are in terms of needs and wants, regardless of nationality or status. Ask students to join in a discussion about what the proper level of responsibility for others is—how important it is to care about other people even when their troubles don't involve us directly.

In conclusion, help students understand that there is much in the world to grieve for, but much to rejoice over as well. We all need to "work for a better world," and every effort counts. Encourage them to take action on social issues because it is morally good, and because working for change can make us feel more positive. Throughout the year, work on building your list of possible actions to take in assuming social responsibility, such as writing letters, newsletters, or articles; joining neighborhood or national organizations; staging demonstrations; raising funds and sending donations; and doing volunteer work. But also dissuade students from feeling overly responsible—particularly as the "gifted youth of tomorrow"—for saving the world.

girls look and dress in ways most conforming to group tastes; popular guys use language adopted by the dominant clique. When popularity depends on conformity to norms, this often excludes the highly gifted student.

But sometimes highly popular people are also lonely. They may have the acquaintanceship of many and the friendship of few. Friendship should provide a refuge from having to perform, and it should respect differences as well as similarities.

Close by summarizing ways to handle aloneness and loneliness. Recap students' observations regarding good friends. What are those good friends capable of doing? How do they do it? How can we all make better friends? How can we, as a group, help each other out?

● DISCUSSION OF GREAT GRIPE #7

Parents, teachers, and even our friends expect too much of us. We're supposed to get A's and do our best all the time.

Purpose

To discuss sources of perfectionism (self, parents, teachers, friends, "society"), feelings associated with perfectionism, and ways to handle perfectionism; to help students understand the difference between perfectionism and the pursuit of excellence.

Preparation

Review the "Perfectionism" section in Chapter 3: Emotional Dimensions of Giftedness (pages 63–66). Make copies of "Perfectionism vs. the Pursuit of Excellence" on page 211.

Procedure

Arrange students in a circle, introduce the topic, and have students help generate an agenda for your discussion. Begin by listing two or three agenda items yourself and then request others. Once the discussion gets going, you may want to let students take turns moderating the discussion. This gives them a chance to practice leadership skills and also helps the group focus on each other, rather than looking to you for answers.

Possible Agenda Items

■ Sources of perfectionism

■ What "failure" is, and what feelings are associated with it

■ How do you define success? What does success look and feel like?

■ What to do about expectations (from teachers, parents, classmates, students themselves, and others)

■ A healthy alternative to perfectionism

Discussion Questions

1. Who tells you that you have to be perfect? How do they say it? If the message isn't verbal, how is it communicated? Why do you suppose these people expect or want you to be perfect?

2. Is it possible to be perfect? In anything? In everything? Some of the time? All of the time?

3. What are your standards or goals? Do you think they are they realistic, or idealistic?

4. What happens when you're less than perfect? How do you feel when you get answers wrong or receive less than an A?

5. How many of you feel anxious about being "good enough"? How many of you worry about your grades?

6. Who do you think should set your performance standards?

7. What can you say to people who expect too much from you?

8. How else can you protect yourself against unrealistically high expectations—your own and other people's?

9. Does anyone here think there might be alternatives to perfectionism—positive, healthy ways to approach achievement and success?

Discussion Guidelines

At the beginning of this discussion, kids will likely need to simply vent about how everyone else expects unreasonable things from them, values them only when they perform well, or "punishes" them in some manner for poor performance. Let students air their views, but also try to get them to articulate how these expectations are conveyed—in other words, guide them to "reality-test" their perceptions. Some of the messages they hear may be ambiguous ("I'm surprised you didn't volunteer for that activity"), some may be unmistakably clear ("I expect a lot more from a gifted kid like you")—and some may be entirely in their heads (a look or gesture that they perceive as registering disappointment or judgment). Periodically summarize for them the sources of their perfectionism and ask how frequently they hear the messages urging them to be perfect.

Get students to explore their intrinsic needs for success and perfection. Introduce the idea that their own expectations may influence how they perceive

One Writer's Vision of Success

In 2013, author George Saunders delivered the convocation speech to Syracuse University's graduating class. In part, his message to the graduates was that, "as a goal in life, you could do worse than: *Try to be kinder.*"

In his speech, Saunders went on to explore success, achievement, and what these big ideas mean—especially alongside the equally big idea of kindness. His advice to the young people in the audience included the following:

"When young, we're anxious—understandably—to find out if we've got what it takes. Can we succeed? Can we build a viable life for ourselves? But you—in particular you, of this generation—may have noticed a certain cyclical quality to ambition. You do well in high school, in hopes of getting into a good college, so you can do well in the good college, in the hopes of getting a good job, so you can do well in the good job so you can . . . .

"And this is actually okay. If we're going to become kinder, that process has to include taking ourselves seriously—as doers, as accomplishers, as dreamers. We *have* to do that, to be our best selves.

"Still, accomplishment is unreliable. 'Succeeding,' whatever that might mean to you, is hard, and the need to do so constantly renews itself (success is like a mountain that keeps growing ahead of you as you hike it), and there's the very real danger that 'succeeding' will take up your whole life, while the big questions go untended.

"So, quick, end-of-speech advice: Since, according to me, your life is going to be a gradual process of becoming kinder and more loving: Hurry up. Speed it along. Start right now . . . Do all the other things, the ambitious things—travel, get rich, get famous, innovate, fall in love . . . but as you do, to the extent that you can, err in the direction of kindness. Do those things that incline you toward the big questions, and avoid the things that would reduce you and make you trivial. That luminous part of you that exists beyond personality—your soul, if you will—is as bright and shining as any that has ever been. Bright as Shakespeare's, bright as Gandhi's, bright as Mother Teresa's. Clear away everything that keeps you separate from this secret luminous place. Believe it exists, come to know it better, nurture it, share its fruits tirelessly.

"And someday, in 80 years, when you're 100, and I'm 134, and we're both so kind and loving we're nearly unbearable, drop me a line, let me know how your life has been. I hope you will say: It has been *so* wonderful."

Consider using Saunders's speech as a starting point to talk with students about how they view success; about if, how, and where they see kindness fitting into being successful; what they dream about and how those dreams are (and are not) connected to traditional ideas about ambition; what they believe comprises the "secret luminous place" in each of them; and any other questions and ideas that are sparked by your conversation.

George Saunders, *Congratulations, By the Way: Some Thoughts on Kindness* (New York: Random House, 2014).

other people's expectations, and that their own internal goals and needs can be more powerful and more fulfilling in the long run.

Some of the clues to perfectionism lie in the emotions that accompany "failure" (in other words, lack of perfection). What are the consequences of poor performance? Do students fear a loss of identity? ("She must not be as smart as we thought," or "Perhaps he's not gifted after all.") Heavy guilt and anxiety suggest a deep need to satisfy parents and teachers, as well as a concern about being valued as a person rather than being valued for high performance. Disappointment and anger suggest a need to satisfy one's own internal standards, and perhaps the inability to admit to certain limitations. ("I can't be gifted if I don't get all A's.") Have students try to name the emotions they feel upon "failing," and ask them to analyze the source of those feelings.

One's defense in the face of perfectionism depends on its source. If parents are the taskmasters, then students need to understand their parents' feelings (a misunderstanding of what perfectionism really is and means? wanting only the best for their children? love and concern? self-aggrandizement?) and find appropriate answers to them. Talk about ways in which students might approach their parents on this topic. What could they say? How might they express their own feelings about their performance and achievements? How could they differentiate between their personal goals and their parents' goals for them? If societal or educators' views are the source, then appropriate responses to them need to be found. Is a particular teacher the problem? (Are you the problem?) If the source

of conflict is partially or predominantly internal, the student needs to learn how to become his or her own "best friend" or supporter rather than taskmaster. Encouragement, support, and careful goal setting can help here.

If time allows, you might read aloud the section on "Perfectionism" on pages 63–66. Read the list of characteristics in the "Perfectionism at a Glance" box on pages 65–66, and invite students to consider which ones describe them.

After students have responded to question 9, distribute the "Perfectionism vs. the Pursuit of Excellence" handout. Ask students to read it, reflect on it, and share their views about what it has to say. Tell them that you gave them this handout because you want them to keep it and refer to it often.

● DISCUSSION OF GREAT GRIPE #8
Tests, tests, and more tests!

Purpose
To give students the opportunity to air their frustrations and worries over tests (and which tests, in particular), and to provide perspective and information about what types of tests they are given, why, and what test scores do and do not mean.

Preparation
If you do not administer the types of tests in question, consult with whomever it is at your school who does. You'll need at least a basic awareness about the tests, including what the tests are designed to assess and how to talk with students about interpreting their scores. Be prepared to discuss IQ tests (and results) in particular, since many gifted kids are familiar with the tests and have a natural curiosity about their own scores. Many

gifted students have taken one or more IQ tests at school, or on their own online.

Procedure

Invite students to talk about tests that they feel are given too often, that they feel are meaningless, or that they find otherwise frustrating. Have them name specific tests if possible. Then ask them to describe what they know, don't know, or would like to know about the tests as well as the scores.

List the Know/Don't Know/Would Like to Know responses in three columns on a board or sheet of paper.

Discussion Questions

1. When you look at the responses listed on the board, are there any that especially stand out to you? What intrigues you? What seems erroneous?

2. On this list, is there one thing in particular that you would really like to know more about? Where would you go for this information?

3. Do you think high test scores equate to having a successful life and future? Why or why not?

4. Can you think of character traits that no test can measure? (Students might suggest things like leadership ability, creativity, oral communication skills, honesty, and so on.)

5. Do you need help learning how to better prepare for tests?

6. Many students, including gifted students, suffer from test anxiety. What do you do to calm yourself before a test, and why is that important?

7. Can you think of better alternatives to measure ability and achievement? What are the pros and cons of these alternatives to tests?

8. If you were a test writer, what would you do to make tests more accurate, meaningful, and (dare we say) fun?

Discussion Guidelines

Make students aware that this conversation isn't about sharing their test scores, but rather about taking the mystery out of the who, what, why, where, and how of tests. The discussion may lead to individual or group research about the nature of tests, especially those that are standardized, such as achievement tests, Common Core State Standards tests, or IQ tests. It may lead you to have small-group sessions on developing test-taking skills, including relaxation exercises. Research tells us that students who are overly anxious at test time typically don't perform as well as they could if they were more relaxed and confident.

An overarching message to get across to students is that they are best off not letting any test score shape how they see themselves—whether their scores are high, low, or in between. Make them aware (if they aren't already) that many tests are culturally or racially biased. In addition, if you're highly creative, or if you don't feel comfortable in the test setting, you aren't likely to do particularly well. (Creative people can often figure out why A, B, C, and D are *all* correct! Unfortunately, they don't get the chance to explain their reasoning.) Finally, tests don't account for varied learning styles.

A Few Final Thoughts

As we mentioned at the beginning of this chapter, talking about the "Great Gripes" has served countless gifted kids and their teachers well for more than three decades. You may also find that, in the course of the conversation, students reveal *other* troubling gripes, or elaborate further on the Eight Great Gripes that we've listed. You can best meet your students' social and emotional needs by being respectful and responsive to those concerns, and by coming up with other activities to address them.

You're likely to find that, sometimes, simply being able to vent about the frustration of perfectionism or meaningless schoolwork is psychologically beneficial. What's even *more* beneficial, though, is if the gifted kids you work with discuss their gripes and then take positive steps to address and remedy them with their classmates, teachers, or parents. That's the purpose of these activities: self-initiated positive change, catalyzed by you, their caring teacher.

Group Guidelines

1. Anything that is said in the group stays in the group. We agree to keep things confidential.

2. We respect what other group members say. We agree not to use put-downs of any kind, verbal or nonverbal.

3. We respect everyone's need to be heard.

4. We listen to each other. When someone is speaking, we look at him or her and pay attention.

5. We realize that feelings are not "bad" or "good." They just are. Therefore, we don't say things like "You shouldn't feel that way."

6. We are willing to take risks, to explore new ideas, and to explain our feelings as well as we can. However, we agree that someone who doesn't want to talk doesn't have to talk.

7. We are willing to let others know us. We agree that talking and listening are ways for people to get to know each other.

8. We realize that sometimes people feel misunderstood, or they feel that someone has hurt them accidentally or on purpose. We agree that the best way to handle those times is by talking and listening.

9. We agree to be sincere and to do our best to speak from the heart.

10. We don't talk about group members who aren't present. We especially don't criticize group members who aren't here to defend themselves.

11. When we do need to talk about other people—such as teachers and peers—we don't refer to them by name unless it is absolutely necessary. For example, we may want to ask the group to help us solve a problem we are having with a particular person.

12. We agree to attend group meetings and our class regularly. If for some reason we can't attend, we will try to let the teacher know ahead of time.

Perfectionism vs. the Pursuit of Excellence

There is a healthy alternative to perfectionism. It's called the Pursuit of Excellence. Here are three ways in which the two differ:

1. **Perfectionism** means thinking less of yourself because you earned a B+ instead of an A. **The Pursuit of Excellence** means thinking about what you might do differently to earn an A next time, if that's what you want. Pursuing excellence also means giving yourself credit for taking on challenging work and for trying something new.

2. **Perfectionism** means being hard on yourself because you aren't equally talented in all sports. **The Pursuit of Excellence** means choosing some things you know you'll be good at—and others you know will be good for you or just plain fun.

3. **Perfectionism** means beating yourself up because you lost the student council election. **The Pursuit of Excellence** means congratulating yourself because you were nominated, and deciding to run again next year—if that's what you want.

How can you become a Pursuer of Excellence? By:

- Determining the sources of your perfectionism
- Reassessing your feelings about failure and success
- Developing tactics for standing your ground against people who pressure you to be perfect
- Learning ways to be easier on yourself so you're free to take risks and try new things

What other ideas do you have for pursuing excellence? For avoiding the perfectionism trap?

_____

_____

_____

_____

_____

Questions and Answers About Friends and Friendship

Q: *Some of my friends seem to resent me, or they're prejudiced against me because I'm gifted. Why is that?*

A: Usually, people have prejudices when they don't understand something or someone. They may feel inferior if they don't have enough good things going on in their own lives. So putting you down may make them feel better about themselves (at least for the moment). Just be yourself, and they may come around—or you may need to start hanging out with other people.

Q: *Does everyone have trouble making friends, or is it just me?*

A: Relax; it's not just you. Some people seem to make friends effortlessly—they're in the right place at the right time with the right social skills. Other people find it difficult to connect because of shyness, circumstances, or whatever. But everyone—whether adept or awkward—has to work at forming and sustaining meaningful friendships.

Q: *I don't have any trouble making friends, so why is there all this talk about gifted people being socially awkward?*

A: It's true that many gifted children and teens make friends easily, but for others it's not so easy. They might perceive themselves as socially awkward, which sabotages their self-confidence. Also, some people assume that because gifted kids are brighter and more intellectually advanced than their peers, they will automatically have problems relating to so-called "normal" kids.

Q: *Does it matter if my friends are two, three, or even four years older or younger than I am?*

A: No! Adults have friendships with people of all ages, so why shouldn't you? What matters is to cultivate friends you can count on and relate to. Sharing the same birth year isn't as important as sharing interests, goals, and values.

→

Questions and Answers About Friends and Friendship, continued

Q: *Is it normal to have just a few close friends?*

A: Yes! Gifted children and teens tend to be more adult-like in their relationships, favoring a few intense relationships over several more casual ones. What's important is to have at least one or two friends that you can rely on. When it comes to relationships, quality matters more than quantity.

Q: *Do I have to conform to be accepted?*

A: It's not a bad thing to go along with the crowd—as long as the crowd is right for you. It's only when you compromise your own values, beliefs, and goals that conformity becomes a problem and can even be dangerous. On the other hand, if you always insist on doing things your way, be prepared for a lonely life.

Q: *I've just met someone I'd like to be friends with, and he asked me what "gifted" means. What can I say that won't alienate him or sound arrogant?*

A: You might begin by asking him what he thinks it means. If he's serious about wanting to know, this could lead to an interesting discussion about your individual points of view. Remember, there are no right or wrong answers about giftedness, and even the experts can't agree on a single definition. By now, you probably have your own ideas about what it is and what it means. Share as much or as little as you want. And sometimes it's enough to simply say that you need extra challenges in school because your brain is often on overdrive!

Q: *How can I cope with "leech" friends—people who rely on me for homework and test answers?*

A: First, ask yourself, "Are they really my friends?" People who like you only for what they can get from you don't qualify as friends. So that's something you'll have to decide. Second, if you feel like helping (with homework, not with test answers), and if you have the time, then go ahead and do it. Otherwise, simply explain that you have your own work to do and you just can't help right now. Maybe the "leeches" will take the hint—or maybe not.

Twelve Tips for Making and Keeping Friends

1. Reach out. Don't always wait for someone else to make the first move. A simple "hi" and a smile go a long way. It may sound corny, but you'll be amazed at the response you'll receive when you extend a friendly greeting.

2. Get involved. Join clubs that interest you; take special classes inside or outside of school. Seek out neighborhood and community organizations and other opportunities to give service to others.

3. Let people know that you're interested in them. Don't just talk about yourself; ask questions about them and their interests. Make this a habit and you'll have mastered the art of conversation. It's amazing how many people haven't yet grasped this basic social skill.

4. Be a good listener. This means looking at people while they're talking to you and genuinely paying attention to what they're saying. (A long litany of "uh-huhs" is a dead giveaway that your mind is somewhere else.)

5. Risk telling people about yourself. When it feels right, let your interests and talents be known. For example, if you love science fiction and you'd like to know others who feel the same way, spread the word. If you're an expert on the history of science fiction, you might want to share your knowledge. BUT...

6. Don't be a show-off. Not everyone you meet will share your interests and abilities. (On the other hand, you shouldn't have to hide them—which you won't, once you find people who like and appreciate you.)

7. Be honest. Tell the truth about yourself and your convictions. When asked for your opinion, be sincere. Friends appreciate forthrightness in each other. BUT...

8. When necessary, temper your honesty with diplomacy. The truth doesn't have to hurt. It's better to say "Your new haircut is interesting" than to exclaim "You actually paid money for THAT?" There are times when frankness is inappropriate and unnecessary.

→

Twelve Tips for Making and Keeping Friends, continued

9. **Don't just use your friends as sounding boards for your problems and complaints.** Include them in the good times, too.

10. **Do your share of the work.** That's right, *work*. Any relationship takes effort. Don't always depend on your friends to make the plans and carry the weight.

11. **Be accepting**. Not all of your friends have to think and act like you do. (Wouldn't it be boring if they did?)

12. **Remember: Friendship is not about competition.** You may have friends who are also gifted and perhaps you are driven to succeed in similar pursuits, which may lead to competition. A certain amount of competitiveness is normal and healthy among friends. However, don't let it prevent you from supporting one other through your challenges and celebrating your accomplishments together. Remind each other periodically that you are in this together, that life is not a race, and that having solid friendships is more important in the long run than winning any competition.

CHAPTER 8

Making It Safe to Be Smart: Creating the Gifted-Friendly Classroom

 A good teacher knows you're smart but doesn't do anything about it. A great teacher is a support system. He or she is a mentor and role model and understands that there's more to life than textbooks.
—Micah, 14

Mrs. Sanders was a remarkable first-grade teacher. She had twenty-eight students in her class, including three who did not speak English and several more whose backgrounds, interests, and abilities made cluster grouping difficult. There are many qualities about Mrs. Sanders worth mentioning here—her varied teaching strategies, her effective use of praise—but most special was what she did at the end of each day.

As the children were preparing to go home—"walkers" on the right, "riders" on the left—Mrs. Sanders made a point to take each child and either squeeze a shoulder, rub a head, or make a funny face to encourage any frowners in the group to smile. Each gesture was accompanied by a verbal statement, such as "Good answer in math today, Mary!" or "Nice high-tops, Jeff!" Each child, each day. A different gesture, a different expression.

Why did she do this each day, with every student? Her answer was simple, straightforward, and indicative of a teacher for whom 110 percent is typical: "I have no idea what happens when the students leave school. Some ride on the bus and get ridiculed; others go home to an empty house; still more rush around from ballet to soccer to who-knows-what. I have no idea, and I have very little control. But I do have control over how each student will remember his or her last moment of the day with me, and that memory will be a fond one."

Mrs. Sanders did admit that on some days, with some children, it was tough coming up with a positive statement. (Once she was overheard saying, "This was a good day for you, Eric. You only yelled twice in class today.") "But they're worth it," she said. "I dig until I find something good."

Even the smallest act can make a big difference. You probably know this from your own experience. Now imagine how effective frequent, deliberate, consistent efforts to reach out, support, and encourage children can be.

This chapter presents activities that will help you create the kind of classroom where students feel welcome and wanted. As you read through them, you may find yourself wondering, "Aren't these ideas good for *most* students? What makes them especially good for gifted students?" In fact, many of the activities *are* good for most (if not all) students. Gifted students may respond to some of them at a depth that other students do not. Still, we challenge you to encourage all of your students to dig deep within themselves and produce work that reveals something about their minds, hearts, and personalities.

Remembering Mr. Walls

by Frank Davies, fourth-grade teacher

Ken Walls was an amazing person. Very unpretentious and not gushy with praise. But his underlying belief was that he treated students with respect and dignity. He encouraged us to follow our interests and would be very flexible in going with individuals' choices. He never shouted or put us down. I knew that he believed in me, and I saw him make some amazing changes in other students, too.

We were about fourteen or fifteen at the time—a bunch of little so-and-sos. Like a lot of kids that age, we just wanted school to be over. Yet, when we were in Mr. Walls's class for that couple of hours a week, my fellow students and I became responsible and responsive, and we took pride in our work.

Ken Walls didn't come down to our level, he invited us up to his. He asked our opinions and yet he was also very strict, as there were very clear boundaries in place in his classroom. But the bottom line was, he liked us and we liked him.

Self-Esteem and School Achievement: A Natural Link

Gifted children are, first and foremost, children. Their feelings, needs, and wishes are more like those of other children than they are different. This being so, the comments that follow may lead you to ask, "But isn't the development of self-esteem good for *all* children?" The answer, of course, is yes.

Still, there are at least three reasons why this section is here, in a book about the social and emotional needs of gifted children.

1. Gifted children—who are often more aware of other people's reactions toward them—may begin to develop their self-esteem at a very early age.

2. Since many gifted students tie their success in school to their worth as a person, early attention to self-esteem enhancement is essential.

3. The belief that perfection is an attainable and expected goal limits some gifted children from giving themselves credit—and experiencing a personal sense of pride and worth—for many of their less-than-perfect achievements.

If you read educational or psychological literature, it's tough to find a writer who does not link self-esteem with school achievement. This is as true in articles in the *Journal of Educational Psychology* as it is in *Family Circle*. No writer (at least none of whom we are aware) states publicly, "Who cares if you think you're worthless? You can still learn, can't you?" Everyone, from everyday people to eminent scholars, seems to agree that attitude affects performance.

Which Comes First?

If there is any disagreement about self-esteem and school achievement, it comes in the form of a chicken-egg conundrum: Which comes first? Does a solid sense of self encourage a person to want to learn more, or does successful learning make an individual gain a more positive sense of self?

An important question, perhaps, and an intriguing one, but we're afraid our response boils down to, "Who cares?" We already know that self-esteem and school achievement occur in tandem, so the question of which precedes which is as meaningless as trying to remember which half of a happily married couple first said "I love you" to the other. If the marriage is working, the point is moot.

A Daunting Task

Franklin Delano Roosevelt once said, "The ablest man I ever met is the man you think you are." Quite an optimistic comment, especially coming from a man whose legs were permanently disabled by polio. When he first contracted the disease, his political career appeared to be over. He went on to become president of the United States.

It's a daunting task, being an educator, bearing the responsibility for shaping both academics and attitudes. Accountability, as defined in today's schools, often measures the easy stuff: the math facts memorized, the commas placed correctly, the historical events accurately sequenced. But the true measure of an educator's teaching performance is not so readily determined.

No computer-scanned bubble sheet measures how our students feel about learning, or their biases toward themselves and others. *These* indexes—which assess the true value of learning and education—elude detection and measurement, sometimes for years. And even if we assessed attitudes and biases (there are self-esteem scales available, for example), we might pick up general trends, but not specific thoughts. For instance, answering "I like to take challenges" on a score sheet is one thing, but signing up for an honors chemistry course where receiving a B is likely is something else altogether.

So, those brave educators wishing to enhance both students' self-esteem and their achievements must be content with knowing only the immediate impact of their actions. Some changes will be noticeable. Others will be stubbornly absent (at least in the short term). But as Mrs. Sanders knows quite well, ripples expand as they leave the central core.

Building Self-Esteem: One Teacher's Approach

A teacher we know very well worked for several years as a resource teacher of gifted students in a rural school district. She worked in four different buildings, seeing about thirty kids at a time, in first through sixth grade (4 schools x 30 students = 120 students per week). A difficult task, even for an expert juggler.

Meeting with each group of students only once per week created some gaps. Projects that were expected to be completed in the interim sometimes got "forgotten." Resource books, outlines, and iPad notes got lost amidst more pressing homework assignments. On a more

personal note, some students' lives went topsy-turvy from one week to the next. Pets died or ran away, best friends moved, new babies arrived, school awards were won. A lot occurred between one Monday and the next that affected students' attitudes and performance.

In an effort to learn more about her students, the teacher introduced "New and Goods," a time period (15 minutes or so) that began each class. During New and Goods, students met in small groups to review the past week. Each child (and the teacher, too) was given the chance to share something new and good that had occurred since their previous meeting. Talking was encouraged, though not required, but most children took advantage and spoke of something real, something personal, something only theirs. Occasionally, as group members became better acquainted and more trusting, a child would ask to share a "new and sad" or a "new and bad." This was allowed. The purpose of New and Goods was to communicate; the content of what got shared was an individual choice.

As the year moved on and the pace became more hectic, class schedules became less predictable. Still, New and Goods began each resource-room meeting. The children demanded it. Having been given the chance to express themselves freely and without criticism (a key point), they were not about to forgo this special time. Projects could wait. First, they wanted to talk about themselves and learn about each other.

New and Goods is just one example of an activity that promotes both self-esteem and achievement. It requires no materials, no budget, and no preplanning; in other words, it's a teacher's dream. What it does require is a belief that listening to what children say is important, and a willingness to take the time to do so within the confines of a classroom schedule.

If you're in a regular classroom setting where you, as a teacher, see your students every day, New and Goods may not seem as necessary. Right?

Wrong! Just as middle-school educators have experienced success with the incorporation of "advisory groups" into the daily or weekly calendar, it's vital to get to know our students from the inside out. (In typical advisory groups, one teacher is responsible for ten to fifteen students, who often stay together as a group for two to three years. Discussions and fun activities are planned for these 20-minute sessions.) With an increased emphasis on high-stakes testing and accountability, advisory groups are not as common as they once were. Yet, where they do exist and are well planned, they can be a great boon to students' self-esteem. Indeed, without this time for more personal interaction, kids may feel lost in a sea of faces. Advisory groups, or classroom-based activities meant to encourage self-exploration and knowledge, are more necessary than ever in this age of rampant testing, prescribed curriculum, and growing electronic "noise."

Invitational Education

If the idea of New and Goods makes sense to you, then you'll probably value the idea of Invitational Education. As defined by the International Alliance for Invitational Education and its founders, William Purkey and Betty Siegel, the theory's basic assumptions are:[1]

1. People are able, valuable, and responsible, and should be treated accordingly.

2. Helping is a cooperative, collaborative alliance in which process is as important as product.

3. People possess relatively untapped potential in all areas of human development.

4. Human potential can best be realized by places, policies, programs, and processes that are intentionally designed to invite development, and by people who consistently seek to realize this potential in themselves and others, personally and professionally.

When teachers communicate to students their belief that the students are capable, learners are more likely to act in ways that prove their competence. Conversely, if teachers tell students—verbally or through nonspoken cues—that they are "as dumb as they come," it's likely that the students will behave in ways that confirm this impression.

An important belief underlying Invitational Education is that most teachers are in the business of building character, not tearing it down. It is the rare educator who sets out for school on Monday morning thinking, "I wonder whose ego I can crush today." Such teachers do exist—every profession has its buffoons and its meanies—but still, it's unusual to find an educator who practices deliberate self-esteem destruction.

Those teachers, counselors, administrators, and other school personnel who do destroy others' love of or desire to learn often do so unconsciously or unintentionally. These unintentional disinviters would argue vigorously that their aims

Invitations Defined

Intentional Inviter: This teacher understands the importance of acknowledging a child's unique existence, and strives to actively support a child's efforts, however small, to improve. *Example:* "If I allow children to post their favorite work on the bulletin board, and to let them use my Teacher's Guide to grade their own homework, they will know that I trust them to do the right thing."

Intentional Disinviter: This teacher actively seeks out ways in which children fail in academic or social settings, and never lets them forget they have found these "chinks in the armor." *Example* (said in front of class): "You know, just because you're 'gifted' doesn't mean you're entitled to anything special. And looking at that C you got on your science project last month, I even question if that 'gifted' label is accurate."

Unintentional Inviter: This teacher sends positive, inspiring messages to students, through words and actions, but doesn't recognize their importance in a child's life. *Example:* "As your English teacher, I can't possibly write comments on every one of your papers—I wouldn't have a life for myself! But I promise to write each of you at least one letter this quarter where I comment on how good your work is. I hope this is okay, and I wish I could do more."

Unintentional Disinviter: This teacher implements strategies or makes comments that make some students go "ouch!" even though the teacher claims there are no negative results from these words or actions. *Example:* "Okay, let's all trade quizzes and we'll correct them together. At the end, when I call out the student's name, just shout out the grade and I'll place it here in my grade book."

are to improve student performance and attitude. What goes awry is this: The "messages" they send that are intended to instill pride or a love of learning are interpreted by individual students as negative and critical.

The following examples of unintentional disinvitation—provided by students themselves—will help clarify this point.

Most likely, those teachers who make public declarations of how "perfect" gifted children are do so to reward high-achieving students and prod others to imitate their academic or social behaviors. We know that at least *some* of these gifted students are embarrassed by this unsolicited attention. Besides, when you're put on a pedestal, the only direction to go is down.

Gifted Kids Speak Out

"My social studies teacher is driving me nuts. She targets me as 'the perfect one' in class by always asking me (whether I've raised my hand or not) what I think about issues . . . as though I'm always supposed to have some outstanding insight. Whenever I hand in a paper, she always makes a point of saying how neat my handwriting is or something, right in front of everyone. This is embarrassing, and people think I'm a teacher's pet even though I don't want to be. This creates an atmosphere where there's a disincentive to do well. I know she doesn't mean to humiliate me, but really, I'm not the only person in class who has a brain and can do well."
—Cora, 13

"I think teachers can, at the very least, keep their expectations normal while recognizing the giftedness of a student. I have one teacher who has ULTRA-high expectations of my performance . . . even in gym class! She uses my results as the benchmark for other people's grades (which doesn't exactly help me in the popularity area). And then, if I make a mistake, she announces it to everyone, which is very embarrassing. It's as though I can't be human."
—Ray, 15

"I never seem to be able to live up to the expectations of my teachers or my family. Everyone keeps telling me how smart and gifted I am, and if I don't meet their expectations, it brings my pride to an all-time low. When this happens, I figure that I can't possibly be as smart as they think I am."
—Melissa, 11

Positive or Negative?

Messages sent, messages received: Sometimes the lines of communication get crossed, and when they do, the end result is often no communication at all.

Donald MacKinnon, a scholar in the field of creativity, once wrote, "The same fire that melts the butter, hardens the egg."[2] He was reviewing the elements of creative environments and discovered that few creative people agree on the ideal setting that prompts original thought. Some adults love loud music, open spaces, and a beer by their elbow. Others demand a quiet room with dim lighting, and herbal tea. The same is true for message sending and receiving: Their impacts are as individual as fingerprints or snowflakes.

The following chart shows how a singular message may have multiple meanings and interpretations. As illustrated by the variety of contexts in which messages are sent and received—social, academic, and other settings—it's easy to see the pervasive nature of the thousands of invitations that we give and get within even a single day. Nonverbal clues—the raised eyebrow, the broad grin, the pat on the back—are as common as spoken statements. Often, they are just as open to interpretation.

Message Sent	Message Received: Positive	Message Received: Negative
Social Messages		
"Great haircut!"	I guess I look pretty good.	I must have looked awful yesterday.
"I would have invited you to my party, but you live so far away. I didn't want you to feel obligated to come."	How considerate! I was spared having to turn down an invitation.	That's only an excuse. If they really wanted me there, I would've been invited anyway.
"Interesting meal: I never would have thought of glazing the chicken with orange juice."	I got their taste buds talking. How exciting!	Everyone hates it. So much for recipe experiments.

➡

Message Sent	Message Received: Positive	Message Received: Negative
Academic Messages		
"There was only one A on yesterday's test. Can anyone guess who got it?"	I'll feel so proud if it's me; I really studied hard.	I'll die if it's me! How embarrassing to be picked out as "Mr. Smarty Pants" in front of your friends.
"What's your opinion, Sally? We can always count on you for the wildest ideas."	The teacher really appreciates my creative ideas.	My teacher thinks I'm weird. She even expects me to act that way when I give my opinion.
"Whoever finishes this assignment first will be my special helper for the day."	I'd love to help out. I'll work as fast as I can!	So, I'm only "special" when I'm fast? Forget it, I'm not into speed! Besides, I'll never finish ahead of everyone else.
Other Messages		
"Of course I trust you, but I never lend my car to anyone. Really, it's not just you."	I can't argue with him if that's his policy for everyone. He'd say no to anyone who wanted to borrow his car.	He doesn't trust me.
"It's okay to be alone sometimes."	My parents understand that solitude is important to me.	If I'm not always on some sports team, my parents will think I'm strange.
"I'll bet you'll be even more successful in life than your sister."	My family really wants me to do well.	I'll never catch up to my sister, so why try at all? I hate being compared to her!

Gifted children are especially apt at picking up the multiple meanings of both blatant and subtle messages, as their sensitivity to people's impressions of them is often quite strong. However, this precocity in perception is not always accompanied by a similarly advanced ability in interpretation. The result can be a misreading of invitations sent by teachers or parents so that the gifted child notes the negative over the positive. For example, a child who is told that report card grades of A's and B's are signs of good work may hear the message as a warning to do better, rather than as an acknowledgment of strong efforts.

These negative misinterpretations are most apt to occur in gifted children who are perfectionists or those whose self-esteem is low. In fact, if individuals believe something about themselves, they are likely to accept as true only those statements that validate their established beliefs or attitudes. Thus, a child who thinks, "I am stupid," will readily accept those messages—intentional or not—that go along with this belief. Likewise, a child with strong self-esteem will be more likely to interpret messages in a more positive way.

Four messages people send to gifted children that can have unintended negative effects are:

1. **"You did a great job on this project, but . . ."** When we couple a compliment with a suggestion to improve, what is usually remembered the most is what comes after the "but," diminishing the impact of the intended compliment.

2. **"I don't care about your grades as long as you try your best."** No adults we know try their best at everything they do. As we all have discovered,

there are some things in life that just take precedence over others. This "try-your-best" statement is a sure way to breed perfectionism as well as limit a child's ability to set priorities.

3. **"This'll be easy for a smart kid like you."** "And what if it isn't?" the child might think. "That means I must really be some big loser, if even a task that is simple to others seems complex to me." When you interpret this message like this, there's no way to feel but low.

4. **"You're not working up to your potential."** This implies that someone else knows the range of another's potential and is somehow keeping it a secret from that person. This statement is a sure way to make someone's efforts seem less than worthwhile. Further, it implies that "potential" has an end point when, in fact, it is an ever-changing set of goals based on personal interests and strengths.

The importance of invitations, and their correct interpretation, has been proved through reams of research and years of human interaction. As adults, we often recall the times in our own childhood when we were either invited or disinvited, and these memories, if powerful enough, can affect our behavior even decades later. A teacher in Gary, Indiana, related the following incident:

When I was in third grade, I raised my hand to answer a question, and the teacher called on me. I gave the wrong answer. To this day, I remember how she reacted. She said, "Oh, Catherine, you're just like an old hen. You cackle and cackle but never produce an egg." I'll remember how hurt I felt then—and now—for the rest of my life.

Invitational Education in Action

If you've read this far, you probably realize the importance of invitational education. But saying "I believe" and taking appropriate actions are two very different things. What follows are specific ways to construct an inviting environment—for yourself and for those you teach.

To us, there are at least six key areas in which educators can provide "invitations" to gifted pupils. In the following sections, we will present ideas for incorporating invitational education in all six of these action areas:

1. Within the curriculum

2. In grading procedures and student evaluation

3. Within the classroom environment

4. In establishing disciplinary procedures

5. Through self-satisfying behaviors that energize you as an educator

6. By explicitly valuing giftedness (and gifted kids)

#1: Invitational Education Within the Curriculum

STRATEGY **Provide Posttests as Pretests**

It is more common than rare that gifted students know portions of the regular curriculum before instruction begins. If teachers allow able students to take the textbook-provided posttest at the *beginning* of a particular unit of study, then curriculum can be adapted to meet the current level of student achievement. It also allows for extension activities and other independent or small-group-work opportunities.

One term for this approach, coined by Joseph Renzulli, is "compacting." Compacting (sometimes called "telescoping") is a way to eliminate or reduce those areas of the curriculum that the student has already mastered, buying time to do other, more innovative or in-depth assignments or projects. Compacting not only prevents many "I'm bored" comments, but it also gives students credit for their past accomplishments and present competence. In her book *Teaching Gifted Kids in Today's Classroom*, Susan Winebrenner presents "Seven Steps to Successful Compacting." You can use these steps—shown below—to help you challenge and support gifted learners.

Seven Steps to Successful Compacting

1. **Identify the learning objectives** or standards that all students must learn.

2. **Give students time to examine** the content to be tested.

3. **Offer a pretest opportunity to volunteers** after explaining the level of achievement needed to pass the pretest. Tell students they may stop the pretest at any time if they realize they will score below the required level. Make sure all students understand that the pretest results will not be formally entered as grades. The pretest simply allows advanced students to demonstrate that they need less direct instruction than age peers on upcoming content.

4. **Have extension activities available** for those who can "compact out" of specific learning activities because they have demonstrated their existing competence with that particular content on a pretest. These extension activities should be connected to the unit of study but not limited solely to the required standards.

5. **Eliminate all standardized test drill, practice, and review** for students who have already demonstrated advanced levels of mastery.

6. **Decide how you will keep accurate records** of the students' compacting experiences. Then instruct students how to keep their own records of their extension activities.

7. **Devise a method for storing compacting documents.** You might use hanging file folders in a plastic crate so all students have a place to store their extension work. All logs, contracts, and other forms related to compacting and extension work should be dated and kept in the same location.

Adapted from *Teaching Gifted Kids in Today's Classroom: Strategies and Techniques Every Teacher Can Use* by Susan Winebrenner, M.S., with Dina Brulles, Ph.D. (Minneapolis: Free Spirit Publishing, 2012), p. 39. Used with permission.

This is easier said than done, of course. And in the short term, it will require more work on your part. You'll need to design some alternative assignments for gifted students (at least initially), and this is an extra effort. However, as time goes on and students become more savvy about the procedures, they can be given the responsibility of designing a replacement curriculum from which they would draw both enjoyment and academic satisfaction.

Also, don't forget to use the services of your school's gifted specialist to help design alternate assignments or locate supplemental resources. Media center specialists can be enormously helpful as well. That's why they're there!

STRATEGY Embrace the World of Online Learning

Gifted students have more options than ever to take charge of their own learning by entering the online classroom. Many educational websites give learners the chance to control the pace, focus, and depth of their study. Encourage students to use the following sites and others by inviting them to locate specific topics on lessons that you are teaching anyway—whether it's calculating pi, interpreting *Jane Eyre*, or saving a local landmark from demolition. Let students do the digging! Naturally, these courses may very well be pursued by students outside of the school day. If so, be sure to note in student records their participation in such offerings. And, should they find an online alternative to the lesson you had planned, consider inviting them to co-teach the class and present the lesson together with you.

The following sites are great places to get started. Explore these and other resources to find the right options for you and your students. (*Note:* Some online courses are free, and others are tuition-based. Your budget may not allow students to take courses that require fees. In this case, parents will have to be approached for their approval.)

Khan Academy (khanacademy.org) features short educational videos on many topics and for students of all ages. Students can use the site to learn, measure their own progress, and work toward individualized goals at their own pace.

MIT + K12 (k12videos.mit.edu) is a collaboration between Khan Academy's founder (Sal Khan) and MIT students. The site presents short videos with a focus on STEM topics (science, technology, engineering, and math).

TED-Ed (ed.ted.com) lessons (inspired by TED Talks) are videos recorded by educators and professionally animated. These lessons cover many topics, organized by theme. The website also features quizzes, questions for further exploration, and additional resources.

Wonderopolis (wonderopolis.org) posts a new "wonder" every day—a thought-provoking question that forms the basis for investigation. Each wonder is accompanied by a video, word list, and other resources. Most wonders also include quizzes. Students can submit their own ideas for wonders to be included on the website.

🖈 STRATEGY Coordinate Student Schedules

Many gifted programs, especially at the elementary school level, operate in a "pull-out" format, where students leave the regular class for a period of time each day or week. Whether you are the "sending" teacher (in the regular classroom) or the "receiving" teacher (in the resource room), be aware of the scheduling dilemmas that are part and parcel of pull-out programs. Try to coordinate tests, special events, and the introduction of important topics so students don't get caught in a bind as they try to serve two (or more) expectations in their different classrooms.

Please don't become one of those teachers who gifted students know "just don't get it." Don't:

- Schedule a party or field trip on the day of the pull-out class.

- "Forget" to give gifted students the homework required when they return from their pull-out class, and then give them zeros for not turning in homework that they didn't know they had.

- Say to the students who return to your class following their gifted pull-out time, "Thanks for returning to *our* world."

- Introduce a major new topic or project on precisely the day that the gifted kids aren't there, then expect them to understand it anyway because "they're supposed to be gifted, aren't they?"

These are all questionable strategies that have been used by some teachers to knowingly or unknowingly subvert gifted pull-out programs and the gifted kids in them.

Gifted students who get pulled from your classroom deserve the same degree of personal and educational respect afforded to students who leave your room for speech therapy, a special class for students with learning differences, and so on. Anything less is discriminatory and inhumane.

🖈 STRATEGY Provide "Instead of" Enrichment, Not "In Addition to" Enrichment

Often, gifted students are told that they can work on special projects or in learning centers only after they have finished their assigned work. This is all well and good, except for those times when the assigned work is little more than a task requiring a rote drill of an already mastered concept.

"Instead of" versus "in addition to" enrichment is seen in these two examples:

- **The "instead of" teacher says,** "Desmond, since you scored 95 percent on both your math and spelling pretests, why don't you use your time to work on another activity instead?"

- **The "in addition to" teacher says,** "Desmond, once you've written your spelling words ten times each and completed these three pages of math seatwork, you may work on your independent project."

"Instead of" enrichment, also known as curriculum streaming (and fitting into the greater practice of differentiation for gifted kids), allows teachers to buy time within the school day for students whose past efforts have proved their competence in basic skill areas.

If the "instead of" enrichment sounds a lot like curriculum compacting, that's because it is the next logical step after compacting has been done. Those students whose curriculum has been compacted can now use their time more effectively by completing extension activities that build on and deepen their existing knowledge and understanding.

STRATEGY Provide Incentives

Many teachers are frustrated by the seemingly haphazard attempts gifted students make when completing simple tasks. For example, when a top math student makes ten computation mistakes on a review worksheet, the student is often chided for making "careless errors." The

Letting Students Go Wild
by Kelly, 22

When I was sometimes asked to write an essay or poem—no topic selected by the teacher—I'd go wild. It wasn't often we were trusted with our own minds to wander where we chose. The time I grew most, intellectually, was during the spring of eleventh grade, when my Honors English class was studying Thoreau. Our class was asked to keep journals. The only limit on our writing was that it was to be about nature. Nature! That's anything! To me it was anything. To Thoreau it was anything. And to my teacher . . . it was anything.

My advice to you is to let your kids (whatever their age) go wild with their own brains. Whether on paper, tablet, computer, or canvas, don't always tell them what to do! Let them use their own ingenuity. Tell them to call forth from their innermost selves the truth that is alive in all of us. Let them define beauty, knowledge, nature, and meaning in their own individual ways. This is why we were all made different! The only way to learn something really worthwhile, I am convinced, is to look inside and try to find out what's alive in there. Most people have never dared to consult themselves, before others, in making their own opinions.

student balks at redoing the assignment with complaints of "I already know this stuff!" The teacher agrees and says, "I *know* you can do the work—just be more careful." Thus begins a cycle of frustration for everyone concerned.

Think how much of an incentive it would be for students if they were told, "There are 50 math problems on this page. Anyone who completes the first 25 examples with no more than two errors does not have to finish the remaining problems."

This comment invites achievement in a way that rewards students who take the time to think about what they are doing, and it offers a "quality discount program" that prods attention to the task at hand. (Also, and not so incidentally, it cuts down on the teacher's grading time while ensuring that students have mastered basic concepts.)

#2: Invitational Education in Grading Procedures and Student Evaluation

📌 **STRATEGY** Get the Red Out

The ubiquitous red pen that is used to grade students' projects and papers is perceived as an instrument of torture by many children, especially those who are either perfectionists or extremely averse to criticism. Able children make the connection early: "The more red marks, the worse my grade."

Solutions? Use any color but red to grade students' papers, or use red ink only to point out pupils' accomplishments or *correct* answers.

📌 **STRATEGY** Let Students Grade Their Own Papers

Every text has a teacher's edition; every workbook has an answer guide. Hand these over to those students who finish their tasks early and allow them to grade their own work.

Not only does this allow students a chance to determine the extent of their knowledge, but it also cuts down on your grading time, so everyone wins. Also, and most important, allowing students to grade their own assignments implies that you trust them to be honest about their errors. And, ironically, when most students are given the chance to cheat, they won't. There's no need to be dishonest when the person in charge respects your right to make errors (and to learn from them).

📌 **STRATEGY** Help Students Set Reachable Goals

Many gifted children select topics of study that are bigger than they are. "I want to study dinosaurs," they say, or "I'd like to learn about chemistry," or "I'm worried about crime in my neighborhood, and I want to do something about it." Great topics, but each is hardly manageable in a six-week independent study.

The first step to success is setting limits in terms of the depth and breadth of the project focus. One approach, called curriculum "webbing," is illustrated on page 232. By constructing such webs (a colleague calls them "spider plans"), students get to see the many facets of a topic that, at first, may have appeared one-dimensional. Then they may pinpoint their specific areas of interest within the broader scope of their initial topic idea

Web Diagram for an Independent Study on Crime Prevention

1. Find out how often police patrol the park.
2. Ask about more lights in park.
3. Ask for more adult supervisors during the days.

1. Find out how to start a neighborhood watch program.
2. Have a neighborhood meeting. Invite police to talk about ways to prevent vandalism.
3. Have a block party so neighbors get to know each other.

1. See if neighborhood organization or city has money for deadbolt locks, lights on garages, and so on.
2. Invite police to check houses and give burglar-proofing tips.
3. Encourage neighbors to tell each other when they're going out of town.

1. Get more trash cans for neighborhood.
2. Start Adopt-a-Sidewalk and Adopt-an-Alley programs.
3. Hand out litter bags for people to put in their cars.

1. Report all graffiti to police right away. Special phone number?
2. Find out if city government has people who clean up or paint over graffiti.
3. Learn what other neighborhoods have done.

and work on a scaled-down version of the original theme.

Limiting one's scope is not the same as lowering one's standards. If a web is well thought out, the student can return to it if the new, trimmed-down project seems too lean. It's easier to build on a firm foundation than on patches of scattered thoughts.

⚓ STRATEGY Post Less-Than-Perfect Papers

Walk into many classrooms (or visit their websites, or Pinterest pages), and you may notice impressive collections of perfect papers. Every spelling paper an A, every coloring page drawn within the lines, each 3-D relief map of the USA complete with all fifty states and a couple of oceans.

But what message does this send to students whose work, while good, is not perfect? And what about the child who may never (or seldom) have a perfect paper but continues to show improvement over time? Doesn't this student deserve to get the accolades of others by seeing his or her work on display?

Tell your students that they have the chance, and the choice, to post projects that make them proud. Remind them that these need not be perfect, and start the ball rolling by posting something of your own that is good, but not great, work. (Remember that graduate paper you got a B-minus on? Now's the chance to show it off.)

Posting less-than-perfect work neither lowers standards nor rewards mediocrity. Instead, it acknowledges an essential truth: Less than perfection is more than acceptable.

One last word in these litigious times: Some states have enacted laws or policies forbidding the posting of any graded

student work on which the student's name appears, citing it as unconstitutional on the grounds of freedom of privacy being violated. Be this right or wrong, it may be a reality in your state. Check with your school's principal to be sure that displaying student work does not constitute a legal violation.

⚓ STRATEGY The BUG Roll

Few would argue the benefits of having some type of Honor Roll in schools. Call it the "Principal's Club" or the "Academic Aces" or whatever other euphemism you choose: It makes sense to reward those students who excel in the business of schooling.

But what about a student like Ben? A smart kid—and everyone knows it—Ben has had grades that fluctuate as wildly as April temperatures in Chicago. Then there's Monchelle, a quiet girl who's not convinced that her mind is as sharp as everyone says. She can do well, but since her grades are seldom top-notch, there's nary a mention of her successes.

Enter the BUG Roll. BUG—an acronym for Bringing Up Grades—gives credit and public recognition to students who improve at least one letter grade between report cards, without letting any other grades fall back. So, if Ben goes from all Cs during his first quarter to a combination of Cs and Bs in the second quarter, he makes the BUG Roll. So would Monchelle, if those B-minuses she was toying with one quarter rose to become B-pluses by next term's end. Neither student is in top form academically, but their progress toward improvement is noteworthy and deserves some public recognition.

If you work at the middle school level, the BUG Roll moniker will seem too childish for emerging adolescents. So change the name to "On a Roll," a homophone for "Honor Roll" that gets the same point across: "Your efforts are noticed and appreciated."

Some schools have added a few modifications to the BUG Roll/On a Roll, such as students needing to attain a minimum average of C to earn list status (going from Fs to Ds doesn't cut it). Other educators require that students go up at least one grade in two subjects in order to earn this recognition.

We believe that any improvement in academic performance is noteworthy and, therefore, we don't support these modifications. However, we also understand that the climate of each school is different, and we would rather see a modified BUG Roll than no BUG Roll at all.

Use the BUG Roll. It can make a difference in the lives of gifted students (and others) who realize that academic success sometimes comes in small steps, not giant leaps. You'll find a reproducible BUG Roll on page 256.

STRATEGY Determine Evaluation Criteria

> "When I was growing up, I always wanted to be somebody, but now I see that I should have been more specific."
>
> **—Lily Tomlin**

It doesn't take a brilliant mind to figure out that if you don't know where you're going, you'll probably end up someplace else. Life in the classroom is like a trip down the interstate. A road map that

Spotlight on External Rewards

Despite Mae West's assertion, too much of a good thing is not always a good thing. Take the case of the preceding two suggestions: the posting of imperfect work and the BUG Roll.

In some ways, educators who use them (and similar methods) are resorting to bribery to get children to perform academically. "Do a good job and we'll let everyone know it" may be how some students interpret either action, especially those who are smart enough to recognize that they deserve to be valued not for their work but for themselves.

This is the main point raised by Alfie Kohn, whose classic book, *Punished by Rewards*, lambastes America's fascination with praise and rewards for work that may, in fact, be meaningless to the child. In a chapter titled "The Trouble with Carrots," Kohn points out four reasons why external rewards have no long-term positive impact:[3]

1. **Rewards punish.** "If you're a good boy, you can have ten extra minutes of recess" is "functionally identical" to a threat, as the student realizes what will be lost—free time—if certain steps aren't followed.

2. **Rewards rupture relationships.** Implementing a "Genius of the Week" program, in which one student is selected as the top boy or girl for the week in a classroom, actually pits students against each other in unhealthy ways and creates a power structure where the teacher wields his or her biases over students.

3. **Rewards ignore reasons.** Did anyone ever ask Ben why his grades are low? (Perhaps the curriculum is meaningless to him; hence, so are his grades.) Or question Monchelle about her relatively low grade achievement? (Maybe she's afraid that if she gets straight A's once, she'll be expected to do it time and again.) In an externally based reward structure, the main core of a problem may never be addressed.

4. **Rewards discourage risk-taking.** According to Kohn, "When we are working for a reward, we do exactly what is necessary to get it, and no more." As a corollary, people who work for the reward are less likely to take chances or experiment with ideas that do not lead directly to the desired result. The objective becomes earning the reward, not learning or testing new thoughts. Risk-taking, and the resultant growth, is scaled back considerably.

Kohn's work is both elegant and controversial—and, some would add, unrealistic. After all, how long would you go to work if you never received a paycheck, even if you loved what you did? Still, his ideas merit attention, especially when considering that gifted children might interpret an externally based reward structure as little more than a thinly disguised bribe to perform work that, intrinsically, does not matter to them.

It is up to you to reach a balance between encouraging students to do work because of the outside benefits or recognition it brings, and allowing them to pursue projects solely because of their passion for a particular subject or topic. And you have your work cut out for you, as this balance often differs from student to student.

clearly marks your intended destination will get you there a bit more quickly and smoothly than just following your nose.

This advice rings true for, among other things, the completion of student projects. Too often, as students embark on adventures in learning, they have only vague ideas of their goals. "I want to learn about outer space" is about as precise a statement as "I think I'll visit Kansas." While the former is significantly bigger than the latter, both are large enough to get lost in unless you add some specificity to your plans.

To guide students through learning excursions that will lead them to places they intended to go in the first place, try using an "Independent Study Guide" like the one on page 257. This outline is designed to encourage students to consider—from the beginning—a project's scope, starting points, possible pitfalls (and "escape routes"), and evaluation criteria.

Of course, some parts of the plan may change as the student learns more about the topic (haven't you ever diverged from your scheduled itinerary?), but it's always easier to switch from a known direction than to set out without one and hope for the best. Not all students need this formal a plan to study a topic, but for those who do, a curriculum road map can save time and energy for both them and their teachers.

🖈 **STRATEGY** **Praise and Critique Separately**

Remember your last job performance evaluation? All "excellents" or "goods," we suspect—except for maybe that one item about turning in lesson plans on time or arriving at school before the students get there. One flaw (maybe two) on an otherwise perfect record. So, what do you remember? Generally, human nature prevails, and we recall the negatives.

As we mentioned earlier in our review of "unintentional disinvitations," our students may have similar reactions. Thus when we tell them, "Your essay was good, *but* you could improve your grammar," or "I like your picture, *but* elephants aren't really blue," they may feel as if they just got kicked in the "but." What they remember is what *should have* been done rather than what *was* accomplished.

When praise is coupled with criticism, it is usually the latter that is retained. Even though both types of comments might be appropriate and important, it's best to mention them at two separate times. "Your essay was well written" or "I like the colors in your picture" is all you need to say for the moment. Suggestions to change or improve can come later.

#3: Invitational Education Within the Classroom Environment

🖈 **STRATEGY** **Keep Private Things Private**

Many teachers are guilty of unintentionally embarrassing their students by classroom actions that should be stopped. For example:

- Do you place a student's name on the board when he or she misbehaves or speaks out of turn?

- Do you have students grade each other's spelling tests, then have them recite the grades out loud for you to record in your grade book?

- Do you announce, "There was only one A on the social studies paper. Can anyone guess who got it?"

Each of these teacher behaviors takes something that belongs to the student and puts it out front for public display.

In the first case, the name-on-the-board strategy is a not-so-subtle attempt to intimidate the student into compliance. The problem is, any stranger (or parent, or principal) who walks into your room knows who "the bad kid" is—something that no one but you needs to know. As an alternative, have any students who act out write their own names on a notepad on your desk. You'll still know who did what and needs to face the consequences, but no one else will be the wiser—which is how it should be.

The two other examples both involve the public display of something intended to be private: a student's level of academic performance. Having kids grade each other's papers and relay the grades to you orally saves time, but what about the child who gets a D, or the superstar speller who got an A for the thirty-eighth time this year? Both might be criticized or ostracized by others outside of your earshot. And what about the "only one A" comment? Again, good intentions gone awry. The child being lauded now might be the child being pummeled later at the bus stop or bullied online for being the teacher's favorite.

It's always a good idea to ask ourselves, "Am I treating my students the way I would have wanted to be treated as a child?" and then act accordingly.

A few final words on the practice of having students grade other students' papers: In 2000, a federal appeals court declared it illegal, saying that it violated the Family Educational Rights and Privacy Act of 1974 (FERPA). In 2002, the U.S. Supreme Court reversed the decision of the appeals court and ruled unanimously that peer grading does not violate FERPA. Legal or not, we don't recommend it.

📌 STRATEGY Establish a Planning Council

In most classrooms, the teacher determines the decor. Prints, posters, bulletin boards, and desk arrangements are all in place as the school year begins, and if changes are made throughout the year, it is due to the teacher's initiative. But students spend almost as much time in the classroom as teachers do. Why not give them a say in how it looks and feels?

Enter the Planning Council (PC). Chaired by the teacher (or a designee), the PC comprises students who are members of the class in question. It is their job to recommend changes in the classroom environment and to implement these suggestions, either by themselves or by "subcontracting" the job to an interested group of students. Of course, the teacher may request that an "environmental impact study" be done prior to any major changes. For example, will putting the desks in clusters instead of rows

create unnecessary talking or congested traffic patterns?

By establishing a PC, you're telling your students in a very real way that *this* classroom is *their* classroom, too. (As the year progresses, PC membership may change to involve as many students as possible.) Successfully implemented, the PC turns the classroom atmosphere from one of factory to one of family. As noted in Chapter 6, this is the atmosphere that most underachievers and selective consumers prefer. Many other students will feel the same.

STRATEGY Take the Classroom Temperature

Moods affect performance, no question about it. But moods are sometimes subtle and secretive, and it is easy to suppress anger behind a calm demeanor or to veil disappointment with a smile. Often, the very students who need the most care and attention are the ones most adept at disguising their moods.

In their article ""Eight Effective Activities to Enhance the Social and Emotional Development of the Gifted and Talented," counselor George Betts and psychologist Maureen Neihart recommend that educators invite students to take their "emotional temperatures." They suggest a rating scale from 1 (low; I don't feel good about life right now) to 10 (high; I feel good about life right now and want to tell everyone how exciting it is).[4]

You could use this 1 to 10 scale. Or, in keeping with the "temperature" metaphor, you might have your students construct

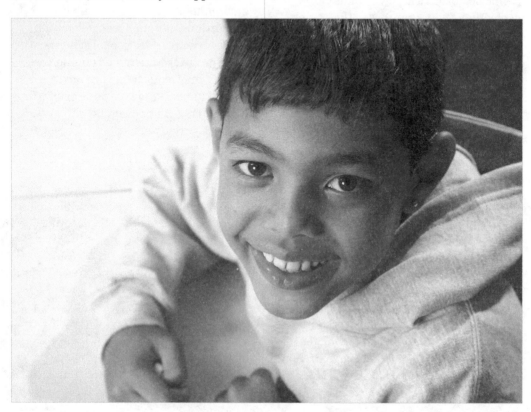

cardboard thermometers with sliding markers. (Make one for yourself, too!) Then have everyone monitor and record their moods throughout the day. For example, a student might have this type of day:

9:00 a.m. 72° (very comfortable). Feeling good after a bus ride seated next to my best friend.

10:50 a.m. 32° (cold and uncomfortable). Picked last (again) for the recess kick-ball team.

12:30 p.m. 95° (very hot and uncomfortable). Everyone lost free time because a few kids were fooling around at lunch. No fair!

1:20 p.m. 78° (feeling a little better). Ms. Fong let us talk about our feelings about the lunchroom problem.

2:45 p.m. 72° (comfortable again). A good end to the day—a B on a test and a surprise popcorn treat!

A simpler (but similar) suggestion is to let students use a color wheel—the k ind found in many board games—to express their moods. Red indicates anger, blue means sadness, green shows joy, and so on.

A mood indicator, whether a thermometer or a color wheel, allows students to monitor their changing emotions throughout each day. It helps them pinpoint and acknowledge the events that get them angry or calm them down. When teachers also participate, this lets students know that we, too, are affected by different moods as the school day unfolds. Imagine—a teacher, and human!

STRATEGY Design Classrooms That Respect Learning Styles and Preferences

Just as people differ about the environment most conducive to creativity, they also vary in their styles and preferences for completing academic tasks. Some students love group projects, where each person participates actively in a cooperative learning venture. Others prefer solitude—a study carrel in a corner, where the outside world *remains* outside. Still others learn most efficiently by reading, lecture, or drill, while their classmates prefer educational games, videos, online classes, or class discussions.

Educational literature is filled with research evidence (backed by common sense) that even gifted students learn in varied ways. Two notable examples are the multiple-intelligences work of Howard Gardner (which, while imperfect, is fodder for productive discussion) and the learning-styles work of Anthony Gregorc. From them and other researchers—and from our own experience as teachers—we've discovered that some kids learn best by listening, others by seeing, and others by actively doing. There is, however, no consensus on which teaching style or setting works best for everyone (or almost everyone).

One thing is certain, though: A classroom designed to allow for both private and group learning through a variety of techniques invites learning more than does a setting in which lecture alone is used to convey lessons. So vary the "menu." It will enhance and enliven any learning environment.

📌 **STRATEGY** **See Each Student as an Individual**

Quickly add this column of numbers—out loud or in your head:

$$
\begin{array}{r}
1,000 \\
40 \\
1,000 \\
30 \\
1,000 \\
20 \\
1,000 \\
10 \\
\end{array}
$$

If you arrived at 5,000, congratulations . . . for being wrong. This is the most common answer given by both kids and adults, even though the correct answer is 4,100. Go back and check carefully; you'll see that we're right.

What's going on here is *patterning*. As you add, the thousands keep increasing—until the end, when they don't. But since you expect the pattern to stay the same, you give an answer that's logical, consistent . . . and wrong.

Try this activity with your students. Place this list of numbers on a board, revealing the numbers one at a time. When the resounding sound of "Five thousand!" emanates from your apt pupils' mouths, let them know this: Lots of people look at gifted individuals and see them as a collective 5,000—easy to interpret, more similar than different from each other, stereotyped as A students who have few friends. Then let them know that

you understand how wrong this notion is, and you intend to look at each of them as an individual 4,100: a unique entity who is a little more complex than may first meet the eye.

You might hang two big, bright posters on opposite classroom walls—one with "4,100" on it, the other with "5,000." Tell your students that they have the responsibility to remind you (and each other) when the tendency to treat one like all (5,000) is apparent.

📌 **STRATEGY** **Help Students Get to Know Each Other**

In any classroom, students will form new friendships. Kids who have been friends in previous years will likely continue their close relationships. And some students will form cliques designed to keep others out.

As a teacher, you can encourage *all* students to be more open to and accepting of each other. One way is by setting aside time for fun activities in which students learn about their classmates and share information about themselves. Of course, by guiding, participating, and observing, you'll learn more about your students, too—an added bonus. Following are five activities that have worked for us.

✏️ **ACTIVITY** **Visual Enigmas**

Almost everyone we know is intrigued by optical illusions—those eye puzzles that cause you to think in new ways about something that looks simple on the surface but is really quite complex. For example, what do you see in the pictures on the next page?

If you see a knight on a horse in the first set of abstract shapes, join the club. It's not there, of course, but in our mind's quest for solving problems, we create an image that reminds us of something we know. The question mark in the other illustration is quite obvious to many, but the black bird—a phoenix—is less so. Again, neither is there, except in our mind's eye, and if our culture did not use the "?" symbol, we probably wouldn't see the question mark at all.

Kids love mind-bogglers like these. You can find many books of optical illusions at your local library; one of our personal favorites is an oldie but goodie, *Can You Believe Your Eyes?* by J. Richard Block and Harold Yuker (New York: Brunner-Routledge, 1989). These visual puzzles are great for filling those extra moments at the end of a unit, a period, or a day. They can also help your students get to know more about each other's lives. Just don't call them "optical illusions." Instead, use the more sophisticated term "visual enigmas," and present them like this.

Give each student a copy of the "Visual Enigmas" handout on page 258. See if your students can decipher any of these complex words (most cannot), and explain to them that each of them— *enigma, quandary, conundrum*—is almost synonymous with the word at the bottom of the page: *mystery*.

After sharing this handout, do what we do: Make up your own visual enigmas using your full name (see the example below), followed by brief descriptions of things about you that interested people may want to know. Then have each of your students take a turn at unraveling the mystery that is him or her, using either a first name or a first and last name (kept separate). Hang the completed enigmas on a window wall and watch as students try to unravel the mysteries of their classmates' lives, discovering important things that make each of them unique.

My Name

Things That Make Me Unique

1. I like to travel to places where people do not speak English.

2. I think the Three Stooges are way funnier than Jim Carrey.

3. I enjoy listening to alternative music that people my age are not supposed to like.

4. The quality I respect most in a person is integrity.

ACTIVITY Welcome to Our School

Every school building has the overlords (students in the school's highest grade) and the underlings (kids in the lowest grade). For example, if you work in a school designed for fourth through sixth graders, the head honchos are generally those sixth graders who learned the ropes of the school long ago—back in fourth grade. This activity brings the oldest and youngest groups just a little bit closer.

Near the end of the school year, have students who will be in the building's highest grade the following year get together to write a student handbook for the incoming youngest students. The goal: to make school a less scary place for students who will soon experience it as a brand-new place. Topics might include:

- The physical layout of the building ("where stuff is")

- How to get along with your teachers

- How to deal with older kids

- Homework policies

- Where to go and who to turn to for help

Once the handbook has been written, edited, and illustrated, make enough copies to give each incoming student a copy at the start of the new school year. (Or post it on the school's website, or provide it as an enclosure in an information packet sent to new students before the school year begins.) Then, during the first few days of school, have representatives from the school's highest grade visit each new classroom to review and explain the handbook, and to let the incoming students know that "if anyone gives you any trouble, come see us."

When the students at one intermediate school created a handbook, here's what they wrote. The final booklet was illustrated by the students.

Welcome to Dodge Intermediate School!

Introduction

Welcome to Dodge! It is a fun school with many opportunities. Dodge is a very nice school (the cafeteria food is even good!) and, until the high school was built, it was the newest school in town.

We bet you have A LOT of questions about Dodge—everyone does! That's why we put this booklet together.

Our most important advice for the first day of school is to just act like yourself. There are TONS of teachers and older kids to ask where to go if you get lost.

So . . . here are our suggestions about having a good year at Dodge. Enjoy fourth grade!

The school is so big! Will I get lost?

Yes, Dodge is bigger than the other schools you went to, but you probably won't get lost because teachers take you around the school a lot. After a week, you'll know where everything is.

Dodge is pretty much a square. The library is the center. Around it are upstairs and downstairs classrooms. There are some other hallways, but your teacher will take you through them.

How do I make the first few days easier?

Here are ideas from Dodge students:

"I practiced the combination to my locker about five times when I first got it so now I know it so well that I can open it in about ten seconds!"

"If you need any help, ask a teacher, NOT a student (at least not the first few days)."

"At first, all the stairs are a pain, but you'll get used to them."

"Just ignore kids who say you are short or whatever. They are SO annoying!"

"If you buy lunch, have your money ready as you stand in line."

How will I ever stay organized?

Keep your desk organized by putting your books on one side and your folders or trapper on the other. Take home all the papers you don't need at school any more. Also, have a folder for each subject (like math, science, and social studies).

→

Always put your stuff back in the right spot, because once it is in the wrong spot you will never have time to put it back where it belongs.

Lastly, clean out your folders once a month and don't clutter up your locker with all kinds of junk and papers.

What can you tell us about teachers and homework?

You're probably wondering if all the good things you heard about the teachers are true. Well, we can't say that all of the teachers are nice, because that will have to be your opinion. But what we CAN say is that every good thing we ever heard about them WAS true. It's NOT true that the teachers are mean, but it IS true that they may be a little stricter than you're used to.

Teachers don't give as much homework as people say they do. But, when you do get homework, you should finish it right after school, because then you'll have the rest of the night to yourself. We know we probably sound like your mother, but doing your homework DOES help.

What other stuff should we know?

Here's what Dodge students say:

"If you want the older kids to like you, don't show off, be snotty, or try to annoy them."

"Do not write on the bathroom walls—ever! The janitor will make you wash it off."

"You can't sit wherever you want in the cafeteria. There aren't fights during lunch, and there is a much larger selection of food than at your elementary school."

"If you have a problem with another kid, tell an adult or (if you can't leave) ignore the person. DON'T FIGHT THEM!"

"Don't worry about the locker rooms—just like the stairs, you get used to them pretty quickly. Also, don't be scared, because the boys and the girls are kept separated."

ACTIVITY Just Like Me

Students have a lot in common with each other, whatever the depth or range of their intellects. After all, humanity being what it is, there is more tying us together than separating us.

In this activity, students first get to express how alike they really are. This is followed by a "personal inventory" that invites them to share other, more detailed aspects of their lives and personalities.

Begin the activity by having students sit in their chairs, at desks or tables, but far enough back that they can stand up readily. Tell them that you're going to read a series of statements aloud. For each statement that's true for them, they should stand up, raise their arms, and exclaim, "That's just like me!" You might use the statements below or create your own. Tip: Be prepared for loudness and laughter.

Stand up and say *That's just like me!* if . . .

- Pizza is my absolute favorite food.

- Someday I'll own a fancy sports car.

- I cry as easily as I laugh.

- I dream in color.

- I want to have more than two kids when I grow up.

- I wish I could be five years old again.

- I want to be twenty-one years old right now.

- My best friend is at least two years older than I am.

- My best friend is at least two years younger than I am.

- I make up my own rules in the games I play.

- Blue is my favorite color.

- I love playing video games.

Afterward, ask the students to take their seats and settle down. Then explain the next part of the activity: Each student will now write a description of himself or herself, using the letters from "Just Like [his or her name]." The letters can appear anywhere in the words. Here's an example for a student named Joe:

well-ad**J**usted
not too h**U**mble
love**S** beaches
Traveler

Laid-back
wr**I**ter
Kind
Easygoing

Jovial
kn**O**wledgeable
Effervescent

You might make this into an advanced vocabulary lesson, challenging students to find difficult synonyms for common words. (For example, "happy" for someone needing an E can become either "elated" or "ecstatic.") Finally! A use for those classroom thesauruses!

Hang these self-portrayals on a classroom wall—or in the hall—so students can see their common bonds through a unique perspective.

ACTIVITY Symbolic Scavenger Hunt

We all remember scavenger hunts from summer camp, school field trips, or birthday parties. No matter what we were told to search for, all scavenger hunts had something in common: They were concrete. We worked our way down a list, looking for specific objects. There usually wasn't much creativity or self-expression involved.

Our "Symbolic Scavenger Hunt" is different. The object of this game is to locate items that symbolize or represent ideas, concepts, or relationships. Students are also asked to locate items that represent *themselves* as people—past, present, and future.

For example, on a field trip to a nature center, Jim had his seventh-grade students do the following:

Find one thing that . . .

- represents mathematical precision in nature
- represents nature's way of recycling
- represents what a friend is
- indicates positive and negative changes
- proves that nature has a sense of humor
- looks like something you might find on another planet
- reminds you of someone you know
- has been changed by human intervention
- is natural, but not native, to this area
- symbolizes the best part of being a kid

- you think no one else will find
- is used or made by an animal
- is living and is older than you are
- is living and is younger than you are
- has been shaped by wind
- has been shaped by water
- represents something you enjoy
- represents the person you are now
- represents the person you once were
- represents the person you will someday be

The students were given forty minutes to locate as many items as possible from this list. They worked in teams of three or four. They were told to write descriptions of the items they found—and not to take anything from nature. Later, when the students returned to the classroom, they reported on their discoveries and why they thought specific items made good symbols.

Not only did students learn something about themselves, they also became careful observers of nature, looking for personal meaning in the trees, plants, and animals they saw. A class discussion of their responses could have gone on forever, as students jumped at the chance to express who they were and what was important to them.

ACTIVITY Who Knew?

If your experience is the same as ours, this activity is one your students will want to repeat. Why? First, because it's fun (and funny). Second, because it reveals something about memorable events in a person's life. Third, because it gives students a chance to stretch the truth legitimately, all in the name of self-disclosure.

Have each student write down five statements about himself or herself. The rules: Four statements must be true, and one must be a lie. Allow ten to fifteen minutes for this. You'll probably find that some students have trouble coming up with legitimate-sounding lies.

You might start by sharing a list of your own. Here are two lists we came up with, followed by two lists submitted by sixth-grade students Melissa and Kent.

Jim's List

1. I had to take over the controls of a small plane when the pilot got sick.

2. I almost drowned when I fell off a boat into the ocean.

3. I attended three colleges before I earned my bachelor's degree.

4. I bought a sports car without knowing how to drive a stick shift.

5. I took my first trip overseas by throwing a dart at a world map and going where it landed.

Judy's List

1. I love dogs of all shapes and sizes, but I can only have a terrier or a poodle because they don't shed. (I'm allergic to animal hair.)

2. I jumped off a sailboat off the coast of Africa, without any idea how I was going to get home. I landed in Mozambique!

3. I have traveled to more than fourteen countries around the world.

4. I speak several languages fluently.

5. I love cheese and have been called a cheesehead.

Melissa's List

1. I almost got lost at the Grand Canyon.

2. I hit my head on four metal bars while falling off a jungle gym.

3. I've been to Canada.

4. I have a sister named Sara who doesn't lie.

5. I know someone who guards the Dalai Lama.

Kent's List

1. I pulled the fire alarm when I thought it said "free."

2. I cried when my fish got flushed down the toilet.

3. I'm scared of my grandmother.

4. I can't bend my big toe backward.

5. I took a knife out of a drawer and stabbed the kitchen wall.

What you find out from this activity is fascinating. You learn about your students' talents, skills, and quirks; you learn about their families and social relationships; you learn about places they've lived and visited, languages they speak or understand, and dreams they aspire toward. Indeed, you learn more from their truth-telling than their lie-sharing.

In case you want to know the lies in the lists: Jim's is #1. Judy's is #4. Melissa's is #4 (her sister lies all the time—according to Melissa, that is). And Kent's is #5 (thank goodness).

More Ways to Promote a Positive Classroom Environment

1. **Grade papers with the number correct, not the number wrong.**

   If a student takes a twenty-item quiz and gets two wrong, don't take the easy route and write "–2" on the paper. Instead, write "+18" or 18/20. A small thing, but it sends a big message: "You did a fine job, and you got a lot more right than you missed."

2. **At least once in a while, write a positive comment.**

   Matt (Jim's son) once received an assignment back from his eighth-grade language arts teacher. Attached to it were two self-sticking notes on which these words were written:

   Matt, I have figured out why I enjoy reading your work so much. You give yourself permission to dream, to think wild thoughts, and to record those thoughts. Remember, Matt, continue dreaming BIG DREAMS and focus on pleasing yourself, your own creative mind. In that way, you'll never stifle yourself or become a robotic writer. —Mrs. Setter

   This was the only extended note from Mrs. Setter that Matt received all year—and it was the only one he needed to receive, for it validated not only Matt's work, but also his sense of self.

   Make yourself a promise to write each of your students at least one special note this year, a note that acknowledges not only what they do but who they are. It might hang on a refrigerator for months—like Mrs. Setter's note to Matt.

3. **Post your own Points of Pride.**

   Several teachers we know hang their high school and college diplomas in their classrooms. Others post positive notes on bulletin boards that they received in previous years from parents or students. Still more bring in trophies won in sports, T-shirts worn in 5K runs for muscular dystrophy, or blue ribbons won for pie-baking or flower-growing at a county fair. (One brave teacher posted "before" and "after" photos of her journey to losing seventy-five pounds.)

   In each instance, these teachers are sharing pieces of themselves and their lives with students. In the process, they are also letting their students know that learning extends beyond the school years and goals continue to be attained, even in adulthood.

#4: Invitational Education in Establishing Disciplinary Procedures

⚑ STRATEGY Avoid Group Punishments

Your students are chatty in general, and your requests for quiet go unheeded— at least by some. Unable to determine exactly which children are responsible for the noise, you give one final warning: "If it's not quiet by the time I count to three, you will all lose your recess. One . . . two . . . three!"

It isn't quiet, so you smugly (or sternly) follow through with your plan: "Okay, that's it. I'll see you all at 10:15."

There, you've done it—ruined recess for everyone, yourself included. Gifted students in particular hate this form of punishment, although all students can see the inequity inherent in punishing en masse. It's easy to see why the nontalkers get upset; after all, it wasn't *their* fault. Yet even those who are "guilty as charged" realize how unfair it is to punish others who are innocent. Some may appear at your desk, repentant and pleading, asking you to lift the punishment from those who are blameless.

Avoid these situations at all costs. It's hard to argue with the logic of a student whose only guilt is by association, or whose sense of justice demands to know why "innocent until proven guilty" applies in the courthouse but not in your classroom.

⚑ STRATEGY Reward Incremental Improvements

Many gifted youngsters are stingy when it comes to giving themselves credit for a job well done. If there's a flaw, they'll find it; if there's a higher grade to be gotten,

they'll wish they attained it. Too few of them notice incremental improvements in performance and, therefore, downplay their efforts until perfection is reached.

Educators can help students enjoy the fruits of their labors by pointing out to them their small successes. Comments such as "Ann, your cursive handwriting is really improving; I noticed it on the poster you designed yesterday," or "Compare these two assignments, Joey. Notice how much more complete this second one is" go a long way toward sharing your satisfaction with day-to-day growth or progress.

⚑ STRATEGY Catch Them Being Good

It's easy for educators to ignore or take for granted situations that neither bother us nor demand our attention. It's quite difficult, though, to tolerate a child who is misbehaving, disturbing others, or causing a general ruckus. In fact, we react strongly and swiftly to point out and curb these actions.

As R.L. Thorndike might say, "How soon they forget." Thorndike's "law of effect" (we all learned about it in Educational Psychology 101) rests on the idea that animals (people included) are likely to repeat those behaviors for which they are rewarded. Thus, if we want to see a particular behavior repeated in someone's repertoire, we reinforce it, and if we want to extinguish a particular behavior, we douse it with feigned ignorance and make believe it isn't there.

However, behaviorists usually work in labs, not schools, and it's easier to ignore rats in a cage than children in a classroom. This behavioristic theory collapses as soon as it confronts a child who perceives negative attention (such as when a teacher chastises a child's behavior) as preferable to no attention at all.

Still, the impact of emphasizing the positive to children can't be argued. Imagine the surprise of a group of first-graders who hear, "I really appreciate the way you are sharing your crayons. It makes my job more pleasant when you behave so well." "Who is this?" they'll wonder. "The teacher from Planet Nice-Nice?"

Yet they'll listen and incorporate this statement into their ever-growing reserve of comments that prove their value, their ability, or their responsibility. Pick on the positive, and see how much more pleasant a place school can become.

🖈 STRATEGY Avoid Fear-Based Discipline

Sometimes, it's easier to learn what to do by seeing an example of what *not* to do. In this case, a second-grade teacher—sweet, kind, and misinformed—presented us with this illustration:

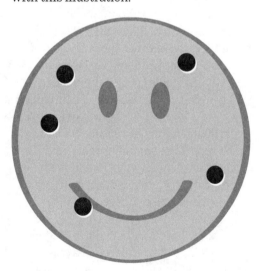

Her explanation? "I went to a workshop where the speaker said that children had to know the reasons they might have lost a special privilege, like extra recess. So, every morning I give each of my students a fresh happy face and, when I catch them doing something wrong, I punch a hole in their face with my paper punch. At the end of the day, we each count how many holes we have in our faces. Anyone with more than five holes cannot go out for extra recess."

Did her plan work? Yes. Negative behaviors diminished. Did her plan respect students or encourage them to pursue new, positive behaviors? Doubtful. Her students behaved out of fear, and all you learn from fear is more ways to avoid punishment.

🖈 STRATEGY Discipline in Private

Nobody's perfect. Every student will misbehave at some time. Every student—even the most able and conscientious—will need an occasional talking-to. When this time comes, discipline in private. Though this is more time-consuming, it's a more personal, respectful, and meaningful way to point out the connection between the child's action and your reaction. Examples:

- *(Said in front of class):* "That's inappropriate language, Sue. We'll talk about it after class."

- *(Said in private):* "Erin, Mike told me how bad he felt when you called him 'stupid' because he's not in the top reading group. Were you trying to make him feel bad?"

- *(Said in private):* "Santo, I was going to stop my lesson when you wouldn't stop talking during math, but I'd rather talk with you privately about your behavior."

Each of these statements conveys respect to the student, and each one encourages the student to forge the connection between actions and consequences. Especially effective with intelligent children (who can see the correlation between their action and your response) and students who seldom get punished (and think it's the end of the world when they do), private disciplining can help students save face in front of their classmates. It also teaches an important lesson that an off-the-cuff public reprimand ("Behave yourself, Margaret! I expect better behavior from a smart girl like you") can never achieve.

#5: Invitational Education Through Self-Satisfying Behaviors

When you read the following strategies, you may tell yourself, "Wait—these are about *me*, not about creating a positive classroom environment for my students." There's an old saying: "If Mama ain't happy, ain't nobody happy." The better you feel about yourself as a teacher (and as a human being), the better you'll be at teaching.

STRATEGY Start (and Maintain) a Feel-Good Folder

Even eternal optimists have their down days. Whether caused by biorhythms, bad karma, or distressing news, every teacher has occasional second thoughts about our chosen profession. *There must be easier jobs,* we think, *not to mention more lucrative.* Still, we persevere. We get through. We find that second wind. And we go on.

To make the journey more manageable, keep track of the "invitations" you have received as an educator. Gather together some of the little rewards of our profession—the happy face drawn by a first grader and given to you as a present; the former sixth grader, now in college, who wrote to you once "just to say thanks"; the note from two parents who appreciated the "shoulder to cry on" you provided when they needed it most. Place them all in a file and label it your Feel-Good Folder. Then, on days that are rougher than you would like, open the folder and reread the messages that meant so much. You'll be surprised at how special those notes still are.

Samples from Our Feel-Good Folders

Dear Judy:

Thank you for writing back to me. You are the only person I know who actually writes nice, decent, long letters. You spend time and make the effort. I really admire that, and you always make me feel good because you really know how to handle things. Gosh, you should be a psychiatrist!

Later . . . Thomas

Dear Judy:

This letter is years late, but I wanted to thank you for all that you have done to help me through your book. My education has greatly improved because I took your suggestions to heart. I've pulled through some tough times because of your encouragement. I've been inspired by lessons instilled from your writing . . . you have really made a difference.

Sincerely, Amie

Jim:

Thank you so much for taking the time to get the names of counselors for my daughter. You always amaze me because you are such a busy person, but you always take time to go the extra mile for someone. Thank you!

Jean

Mom and Dad,

I'm in Positano, on the Amalfi Coast. I can't believe you sent me on this trip, and here I am, at a place between heaven and Earth (I don't know which is closer), thanks to you.

Love, Matt

Jim:

Please keep writing. Your articles are like "word candy" to me. I keep chewing on them for a long, long time.

Doris

STRATEGY Leave School at School

Anyone who thinks that education is an 8 a.m. to 3 p.m. job, or an occupation chosen by those who appreciate summer too much to work, need to have their eyes opened and their mouths closed. In any human services career, teaching included, your job follows you home (where you get endless emails from parents) to the mall (where you see your students) and on vacation ("Hey, isn't that Mrs. Jackson over there in the bikini?").

This reality isn't necessarily stressful, but if you find yourself talking about your job to people who aren't involved in education—spouses, neighbors, grandchildren—you might need to learn how to leave school at school. Because this is easier said than done, here are some tricks you can try:

- Grade papers or plan tomorrow's lessons before you leave the school building. On some days, leave school empty-handed.

- Plan an exercise routine—at least thirty minutes three times a week—and stick to it! It could be as serious as racquetball or as leisurely as a walk around the neighborhood.

- Splurge occasionally. Have a massage. It's so invigorating and therapeutic that the seventy-five dollars you spend ought to count as a medical tax deduction.

- Make a "school conversation schedule." Promise yourself that you'll talk shop with colleagues or family for only thirty minutes a night. After that, all talk of school is *verboten*. (Even better: Attach a twenty-five-cent penalty for every infraction of this rule. With luck and a little effort, the penalty pot will be empty and you will be happier.)

STRATEGY Avoid Comparing Yourself to Others

How frequently we downplay our efforts and accomplishments by comparing them with those of our colleagues! In our attempts to become "superteacher," we look around us and see what others have done that we have not. Educators' worst enemies are often themselves. To break this cycle of accomplishment and disappointment, we need to learn a lesson we so often teach our students: Compare your efforts *today* with *your own* efforts of yesterday or last week or last year, never with the efforts of the person down the hall. Remember: You're not the teacher next door, and that's okay.

STRATEGY Know That You Don't Have Total Control

This vital understanding—that you don't have control over your students' lives—is the one taught so well by Mrs. Sanders, the teacher we met at the beginning of this chapter. An excellent educator and a caring individual, she realizes the limits of her powers. She knows too well that the lives of her students are not always easy or pretty. She acknowledges that some pupils enjoy homes of privilege, while others are never free from want—physical, environmental, or emotional.

Still, she goes on . . . because she *can* help and she *does* help, every day between 8 a.m. and 3 p.m., in a place called a classroom.

So do you.

The Magic of Teaching

by Scott Stuart, fifth-grade teacher

I believe that educators are yearning to get back in touch with their "first love." I think that for people to go into teaching in the first place, they had to be called by a dream. A dream that they could make a difference. Educators need to be encouraged to capture that dream once more. Sure, there are difficulties and walls to climb, but the "raw materials"—our students—often have no awareness of the pressures with which we deal. We don't have to transfer them on! Even though we fight the politics of schools, we can still enjoy the pleasure of seeing children grow and develop. I think that is the magic of teaching.

#6: Invitational Education by Explicitly Valuing Giftedness (and Gifted Kids)

STRATEGY Tabula Rasa

The Latin phrase *tabula rasa* translates as "clean slate," which is exactly what your students are to you when they enter your classroom for the first time. So why not use some time early in the school year to get to know your students better?

This open-ended activity can lead to much discussion about the high points and hurdles of giftedness. At the same time, you can respond to students'

comments, concerns, and desires in a way that lets them know you place value on giftedness in general, as well as on them as individuals.

Here are some sentence starters your students can complete with the first thoughts that enter their minds. If helpful, emphasize to your students that these first, don't-worry-about-how-they-sound thoughts are likely to be their most honest, unfiltered ideas, and therefore will be the most interesting and useful to explore.

Ask students to first jot down their responses to these open-ended statements privately, then discuss them as a group:

1. When I hear the word "gifted," I think . . .

2. The biggest misconceptions people have about being gifted are . . .

3. When I get an A in school . . .

4. When I *don't* get an A in school . . .

5. I expect myself . . .

6. If I could convince my teachers of one thing . . .

7. If I could convince my non-gifted friends of one thing . . .

8. If I could convince my parents of one thing . . .

9. The best part of being gifted is . . .

10. The worst part about being gifted is . . .

11. If I could change one thing about my life . . .

12. *Add your own sentence stems, or invite students to propose their additions.*

After holding this conversation, we suggest you collect and copy each student's completed Tabula Rasa answers and hold onto them until near the end of the year. Then give them a new, blank Tabula Rasa sheet to complete, followed by the copy of the one they did initially. Compare the answers—were they the same? Different? More optimistic? Less optimistic? Taking the time to do an activity like Tabula Rasa (twice!) is proof positive to your students that you care about their lives both inside and outside of school.

🖈 **STRATEGY** The 7 "Dreadly" Sins

An article titled "Back to School Blues: Why Gifted Teens Dread Returning to School" lists seven fears that lie behind this "dread."[5] These seven worries are:

1. I will fail.

2. I really am *not* gifted.

3. I won't find any friends.

4. I will be bored—once again.

5. I will have to fake it and dumb myself down.

6. I will have more battles with my parents.

7. It's all about college . . . and pressure.

A great way to show support for your gifted students is to share these "dreads" with them and invite them into a casual conversation in a private space at school (perhaps during the lunch period or after school) to review how personally relevant or irrelevant students find each one. Our hunch is that this initial discussion will extend into several more sessions, because many gifted kids—especially teens—seldom have the chance to express their views and feelings about matters like these. In addition, these chats will help your students know that you are interested in their academic and personal lives, and that you understand that gifted kids face ups and downs like everyone else while also confronting unique challenges.

Invite students to share their experiences with these solutions, and also to help each other brainstorm solutions to these issues. In addition, as much as you are able to do so, encourage them to meet on their own, without you in the room, to discuss these and other issues that arise when giftedness and adolescence collide.

(*Note:* Except for #7, many of these "dreads" may very well be experienced by younger gifted students, too. Why not find out?)

A Final Thought

The invitations to learn that we give our students on a minute-by-minute, day-to-day basis are very efficient ways to enhance both achievement and self-esteem in the classroom. Students who feel good about themselves as human beings, not just scholars, grow to become young people in touch with both their hearts and their minds, and eventually adults who are as willing and able to *care* deeply as they are to *think* deeply.

BUG ROLL

CONGRATULATIONS,

_____!

You "**B**rought **U**p your **G**rade" in

_____

and didn't go down in any subject.

KEEP UP THE GOOD WORK!

Teacher's Signature: _____

Date: _____

Independent Study Guide

As you prepare to do an independent project, think about the nine important points below. In an outline, list, table, or other format, write down your ideas, plans, and expectations for each point. While you work on your project, check in with this preparatory guide regularly to make sure you're still on track.

1. **Your subject area, broadly defined.** *Examples:* Dinosaurs; chemistry; jobs of the future. Create a web diagram for your subject area.

2. **Your subject area, narrowly defined.** Select one or more topics from your web diagram. Write a sentence or two about what you'd like to learn.

3. **Resources you could use.** Describe what they are and where you can find them. *Examples:* Printed resources, including specific books; human resources; Internet resources; other resources such as museums.

4. **Personal evaluation.** How will you know you've achieved your goals for this project?

5. **First steps.** List the first five things you will do to begin your project. As you complete this list, add more items. *Example:* Locate two books and three websites on my topic.

6. **Possible problems and solutions.** Write at least three things that could go wrong with your project. Think of ways to overcome these problems and write those, too.

7. **Sharing your work.** What form will your project take? A report? Movie? Website? Demonstration? Explain what type of project you will do and who will see your results.

8. **Timeline.** Write the dates when you expect to complete each stage of your project.

9. **Project approval.** Have your teacher sign off on your plan.

Visual Enigmas

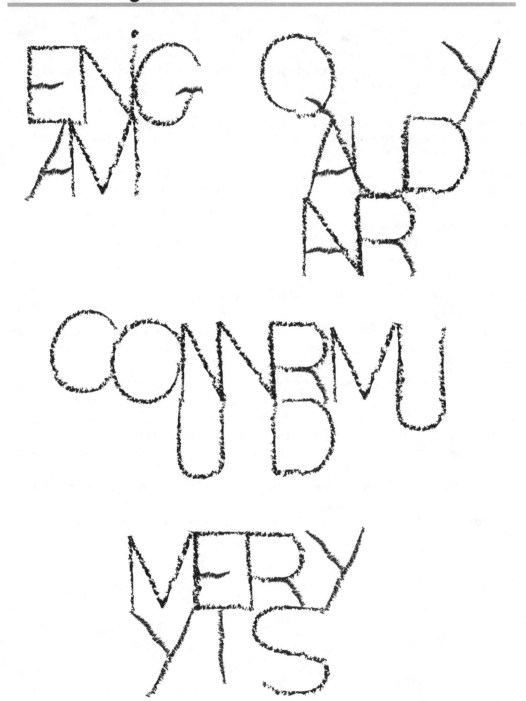

Afterword

> Be open to learning new lessons
> even if they contradict the lessons
> you learned yesterday.
> **—Ellen DeGeneres**

We know that, even after reading this book, you won't have *all* the answers. As a matter of fact, we suspect you might even have some new questions.

But we also know (just as you do) that questions are part of the job. The work you do—helping gifted kids not only in reaching their academic goals but also in the lifelong project of being happy and healthy—is full of twists and turns, challenges and joys. *Plus* plenty of questions.

One more thing we know? The answers and solutions you want won't always be easy to find.

That's why we commend you for remaining committed to seeking out as many answers as you can. It's also why we wrote this book, and why we've updated it to address newer questions that are part of being a teacher today. In turn, we hope the strategies, ideas, and encouragement in these pages help you on your way, and that they give you new perspectives, exciting ideas, and more than a few answers.

We wish you well on this important fact-finding mission, and in all you do. Thank you for letting us be a part of it.

—Judy and Jim

Notes

Chapter 1

1. "Giftedness and the Gifted: What's It All About?" *ERIC Digest* #E476 (Reston, VA: ERIC Clearinghouse on Disabilities and Gifted Education, 1990).

2. Elizabeth McClellan, "Defining Giftedness," *ERIC Digest ED* 262519 (Reston, VA: ERIC Clearinghouse on Disabilities and Gifted Education, 1985).

3. Christopher Ferguson, "Not Every Child Is Secretly a Genius," *Chronicle of Higher Education* (June 14, 2009): p. 39.

4. Tracy L. Cross, "The Lived Experiences of Gifted Students in School, or On Gifted Students and Columbine," *Gifted Child Today* (January 2000).

5. Ibid.

6. Linda Kreger Silverman, Ph.D., "The False Accusation of Elitism" (Denver, CO: Gifted Development Center).

7. Dan Sheridan, "Scant School Accommodation for State's Brightest Children," *Boston* (October 1999): p. 81.

8. J.J. Gallagher and S.A. Gallagher, *Teaching the Gifted Child* (Boston: Allyn & Bacon, 1994), pp. 91–92.

9. Neil Daniel, "New Questions About Talented People," *Gifted Students Institute Quarterly* 10:15 (1985).

10. Carolyn Coil, "My View: Ten Myths About Gifted Students and Programs for the Gifted," *Schools of Thought: CNN*, schoolsofthought.blogs.cnn.com/2012/11/14/ten-myths-about-gifted-students-and-programs-for-gifted (2012). Used with permission.

11. Reported in June Cox, Neil Daniel, and Bruce O. Boston, "Executive Summary," *Educating Able Learners: Programs and Promising Practices* (Austin, TX: University of Texas Press, 1985).

Chapter 3

1. Susan Daniels and Michael Piechowski, eds., *Living with Intensity: Emotional Development of Gifted Children, Adolescents, and Adults* (Scottsdale, AZ: Great Potential Press, 2008), p. 14.

2. Howard Gardner, *Frames of Mind: The Theory of Multiple Intelligences* (New York: Basic Books, 1993), pp. 73–77.

3. Ruth Duskin Feldman, "The Promise and Pain of Growing Up Gifted," *Gifted/Creative/Talented* (May/June 1985): p. 1.

4. Ibid.

5. Jean Sunde Peterson, *The Essential Guide to Talking with Gifted Teens: Ready-to-Use Discussions about Identity, Stress, Relationships, and More* (Minneapolis: Free Spirit Publishing, 2008), p. 32.

6. Howard Gardner, *Frames of Mind: The Theory of Multiple Intelligences* (New York: Basic Books, 1993), p. 13.

7. Amy Bisland, "Gifted Students with Disabilities: Are We Finding Them?" *Gifted Child Today* (2004); Linda Kreger Silverman in an email exchange with Dan Peters (2012).

8. Judy Galbraith, M.A., and Jim Delisle, Ph.D., *The Gifted Teen Survival Guide* (Minneapolis: Free Spirit Publishing, 2011), p. 236.

Chapter 4

1. National Association for Gifted Children, *State of the Nation in Gifted Education: Work Yet to Be Done.* Washington, DC, 2013.

2. Leta S. Hollingworth, *Children Above 180 IQ: Stanford-Binet Origin and Development* (New York: Arno Press, 1975; reprint of the 1942 edition).

3. A. Kathnelson and L. Colley, "Personal and Professional Characteristics Valued in Teachers of the Gifted," unpublished paper presented at California State University, Los Angeles, 1982. See also Barbara Clark, *Growing Up Gifted*, p. 370.

4. Jack Canfield and Harold Clive Wells, *100 Ways to Enhance Self-Concept in the Classroom* (Englewood Cliffs, NJ: Prentice-Hall, 1993).

5. Judith Wynn Halsted, "Guiding the Gifted Reader," *ERIC Digest #E481* (Arlington, VA: The Council for Exceptional Children, 1990).

6. Ann Camacho, ed., *Bookmarked: Teen Essays on Life and Literature from Tolkien to Twilight* (Minneapolis: Free Spirit Publishing, 2012), pp. 2 and 194.

Chapter 5

1. Chester E. Finn and Jessica A. Hockett, *Exam Schools: Inside America's Most Selective Public High Schools* (Princeton: Princeton University Press, 2012), pp. 1–2.

2. Linda Kreger Silverman, "The Gifted Individual," *Counseling the Gifted and Talented*, Linda Kreger Silverman, ed. (Denver: Love Publishing Co., 1993), p. 3.

3. Judy Galbraith, M.A., and Jim Delisle, Ph.D., *The Gifted Teen Survival Guide* (Minneapolis: Free Spirit Publishing, 2011), p. 134.

Chapter 6

1. Joseph S. Renzulli, Brian D. Reid, and E. Jean Gubbins, *Setting an Agenda: Research Priorities for the Gifted and Talented for the Year 2000* (Storrs, CT: National Research Center for the Gifted and Talented, 1991).

2. Thomas P. Hébert and F. Richard Olenchak, "Mentors for Gifted Underachieving Males: Developing Potential and Realizing Promise," *Gifted Child Quarterly* 44:3 (2000): pp. 196–207.

3. Barbara Kerr, "Gender and Genius," speech delivered at the College of William and Mary, March 7, 2000. Retrieved from education.wm.edu/centers/cfge/_documents/resources/articles/gendergenius.pdf (accessed Oct. 2, 2014).

4. Jerald Grobman, "Underachievement in Exceptionally Gifted Adolescents and Young Adults: A Psychiatrist's View," *Journal of Secondary Gifted Education* 17:4 (2006): pp. 199–210.

5. Jane B. Raph, Miriam L. Goldberg, and A. Harry Passow, *Bright Underachievers* (New York: Teachers College Press, 1966); Gary A. Davis and Sylvia B. Rimm, *Education of the Gifted and Talented* (Needham Heights, MA: Allyn & Bacon, 1998).

6. S.P. Marland, *Education of the Gifted and Talented: Report to the Subcommittee on Education, Committee on Labor and Public Welfare* (1972), p. 25.

7. National Commission on Excellence in Education, *A Nation at Risk: The Imperative for Educational Reform* (1983), pp. 8, 18–19, 28.

8. U.S. Department of Education, Office of Educational Research and Improvement, *National Excellence: A Case for Developing America's Talent* (1993), pp. 1, 11, 13.

9. Nicholas Colangelo, Susan G. Assouline, and Miraca M.U.M. Gross, *A Nation Deceived: How Schools Hold Back America's Brightest Students* (Iowa City: University of Iowa, 2004), p. 1.

10. Ibid., p. 3.

11. National Association for Gifted Children, *State of the Nation in Gifted Education: Executive Summary* (Washington, DC, 2011).

12. Jim Delisle, "The Gifted Underachiever: Learning to Underachieve," *The Roeper Review* 4:4 (1982): pp. 16–18.

13. Jane B. Raph and Abraham J. Tannenbaum, *Underachievement: Review of Literature* (New York: Teachers College, Columbia University, 1961).

14. C. Asbury, "Selected Factors Influencing Over and Underachievement in Young School-Age Children," *Review of Education Research* 44 (1974): pp. 409–428; Avner Ziv, *Counseling the Intellectually Gifted Child* (Toronto: The Governing Council of the University of Toronto, 1977).

15. Sally M. Reis and D. Betsy McCoach, "The Underachievement of Gifted Students: What Do We Know and Where Do We Go?" *Gifted Child Quarterly* 44:3 (2000): pp. 152–170.

16. See, for example: Jean A. Baker, Robert Bridger, and Karen Evans, "Models of Under-achievement among Gifted Preadolescents: The Role of Personal, Family, and School Factors," *Gifted Child Quarterly* 42:1 (1998): pp. 5–15.

17. Kyung Hee Kim, "Underachievement and Creativity: Are Gifted Underachievers Highly Creative?" *Creativity Research Journal* 20:2 (2008): pp. 234–242.

18. Gary A. Davis, Sylvia B. Rimm, and Del Siegle, *Education of the Gifted and Talented* (Upper Saddle River, NJ: Pearson, 2011).

19. Barbara Clark, *Growing Up Gifted: Developing the Potential of Children at Home and at School* (New York: Pearson, 2013).

20. Joanne Rand Whitmore, *Giftedness, Conflict, and Underachievement* (Boston: Allyn & Bacon, 1980), pp. 256, 265, 271.

21. Abraham J. Tannenbaum, *Gifted Children: Psychological and Educational Perspectives* (New York: Macmillan, 1983), p. 210.

22. Cynthia Dowdall and Nicholas Colangelo, "Underachieving Gifted Students: Review and Implications," *Gifted Child Quarterly* 26:4 (1982): p. 179.

Chapter 7

1. A list of the "Six Great Gripes of Gifted Kids" first appeared in the original edition of *The Gifted Kids' Survival Guide: For Ages 10 & Under* by Judy Galbraith (Minneapolis: Free Spirit Publishing, 1984).

2. Judy Galbraith, M.A., and Jim Delisle, Ph.D., *The Gifted Teen Survival Guide* (Minneapolis: Free Spirit Publishing, 2011), p. 201.

Chapter 8

1. International Alliance for Invitational Education, invitationaleducation.net.

2. Donald W. MacKinnon, *In Search of Human Effectiveness: Identifying and Developing Creativity* (Buffalo, NY: Creative Education Foundation, 1978), p. 171.

3. Alfie Kohn, *Punished by Rewards: The Trouble with Gold Stars, Incentive Plans, A's, Praise, and Other Bribes* (Boston: Houghton Mifflin, 1993), pp. 49–67.

4. George T. Betts and Maureen Neihart, "Eight Effective Activities to Enhance the Social and Emotional Development of the Gifted and Talented," *Roeper Review* (1985), pp. 18–23.

5. Gail Post, "Back to School Blues: Why Gifted Teens Dread Returning to School," Gifted Challenges Blog. giftedchallenges.blogspot.com/2014/08/back-to-school-blues-why-gifted-teens.html. August 14, 2014 (accessed Dec. 9, 2014).

Resources

Books

The Autonomous Learner Model: Optimizing Ability by George T. Betts and Jolene K. Kercher (Greeley, CO: ALPS Publishing, 1999). This revised edition of a classic shows teachers and gifted coordinators how to plan gifted programs for grades six and up that focus on the emotional as well as the cognitive abilities of students.

Bookmarked: Teen Essays on Life and Literature from Tolkien to Twilight edited by Ann Camacho (Minneapolis: Free Spirit Publishing, 2012). In this collection of writings, young people from a wide range of backgrounds reflect on how words from literature connect with them and influence their lives, goals, and personal philosophies.

Crossover Children: A Sourcebook for Helping Children Who Are Gifted and Learning Disabled by Marlene Birely (Reston, VA: Council for Exceptional Children, 1995). Resource material and information for helping twice-exceptional kids.

Developing Talent in Young People by Benjamin Bloom (New York: Ballantine, 1985). This is one of the classics in the field of teaching and raising gifted and talented children. Through biographies of noted athletes, scientists, artists, and more, Bloom examines the experiences at home and in school that cause young people to excel to extraordinary levels of performance. He then concludes by elucidating how these practices can impact the lives of other children with less eminent talents.

Dumbing Down America: The War on Our Nation's Brightest Young Minds (And What We Can Do to Fight Back) by James R. Delisle (Waco, TX: Prufrock Press, 2014). A provocative review of the ways that gifted children are being shortchanged in America's schools, and what can be done to reverse this trend.

Emotional Intelligence by Daniel Goleman (New York: Bantam, 1995). A well-researched volume that looks at the link between intellectual and emotional intelligence and examines the inner characteristics of people who excel in life.

Emotional Intensity in Gifted Students: Helping Kids Cope with Explosive Feelings by Christine Fonseca (Waco, TX: Prufrock Press, 2010). Fonseca reviews why gifted kids have such extreme behaviors and provides strategies to teach these students how to live with the intensities that many of them feel.

The Gifted Teen Survival Guide: Smart, Sharp, and Ready for (Almost) Anything by Judy Galbraith, M.A., and Jim Delisle, Ph.D. (Minneapolis: Free Spirit Publishing, 2011). A guide for older gifted kids with strategies, practical how-to's, and surprising facts (as well as essays and quotes from teens themselves) on how to survive and thrive as a gifted teen.

The "I" of the Beholder: A Guided Journey to the Essence of a Child by Annemarie Roeper (Scottsdale, AZ: Great Potential Press, 2007). In this classic book by one of the pioneers of gifted child education, readers will learn about how to identify and understand gifted children better through the lens of direct observation. An added bonus is a final chapter, "Growing Old Gifted," which is a rare exploration of giftedness in the elderly.

Living with Intensity: Understanding the Sensitivity, Excitability, and the Emotional Development of Gifted Children, Adolescents, and Adults edited by Susan Daniels and Michael Piechowski (Scottsdale, AZ: Great Potential Press, 2009). This book provides a solid background on the theories underpinning the emotional lives of gifted individuals throughout the lifespan. Applying these theories to best practices for teaching and raising gifted children is also reviewed.

Some of My Best Friends Are Books: Guiding Gifted Readers from Preschool to High School by Judith Wynn Halsted (Scottsdale, AZ: Great Potential Press, 2009). Offers many excellent suggestions for literature appropriate for gifted kids.

The Survival Guide for Gifted Kids: For Ages 10 & Under by Judy Galbraith, M.A. (Minneapolis: Free Spirit Publishing, 2013). A straightforward, friendly guide for younger gifted kids that explains what giftedness is all about, how to make the most of school, and how to socialize successfully.

Teaching Gifted Children in Today's Preschool and Primary Classrooms by Joan Franklin Smutny, Sally Yahnke Walker, and Ellen I. Honeck (Minneapolis: Free Spirit Publishing, 2016). Designed to help teachers identify, nurture, and challenge the younger gifted child (ages 4–9).

Teaching Gifted Kids in Today's Classroom: Strategies and Techniques Every Teacher Can Use by Susan Winebrenner, M.S., with Dina Brulles, Ph.D. (Minneapolis: Free Spirit Publishing, 2012). A classic for teaching gifted kids, loaded with references and resources.

Organizations and Websites

2E Twice Exceptional Newsletter
2enewsletter.com
This organization supports parents, educators, and others who help 2E (twice-exceptional) children reach their potential.

Council for Exceptional Children
www.cec.sped.org
A complete database of research and intervention methods for children who are gifted, twice-exceptional, or have other special education needs.

Coursera

coursera.org

Through partnerships with universities and other organizations, Coursera offers free online courses on many subjects.

Davidson Institute for Talent Development

davidsongifted.org

The Institute seeks out profoundly gifted young people and supports their educational and developmental needs. They host an array of resources for educators, and the database on their website is a deeply comprehensive and searchable listing of valuable information and resources for teachers and parents.

Education Resources Information Center (ERIC)

eric.ed.gov

This digital library of educational literature covers topics including gifted education and twice-exceptional learners.

The Gifted Child Society

gifted.org

This nonprofit organization provides training for educators, assistance to parents, and educational enrichment and support services for children.

Hoagies' Gifted Education Page

hoagiesgifted.org

The site contains a wide variety of resources, links, articles, and information for gifted kids, their educators, and their parents. A valuable and friendly website.

iTunes U

apple.com/education/itunes-u

This site allows teachers to create and manage customized learning experiences, giving students the chance to work at different paces and on different topics of interest. At the same time, students can gather materials, notes, and more as they learn about a subject or prepare a project.

Khan Academy

khanacademy.org

This website features short educational videos on many topics and for students of all ages. Students can use the site to learn, measure their own progress, and work toward individualized goals at their own pace.

MIT + K12

k12videos.mit.edu

A collaboration between Khan Academy's founder Sal Khan and MIT students, this site presents short videos with a focus on STEM topics.

MoMA Learning

moma.org/learn/moma_learning

This site from the New York Museum of Modern Art gives students a chance to explore and study art history independently.

National Association for Gifted Children (NAGC)

nagc.org

A national advocacy organization for parents and educators that addresses the needs of gifted and talented children. The website is a comprehensive resource and features easily accessible links to every state's gifted organization.

Supporting Emotional Needs of the Gifted (SENG)

sengifted.org

Helps parents identify giftedness in their children, helps children understand and accept their unique talents, and provides a forum for parents and educators to communicate.

TED-Ed

ed.ted.com

This website—inspired by TED Talks—offers educational videos recorded by educators and professionally animated. The website also features quizzes, questions for further exploration, and additional resources.

Twice-Exceptional/2E Network LA

groups.yahoo.com/neo/groups/2E_Network_LA/info

This network, based in Los Angeles, provides advocacy and resources for twice-exceptional students and their families. The organization can also be found on Facebook at facebook.com/2E.Network.LA and on Meetup at meetup.com /Twice-Exceptional-2E-Network-LA.

Wonderopolis

wonderopolis.org

Each day, this site posts a new "wonder"—a thought-provoking question as a basis for investigation. Each wonder is accompanied by a video, word list, and other resources.

Index

Page numbers in **bold** refer to reproducible pages.

Photo credits: Page 1: © Monkey Business Images | Dreamstime.com • Page 3: © Lisa F. Young | Dreamstime.com • Page 7: © Anatoliy Samara | Dreamstime.com • Page 12: © Photographerlondon | Dreamstime.com • Page 15: © Monkey Business Images | Dreamstime.com • Page 22: © Dmitriy Shironosov | Dreamstime.com • Page 27: © Dmitry Kalinovsky | Dreamstime.com • Page 44: © Dmitriy Shironosov | Dreamstime.com • Page 47: © Sonya Etchison | Dreamstime.com • Page 54: © Lorraine Swanson | Dreamstime.com • Page 56: © Monkey Business Images | Dreamstime.com • Page 60: © Rimma Zaytseva | Dreamstime.com • Page 62: © Mamahoohooba | Dreamstime.com • Page 69: © Lisa F. Young | Dreamstime.com • Page 72: © Monkey Business Images | Dreamstime.com • Page 78: © Tyler Olson | Dreamstime.com • Page 80: © Robert Kneschke | Dreamstime.com • Page 85: © Monkey Business Images | Dreamstime.com • Page 91: © Darya Petrenko | Dreamstime.com • Page 94: © Tyler Olson | Dreamstime.com • Page 99: © Alexander Raths | Dreamstime.com • Page 104: © Andres Rodriguez | Dreamstime.com • Page 111: © Hongqi Zhang (aka Michael Zhang) | Dreamstime.com • Page 116: © Digitalpress | Dreamstime.com • Page 120: © Szefei | Dreamstime.com • Page 123: © Dmitriy Shironosov | Dreamstime.com • Page 128: © Mamahoohooba | Dreamstime.com • Page 134: © Darrinhenry | Dreamstime.com • Page 137: © Getty Images • Page 143: © Aman Ahmed Khan | Dreamstime.com • Page 156: © Sepy67 | Dreamstime.com • page 159: © Ian Allenden | Dreamstime.com • Page 165: © Tyler Olson | Dreamstime.com • Page 172: © Monkey Business Images | Dreamstime.com • Page 177: © Monkey Business Images | Dreamstime.com • Page 179: © Monkey Business Images | Dreamstime.com • Page 183: © Syda Productions | Dreamstime.com • Page 188: © Monkey Business Images | Dreamstime.com • Page 192: © Milosljubicic | Dreamstime.com • Page 201: © Godfer | Dreamstime.com • Page 204: © Flashon Studio | Dreamstime.com • Page 209: © Anatoliy Samara | Dreamstime.com • Page 216: © Tom Merton/Digital Vision/Getty Images • Page 219: © Jonathan Ross | Dreamstime.com • Page 225: © Wong Chee Yen | Dreamstime.com • Page 228: © Photographerlondon | Dreamstime.com • Page 233: © Monkey Business Images | Dreamstime.com • Page 237: © Andreykuzmin | Dreamstime.com • Page 238: © Darrinhenry | Dreamstime.com • Page 246: © Anatoliy Samara | Dreamstime.com • Page 251: © Monkey Business Images | Dreamstime.com • Page 253: © Monkey Business Images | Dreamstime.com • Page 256: © Iryna Yermak | Dreamstime.com • Page 259: © Yanlev | Dreamstime.com • Pattern on Gifted Kids Speak Out sidebars: © Oxana Lebedeva | Dreamstime.com and © Cienpies Design / Illustrations | Dreamstime.com